# THE REMINISCENCES OF SIR MUHAMMAD ZAFRULLA KHAN

Interviews Conducted
By
Professors Wayne Wilcox
And Aislie T. Embree
For Columbia University

With an Introduction
by
Prof. Dr. Pervez Perwazi

2004

"Copyright in the underlying English-language oral history upon which this publication is based is owned by Columbia University in the City of New York. Columbia University has not reviewed this publication to determine whether it is an accurate translation of the interview.

No material from this publication may be reprinted without obtaining the approval of the Columbia University. Requests to quote material from the publication should be submitted to the Oral History Research Office of Columbia University."

First published by the Oriental Publishers in June 2004.
Oriental Publishers, P.O. Box 96512, 2414 Major Mackenzie Drive, Maple, Ontario, L6A 1B0, Canada.

Main entry under title: Reminiscences of Sir Muhammad Zafrulla Khan. Based on interviews by Prof. Wayne Wilcox and Prof. Aislie T. Embree of Columbia for Columbia University.
(IX) 256p. includes index.
Original Title in English: Reminiscences of Sir Muhammad Zafrulla Khan.

ISBN — 0 973327 1 9

Notes=* 1 Khan Muhammad Zafrulla Sir, 1893-1985. 2. India - History 1917-1947. 3. Pakistan - History 1947-1985. 4. India. Politics and Government. 5. Pakistan Politics and Government. 6. Muslim-India History. 7. India History Partition. 8. Pakistan History Partition. 9. All India Muslim League History. 10. Pakistan Movement History. 11. United Nations 1947-1954. 12. Judge International Court of Justice 1954-1961 and 1964-1973. 13. United Nations 1962-1963. 14. Vice President International Court of Justice 1958-1961. President International Court of Justice 1970-1973.

I. Perwazi, Pervez, 1936-. II. Reminiscences of Sir Muhammad Zafrulla Khan. III. Based on interviews of Prof. Wayne Wilcox and Prof. Aislie T. Embree in 1962-1963.

Cover Design by Nabeel Ahmad Rana (Nabeel@Canada.com)

Published by Oriental Publishers, P. O. Box 96512, 2414 Major Mackenzie Drive, Maple, Ontario L6A 1B0, Canada.

Printed at the Fazl-i-Umar Press, Chauncey, OH 45719, USA.

# DEDICATION

*I dedicate this book to Mr. Kunwer Idrees, my revered teacher and a great admirer of Sir Zafrulla Khan.*

# CONTENTS

|  | Page |
|---|---|
| Preface | vii |
| Acknowledgement | ix |
| Introduction | xi |

**INTERVIEW, MARCH 31, 1962**      1

Biographical Sketch, The Khilafat Movement, Unionist Party, Sikander-Jinnah-Khizr, Cabinet Mission Plan, Two Muslim Leagues, Political Career, Simon Commission, Delhi Conspiracy, Round Table Conferences, President of All India Muslim League Session, Working of Viceroy's Executive Council, etc. etc.

**INTERVIEW, MAY 12, 1962**      50

Third Round Table Conference, First Commonwealth Relations Conference, Membership of the Viceroy's Executive Council.

**INTERVIEW, MAY 19, 1962**      73

Membership of the Viceroy's Executive Council.

**INTERVIEW, JUNE 2, 1962**      89

Viceroy's Executive Council, The Coronation of King George The VI, Imperial Conference.

**INTERVIEW, JUNE 16, 1962**      107

1937 Elections, War Supply, Supreme Court of India, Agent General to China, Dominion Minister's

REMINISCENCES OF SIR MUHAMMAD ZAFRULLA KHAN

Conference, Last Session of League of Nations, Pacific Relations Conference at Mont Tremblant.

**INTERVIEW, JUNE 30, 1962**                        **131**

To England in 1943, Commonwealth Relations Conference, 1945, Chaudhry Rahmat Ali.

**INTERVIEW, JULY 7, 1962**                         **141**

Sir Khizr Hayat Khan, Partition and the Boundary Commission.

**INTERVIEW JULY 28, 1962**                         **161**

Advisory Role, to UN for Pakistan's Membership, Pakistan's Foreign Minister, on Liaqat Ali Khan and Quaid-e-Azam Muhammad Ali Jinnah, The Kashmir Dispute and the UN.

**INTERVIEW, SEPTEMBER 15, 1962**                   **173**

Kashmir, Sheikh Abdullah, UN and Pakistan's Role, 1948-1954, ICJ, Its Working and Jurisdiction, etc.

**INTERVIEW, SEPTEMBER 22, 1962**                   **197**

Again in the UN in 1962, Disarmament Issue, South African Issue.

**INTERVIEW, OCTOBER 26, 1963**                     **213**

President of the UN General Assembly, 17th Session and Particular Issues, Travels during Presidentship, Back to ICJ.

**INTERVIEW, NOVEMBER 17, 1963**                    **232**

Comparing the League of Nations and the UN, Munir Enquiry Commission etc.

**INDEX**                                           **247**

vi

# PREFACE

This memoir is the result of a series of tape-recorded interviews conducted by Professors Wayne Wilcox and Aislie T. Embree with Sir Muhammad Zafrulla Khan in New York City during 1962.

Only minor corrections and emendations have been made, and the reader is enjoined to bear in mind, therefore, that he is reading a transcript of the spoken, rather than the written, word.

Columbia University

# ACKNOWLEDGEMENTS

I am grateful to Jessica Weiderhorn of the Columbia University Oral History Department for her cooperation to get permission from the University to publish the Reminiscences of Sir Zafrulla Khan.

I am also indebted to my teacher, Mr. Kunwer Idrees of Karachi, for extending a helpful hand to make this publication possible. The following friends helped me in various ways: Mr. Naseem Mahdi, Dr. I.U. Mangla, Dr. Safee Chaudhry, Col. Raja Aslam, Mr. Hidayatullah Hadi, Mr. Nabeel Ahmad Rana, Ch. Ehsan Elahi, Mr. Farhan Khokhar, Professor Dr. Basharat Munir Mirza, Prof. Mubarak Ahmad Ansari, and Ms. Amatur Rafique Rahat. Last, and not the least, Mr. Abdool Hamid Abdool Rahman for editing the transcript and crossing the "T"s and dotting the "I"s, and Mr. Muhammad Ismat Pasha for his help in the word processing of the text in various stages of preparation of the book.

Pervez Perwazi

# INTRODUCTION

The incident took place at the concluding session of the International Writer's Conference at Stockholm in 1994. As soon as I left the stage, after having presented a paper on Pakistan's literature, a Morrocan writer came running to me and introduced himself, "I am Zafrulla - Zafrulla Alejabi. I am so pleased to meet a Pakistani writer. You know my name is very unusual for that of a Morrocan, but my parents named me after some famous Pakistani diplomat who was our only supporter at the UN in the late forties and early fifties. We owe our independence to his efforts. Many boys were named after him. I am one of those proud boys and I have for the first time met a Pakistani. I wanted to express my gratitude, so I came running to you. Can you please tell me something about that famous Zafrulla, because we don't know much about our benefactor, our hero, after whom I was named." He was too sentimental. We sat together after the session was over and talked about his hero and my fellow Ahmadi compatriot. He was pleased to know that I knew Zafrulla and had had the chance to meet him personally and that I had shaken his hand many times. He grabbed my hand and held it in esteem as long as we were there. Now that I have the task of writing an introduction to the Reminiscences of a famous man - the man, mere mention of whose name generates awe and respect. Mothers name their children after him to express their gratitude, and here I am, an unknown, unfamiliar person, venturing to introduce Sir Zafrulla.

Obviously, this is an "adventure in self expression." Sir Zafrulla began his political career in 1917, when he was appointed head of the Ahmadiyya delegation to present the point of view of the Ahmadiyya Muslim Community before the Montague-Chelmsford Commission. He was elected to the Punjab Legislative Assembly in 1926. He joined the Unionist Party of the Punjab and worked his way up under the able guidance of Sir Fazle Hussain. He was a member of the Round Table Conferences on India's future Constitution which were held in the years 1930-32. He proved his mark and won respest of all and sundry. Mr. Musarrat Hussain Zuberi, ICS, in his autobiography, "Voyage Through History" has recorded a conversation he had with Sir Samuel Hoare as follows: "Sir Samuel, in the perfect English way, was "pleased" to meet me. When his lead in the poll during counting was reported, he relaxed and took some personal interest in me, asking personal questions. He was keen to know whether allottment to the province had been done and where I was to be posted. When he heard I was going to the Punjab, he smiled his big ... smile and said, "You are lucky." "Why it is so lucky?" I asked. His remark astonished me and does even today: "Because Sir Zafrulla comes from that province and you are lucky to go to that province," and then added: "You know, Sir Zafrulla was here for the Round Table Conference and we still write to each other." My reaction was not very polite. "There were so many others better known and more experienced like Sir Tej Bahadur Sapru, Mr. Jinnah, Sir Srivnivas Shastri." He cut me out: "Oh, as for that, there was the Aga Khan too; but no one made such tremendous impression as Sir Zafrulla did." I could not afford to further contradict the Secretary of State for India and changed the topic."[1]

By the time of the Second Round Table Conference, he had become so eminent that he was appointed to the Viceroy's Executive Council to officiate for Sir Fazle Hussain during the latter's absence on leave for four months. Later, he was appointed, at a relatively very young age, as a member of the Viceroy's Executive Council for a full term of five years. He was re-appointed for anther term of five years after the expiry of the first term. Shortly after the beginning of the second term, he chose to quit the political arena and, apparently, to shut himself in the backwaters of the Federal Court of India. The Viceroy reluctantly allowed him to join the Court. Immediately afterwards, the Viceroy asked him to go to China as India's first Agent General for a short period of six months, which he did. He preferred the Federal Court because he had perceived divine indications that he should do so. The Viceroy, Lord Wellingdon, offered him the chair of the Chief Justice of the Punjab High Court and he refused because he did not want to see the Governor of the Punjab in that matter. The Governor was hostile towards the Ahmadiyya Muslim Community. He also declined the offer to be a Privy Councillor. Mr. Nehru, as the interim Prime Minister of India, nominated him on the International Court of Justice (ICJ), he was not elected. Had he been elected to the ICJ, he would not have been able to render the tremendous service which he did to the

## REMINISCENCES OF SIR MUHAMMAD ZAFRULLA KHAN

cause of Muslims, during the late forties and early fifties. What a pity that after his first term at the ICJ, one of his own countrymen canvassed against his re-election. He was elected and retired as the President of the ICJ. He was the only person to be elected the President of the UN General Assembly at New York and the International Court of Justice at the Hague.

He was not a "yesman." He was known as the dissenting Judge at the Federal Court of India and was always outspoken and straight. At the Round Table Conferences, he was such a courageous spokesman of India's cause that Mr. Chintamoni sent him a chit saying: "In this gathering of reactionaries, it is so refreshing to hear someone speak out with courage." [2]

These are the Reminiscences of the man who rendered invaluable services to the cause of Muslims. He never wanted political eminence, but was granted enviable political and judicial prominence by the sheer grace of Allah, The Almighty. His entry in the International Who's Who reads as follows: "Sir Mohammad Zafrullah Khan, KCSI, BA, LLB; Pakistani politician and diplomatist; born 6 February, 1893; Educated at Government College, Lahore, and King's College, London; Barrister-at-Law (Lincoln's Inn); Advocate Sialkot, Punjab 1914-16; practised Lahore High Court, 1916-1935; Member, Punjab Legislative Council, 1926-35; Delegate, Indian Round Table Conference, 1930, 31, 32; Delegate, Joint Select Committee of Parliament on Indian Reforms, 1933; President, All India Muslim League, 1931; Member, Governor General Executive Council, 1935-41; Leader, Indian Delegation to the Assembly of League of Nations, 1939; Agent General of India in China, 1942; Judge, Federal Court of India 1941-47; Constitutional Advisor to H.H. The Ruler of Bhopal, June-December 1947; Leader, Pakistan Delegation to Annual Session of the United Nations General Assembly, September-November, 1947; Minister of Foreign Affairs and Commonwealth Relations, Government of Pakistan, 1947; Leader, Pakistan Delegation to UN Security Council on India-Pakistan Dispute, 1948-54, and to Sessions of United Nations General Assembly, 1947-54; Leader, Pakistan Delegation to San Francisco Conference on Japanese Peace Treaty, 1951; Leader, Pakistan Delegation to SEATO Conference, Manila, 1954; Judge, International Court of Justice, The Hague, 1954-61, 1964-73, Vice President, 1958-61, President, 1970-73; Permanent Representative of Pakistan to United Nations, 1961-64; President, 17th Session of the UN General Assembly,

**1962-63.** Honorary Bencher, Lincoln's Inn; Fellow of London School of Economics; Honorary LL.D. (Cambridge); Honorary Fellow, Delegacy of King's College, London; LL.D., Universities of Columbia, Denver, California (Berkeley), Long Island; Honorary D.C.I., Beaver College, Penn. Publications: Islam: Its Meaning for Modern Man, 1962; The Qur'an (translated into English), 1970. He died at Lahore on September 1, 1985 and was buried at Rabwah, Pakistan, according to his will."

Much has been written about Sir Zafrulla's achievements and much would be written in future, but I presume he has not been accorded that recognition which was his due. The foremost cause was his beliefs. He was and remained a devout member of the Ahmadiyya Muslim Community. He never ever wavered in his attachment to the Community. He never tried to conceal his affiliation with the Ahmadiyya cause. When the Secretary of State for India and the Viceroy wanted him to be appointed to the membership of the Viceroy's Executive Council, he told them that he belonged to the Ahmadiyya Muslim Community and that other Muslims had certain ideological differences with him. They chose him despite knowing of these differences. The Secretary of State for India circulated a memorandum dated February 15, 1945, to the India Committee, and added that: "Sir Zafrulla is an intelligent Punjabi and represents the balanced Muslim viewpoint. Unfortunately, he belongs to a Community with whom the orthodox Muslims have some disagreement."[3]

Prof. K.K. Aziz has written: "Zafrulla possessed an acute intelligence which pierced the façade of every pretence, legal fraud, political duplicity and diplomatic subterfuge. His mind was as clear as a mirror and reflected the truth of what he contemplated. His immense capacity for hard work laughed to scorn the obstacles of short notices and knotty problems. In a court of law, as in a legislature or in international forums, he built up his case step by step, one argument succeeding another in perfect sequence, one point clarifying or elaborating its predecessor, with the artistry of a master mason putting up an edifice of elegance and classical proportions. Reason and logic supplied the solid foundation which convinced the sceptical. The fluency of the language imparted meaning and substance to the argument. His own belief in the rightness of the cause he was upholding taught words to fall into line like soldiers on parade. Dialectics poured out in solid reality, not as florid gestures. His reasoning was not a desire dressed in a little rationality, but the truth presented in its naked splendour. It was essence clothed by thought. He was not a man of brittle loyalties or icy arrogance or empty mime, interested in keeping the part top spinning or in the small change of debate. He was bred in a different stable. He wedded the logic of facts with the logic of disputation and debate with rare skill, and believed in the sovereignty of discussion. If he walked in the sunshine of fortune and fame all his life, he walked demurely, modestly, humbly. The sweet smell of triumph did not ruffle his calm. The foam and froth and the bubble of worldly success neither seduced his self respect, nor corrupted his simplicity, nor poisoned his humanity. Zafrulla worked hard, long, diligently, and selflessly both for his country and for the nationalist movement which created it. We, the Muslims of Pakistan, have thrown him outside the pale of our religion. We should not also cast him out of our memory. A nation which forgets its great men gradually ceases to produce them."[4]

I am proud that I have been able to present the Reminiscences of Sir Zafrulla Khan, with the courtesy of the Columbia University Oral History Department. May Allah accept this humble effort and make it useful for the generations to come.

**Pervez Perwazi**

*Former Professor, T.I. College, Rabwah, Pakistan*

*Former Visiting Professor at the Osaka University of Foreign Studies, Osaka, Japan*

*Former Professor Research Associate, Uppsala University, Uppsala, Sweden*

*Member of the Swedish Writers' Union, Stockholm*

*References*

[1] *A Voyage Through History*, Musarrat Hussain Zuberi, vol. 1, 2nd. Ed., The Hamdard Foundation, Karachi, January 1987. p. 260.

[2] *Tehdith-e-Nemat*, Sir Zafrulla's Urdu Autobiography. p. 273.

[3] *Sir Zafrulla's Contribution in India's Freedom Movement*, Dr. Pervez Perwazi, Oriental Publisher, Toronto, 2001. p. 35.

[4] *Remembering Some Great Men*, Prof. K.K. Aziz, Vanguard, Lahore, 2002. p. 83-84.

# INTERVIEW WITH SIR ZAFRULLA KHAN

Prof. Wayne Wilcox, New York City

## MARCH 31, 1962

**Khan**: I was born at Sialkot, which is now in Pakistan, and then, of course, was India, on February 6, 1893. My father was a lawyer in Sialkot. I went to school at Sialkot. My connection with America began long ago, as I matriculated in 1907 from the American United Presbyterian Mission High School at Sialkot.

The family belongs to a place called Daska, about 16 miles from Sialkot. We are what are known in that part of the world as a landholding family, so that our roots are in the land. I come from a farming family that cultivated land. My grandfather and father did not cultivate it with their own hands, but our interest was in land - my grandfather's younger brother was a cultivator, so was my father's younger brother, my uncle - so it might be said that I have the background of a peasant. That is why, perhaps, whenever I am in a big town like London, and now in New York, towards the evening when the shades of night are falling, I long to be out in the open.

From Sialkot, I went to college at Lahore Government College, where I graduated in 1911, in four years' time from my matriculation, which was the normal period. My subjects for my degree examination were English, History, Economics and Arabic.

I then proceeded for my law studies to England, where I joined King's College, London, for my Bachelor of Law's degree from the University of London and was entered at Lincoln's Inn for being called to the Bar. I was called to the Bar in June, 1914, but had to stay on for my Bachelor of Law's degree examination in October, 1914, which means that I was in England at the beginning of the First World War.

My three years' stay in England, therefore, coincided with the three last peace years in Europe and in a sense, in the world. At that time, England was undoubtedly at the top of the world; America was coming along, but everyone looked to London as the centre in many respects; it certainly was the financial and economic centre, and, I think in a sense, also the intellectual centre of the world. Thus it was fortunate that during the formative years of my life I had the opportunity of observing some facets of life in the British Isles at that time, and of registering impressions of it.

My hobby, while I was in England, now that I look back upon it, apparently was travel. During vacations I always went on trips, and before I went home in October, 1914, I had travelled practically all over Europe, with the exception of the Iberian Peninsula and the Balkans. I had been as far afield as St. Petersburg, as it then was, in the summer of 1913, one year ahead of the war. It was also the tricentenary year of the Romanov dynasty. In Finland, I went all through the lakes up to the North, and did a very rash thing: I shot the rapids in the Ulea River. From England I had travelled from Harwich across the North Sea to Gotebourg, Sweden. From Gotebourg I went by river steamer through the lakes and the Gotha Canal on to Stockholm. These were all very delightful experiences which I often recall, but nothing seems to have been the same again after the First World War.

I returned to India, as it then was, in October, 1914. We travelled by the ill-fated S.S. Arabia, which was one of the mail steamers of the Peninsular and Oriental Company. The German destroyer, Emden, was then operating in the Arabian Sea. It had already sunk several vessels. We made the voyage all right, but on a subsequent voyage the Arabia, like so many other vessels, was sunk by the Emden in the Arabian Sea.

I arrived home some time in November and started practice with my father at Sialkot in the beginning of 1915. My father was then at the top of the civil practice at Sialkot. Occasionally, he took on criminal work, but his natural bent was towards civil work, out of which he preferred to do cases relating to land. He told me that I could best use my time with him by making myself familiar with the system of land records and the method of tracing the history of every plot of land backwards to 1855, i.e., almost to the advent of the British administration into that part of India. That was one great benefit that I derived from my association with considerable influence over my outlook on life, particularly over my religious views.

In August, 1916, I moved to Lahore, which was the capital of the Province and where the High Court of the province had its seat. My

## REMINISCENCES OF SIR MUHAMMAD ZAFRULLA KHAN

move to Lahore was connected with an offer that I received from the proprietor of Indian Cases, which was at that time the biggest law journal and law reporter in India. It reported the judgments of all the provincial High Courts and also the judgments of the Judicial Committee of the Privy Council on cases from India. The proprietor was the late Chaudhri Sir Shahabuddin, who subsequently became and remained for a number of years the Speaker of the Punjab Legislative Council, which was set up under the Montagu-Chelmsford Scheme of Reforms, under the system known as Dyarchy. He too belonged to the Sialkot district, knew my father very well and was a friend of his. He had known me since my childhood, and he suggested that I should go to Lahore and work with him and then decide what I would prefer out of the various opportunities that might become available. So I moved to Lahore and started working as Assistant Editor of Indian Cases. Within three months he put me in charge of the editing side of Indian Cases, and I, in effect, became the Editor, relieving him of the greatest part of the editorial work.

He encouraged me not to turn down any briefs that might be offered to me, but advised that I should be discriminating in selecting the cases I would accept. He was in many other ways extremely helpful to me. He was himself a lawyer, and had had, if not a very voluminous practice, considerable experience in handling important cases. His advice to a youngster just entering the profession was extremely valuable.

In 1919, I was also appointed part-time lecturer in the University Law College in Lahore. This came through the interest in me of the late Sir Fazle Hussain, who was a Fellow of the University, and was a member of the Law College Committee. When a couple of vacancies occurred among the part-time lecturers and he knew that one of the vacancies would be filled by the appointment of a young Muslim lawyer, he suggested that I should apply and was instrumental in my being given the appointment. That was of considerable help, not so much financially - the emoluments were not substantial - but in bringing me in closer contact with legal circles and, I suppose, giving me more confidence at that stage of my career.

The teaching, which was committed to me, though of interest to me, did not really amount to much. When we sat down before the beginning of the term with the Principal of the college to decide what subjects should be allotted to whom, I did not put forward any claim to speciality in any subject and so two remnants were left to me. I call them remnants because nobody else was interested in those subjects. One was Roman law, and the other Criminal Procedure. There was no connection between the two, except, as I have said, that nobody else seemed to be keen on taking them on. So, when the Principal turned to me and asked whether I would take them on, I signified my assent.

The teaching of these two subjects was, perhaps, easier, in a way, than the teaching of other subjects for there was little change by way of amendment in the criminal law and, of course, none could take place in Roman law. Thus the preparation that I made in the first year proved adequate during the five years that I taught in the University Law College.

The hours were convenient: 8:30 to 10:00, so that one was free by the time the courts started, and I could attend to any work in court or go back to my editorial work.

Gradually both my interest in, and my own inclination towards, my practice increased; but for some years my income remained steady, for, I first gave up the law lectureship and then gave up the editorship of the Indian Cases and concentrated more and more on my practice.

In the meantime, I had begun to be interested in public affairs. I do not think I have at any time been much of a politician in the strict sense of the word, which will perhaps be appreciated as my career unfolds itself. My first contact with public life was in November or December, 1917, when the then Secretary of State for India, Mr. Edwin Samuel Montagu visited India and along with the then Viceroy, Lord Chelmsford, received representative deputations on behalf of different associations, societies and communities in India bearing on the next steps on Constitutional Reforms in India.

On the 20th of August, 1917, Mr. Montagu had made a declaration in London with regard to the advance that was contemplated, and he came over later to India in October or November to hear Indian views at first hand. I led the delegation of the Ahmadiyya Community and read out our address, setting forth our views.

The result of the consultations that Mr. Montagu and Lord Chelmsford held together and with the leading public men in India was the Montagu-Chelmsford Scheme of Reforms, which was subsequently put into effect as the System of Dyarchy.

Briefly, it amounted to this: In the provinces a system of partially-responsible self-government was introduced. Each province had a legislative council composed of elected members to whom the ministry would be responsible for the subjects which would be committed to the care of ministers. These were, for instance, education, health, lands, forests, public works, and the like which were known as nation-building departments. While certain key departments, like law and order, finance, and revenue were entrusted to "executive members." The nomenclature was adopted for the purpose of indicating that ministers would be responsible to the legislature and would continue in office only so long as they had the confidence of the legislature, and that the "executive members" would be appointed for fixed terms of five years. Though the conduct of their departments would be criticized and token cuts could be proposed and carried against them which meant on those particular matters the legislature did not approve of their policies or of their conduct of their departments, they could not be turned out of office by a vote of the Legislature. The two sides had to work together under the Governor and had to find a way to make the system run.

It was subsequently admitted that dyarchy had justified itself in the Punjab, for it had worked smoothly, there had been no deadlocks, and the Punjab from being one of the backward provinces of India, steadily rose under this system of dyarchy to a position that could compare favourably with some of the older and bigger provinces, particularly in the matter of education. A great part of the credit for making dyarchy work in the Punjab was due to the late Sir Fazle Hussain, who became the Minister of Education, when the first government under dyarchy took office in January, 1921. At that time the Ministry was composed of two eminent men who were selected on their individual merits, Sir Fazle Hussain and Lala Harkishen Lal. Later, through the efforts of Sir Fazle Hussain, a political party was organized in the Punjab, known as the Unionist Party which was able to hold office for the greater part of the period until 1947, when on independence the greater portion of the Punjab became part of West Pakistan.

The Unionist Party was, of course, a political party, but was constituted on the basis of economic interest. It represented mainly the rural and agricultural interests. It was composed of Muslims, Hindus and Sikhs, so that it cut across the communal divisions and had this healthy quality, that it concentrated on the economic development of the province with due regard to the interests of the

## REMINISCENCES OF SIR MUHAMMAD ZAFRULLA KHAN

rural and agricultural classes, and particularly, of the backward classes. It showed itself ready to vote taxation the main burden of which would be borne by the interests which it represented. For instance, it raised the land revenue and the water rates in the canal irrigated areas, for it knew that the additional revenue would be applied towards development of education in rural areas, of rural communications, hospitals, dispensaries, and so on. Not that urban areas were neglected, but the sharp contrast between the two which had hitherto prevailed was reduced, and attention began to be paid to rural areas also. So that one might say that the Unionist Party set up a record of constructive cooperation, and, as I have said, there was no serious friction between the reserved portion of government and, what was called, the transferred portion of government. As already indicated, the transferred subjects were those subjects which were in the charge of ministers; the reserved subjects were subjects in the charge of executive members. Members and ministers worked smoothly together in the Punjab.

I have made mention of Sir Fazle Hussain, I should also mention the late Sir Muhammed Shafi. He was also a lawyer, like Sir Fazle Hussain, and was senior to him by several years at the Bar. He was a very successful advocate and until the emergence of Sir Fazle Hussain into the field of politics and public life, Sir Muhammed Shafi had been the acknowledged leader of the Muslims of the Punjab and had led in the All India Muslim League also. The League had been founded in 1906 by men like His Highness the Aga Khan, Syed Amir Ali, Musa Abbas Ali Beg, the Nawab of Dacca, and had its branches in the provinces. I doubt, however, whether Sir Muhammed Shafi possessed the finesse and acumen that were needed in a political leader, although he had a charming personality and was very hospitable, courteous, and popular and was well liked. He held an acknowledged position at the Bar. He was, in my view, a much better advocate than Sir Fazle Hussain but not nearly so dynamic and penetrating a politician as Sir Fazle Hussain proved to be.

When Sir Fazle Hussain entered political life, shortly after he had moved to Lahore as a lawyer, Sir Muhammed Shafi's leadership became more and more confined to legal circles and to the Bar and the political direction of the community and, later, of the Unionist Party was taken over by Sir Fazle Hussain. Sir Muhammed Shafi, as a matter of fact, never entered the provincial legislature, though on account of his experience and eminence, he was later appointed a member of the Viceroy's Executive Council, the highest office, then and right up to Independence, open to any Indian. He held that office with distinction for five years.

**Question:** *Would you care to make any broad comments on the Khilafat Movement?*

**Khan**: The Khilafat Movement, during the years that it captured the imagination of the Muslims of India and even engaged the interest of Mr. Gandhi, was most active in the United Provinces of India, what is now called Uttar Pradesh. Its leading spirits were the two famous Ali brothers, Maulana Mohammad Ali and Maulana Shaukat Ali. It never caught on in the Punjab to any remarkable degree, though it must be said that Muslims all over India were greatly agitated and supported the Khilafat Movement. The central idea behind the Khilafat Movement was to give whatever support was possible and to make whatever effort one could, through the British Government or by embarrassing the British Government, and by sending direct contributions to Turkey, to procure for Turkey better terms than had been imposed upon it in consequence of its having fought on the wrong side in the First World War.

The name "Khilafat" was given to the movement to stimulate the religious interest of the Muslims as the Sultan of Turkey had traditionally occupied for centuries the position of the Khalifa, that is to say, the spiritual head of Islam. Not that the whole Muslim world accepted him as such; but the bulk of the Sunni Muslims looked upon him as Khalifa and accorded him honour and respect. This had no practical effect upon anybody's life, but it invested the Sultan with a certain degree of prestige. Even those sections of the Muslims of India like the Shias, for instance, who could not, from the religious point of view, accept anybody as a Khalifa outside their own Imams; and the Ahmadis who could not accept anybody as their religious leader outside their own Movement, lent their support to the Khilafat Movement, because Turkey did represent the secular strength and prestige of Islam to a large degree. Thus, delegates from all sections of Muslims of India attended Khilafat Conferences and Khilafat Movement continued to grow in strength until it sort of merged itself into, or, at least, became a parallel organization to the Congress, in alliance with the latter, in support of its political objectives. It was a very adroit move on the part of Mr. Gandhi to win the two Ali brothers over to the Congress by expressing his sympathy with the Khilafat Movement.

## REMINISCENCES OF SIR MUHAMMAD ZAFRULLA KHAN

Later, when the young Turks themselves upset everything by abolishing the Khilafat altogether, the Movement gradually lost its *raison d'etre* in India.

I did not take any active part in the Khilafat Movement myself. For one thing, I was rather young at that time; and for another, from the religious point of view, the Ahmadiyya Movement did not look upon the Turkish Sultanate as representing the Khilafat. Nevertheless, in one of the Khilafat Movement Conferences in Allahabad, an Ahmadiyya delegation, which was led by me, made it quite clear that we were in full support of the objectives of the Movement without accepting the claim or the position of the Sultan as spiritual head of Islam.

**Question:** *Mr. Ambassador, I would like to explore with you the demise of the leadership or the end of the leadership of Sir Fazle Hussain and the Unionist Party in the Punjab and to that end to talk about two personalities: Sir Sikander Hayat Khan and Sir Khizr Hayat Khan. I wonder if you would make any general remarks about these people, the way they found themselves in leadership of the Unionist Party, and if you would care to comment on Azim Husain's commentary on what happened to the Unionist Party after these parties took over and Fazle Hussain's old ideology left.*

**Khan:** Sir Fazle Hussain's exit from a direct participation in Punjab politics took place, I believe, in 1930, when he accepted the membership of the Governor General's Executive Council at the Centre. He took over the portfolio of Education, Health and Lands. From 1930 to 1935, he served with the late Lord Halifax who, as Lord Irwin was Viceroy when Sir Fazle Hussain joined the Council, and with Lord Willingdon, who succeeded Lord Irwin.

So the question arose who should take his place as the leader of the Unionist Party in the Punjab. While Sir Fazle Hussain was himself leading the Party, one of his principal coadjucators had been Chaudry Chhotu Ram from the Rohtak District of the Punjab. He was a very respected personality among all sections of the Unionist Party, which included Sikhs, Hindus and Muslims.

But as the majority of the Party was Muslim, it was politic and perhaps necessary that the leader should be a Muslim, though Chaudhri Chhotu Ram was, after Sir Fazle Hussain went up to the Center, respected and looked up to as a sort of joint leader of the Party, along with Sir Sikander Hayat Khan, who took up the leadership in succession to Sir Fazle Hussain.

## REMINISCENCES OF SIR MUHAMMAD ZAFRULLA KHAN    9

Sir Sikander Hayat Khan was a scion of an aristocratic family from the District of Campbellpur in the northwestern part of the Province. His father was a very well-known personality in the early British days. He was, in fact, orderly officer to General John Nicholson at the time when Nicholson took Delhi after the Mutiny. As is well-known, Nicholson was shot down outside the Kashmiri Gate just at the moment of his victory, and he fell into the arms of his orderly officer, Sardar Muhammad Hayat Khan, and expired in that position. Nawab Muhammad Hayat Khan was given a civilian judicial appointment, and, I believe, rose to be District and Sessions Judge. He had a large family. The eldest son also rose to be District and Sessions Judge, and out of the younger sons two rose to great eminence: Nawab Liaquat Hayat Khan, who became Prime Minister of Patiala and held that position for several years; and Sir Sikander Hayat Khan, who became the leader of the Unionist Party and in that capacity led the Party in the Punjab Legislature and became Revenue Member in the Punjab Government.

**Question:** *May I just interrupt long enough to ask how it was that the Chief Ministers of the Punjab States were appointed, Liaquat Hayat Khan at Patiala and, I think, Sir Sikander at one time in Bahawalpur?*

**Khan**: Well, they were appointed at the discretion, at least ostensibly, of the ruler, but in actual fact the ruler always cleared the appointment with the Resident or Agent - as he was sometimes called - of the suzerain power. It was only a person who was acceptable to the Resident or Agent who was appointed. But as I have said, the family was eminent and well liked in those circles; they were completely loyal to the British. Later, in 1937, when the elections took place under the New Government of India Act and dyarchy was replaced by responsible government in the Provinces, Sir Sikandar Hayat Khan became the Chief Minister of the Punjab. As you have reminded me, he was for some time Chief Minister of Bahawalpur earlier, but that office he did not hold for long.

He led the Party very skilfully and was devoted to this principle of working in partnership with the representatives of other communities in a political party based on economic considerations rather than on communal divisions. He did have some difficulty with Mr. Jinnah, but I believe they came to an understanding that Sir Sikandar Hayat Khan could continue in the Punjab as leader of a political party based on economic considerations and continue to lead the Unionists, but that he would lend his full support to the concept of Pakistan at the Centre. In the Muslim League organization and leadership, he supported Mr. Jinnah, and there was, after that understanding, no trouble between them.

On the death of Sir Sikandar Hayat Khan, Sir Khizr Hayat Khan took his place. In my view, Sir Khizr Hayat Khan proved a much shrewder and abler man than Sir Sikandar Hayat Khan, but opinions differ. I think he also showed greater courage when he found himself confronted with a difficulty. He led the Party, but in the meantime the Muslim League had been growing in power, and Sir Khizr Hayat Khan had to face a difficult position. He was nevertheless able to form and continue a government on Unionist principles, but the communal proportions, in the Party membership in the Legislature underwent a big change. Later, I believe, it even became a coalition government rather than a Unionist government. So that when Independence drew near, in the last year or so, though Sir Khizr Hayat Khan continued to be Chief Minister, he could do so only with the support of a Party which in the Legislature was composed mainly of non-Muslims. To that extent his position was much weaker than that of Sir Sikandar Hayat Khan. But this also lent him a certain element of strength in one respect. He could rely on the majority of his Party to give him undivided support to the extent to which he might find it necessary to resist Mr. Jinnah's efforts to control the Provincial Ministry. Having in his Party comparatively few Muslims he was not wholly dependent upon their support to continue as head of the Party.

In the end Mr. Jinnah and Sir Khizr Hayat Khan had a battle royal over the question of the allegiance due from the Provincial Party in power to Mr. Jinnah. There was, first, a direct conflict between the Muslim League and Sir Khizr Hayat's Government. The Muslim League embarked on a course of non-violent non-cooperation which touched off a great emotional wave in support of the Muslim League; though the movement did not succeed in displacing the government, it certainly greatly strengthened the position of the Muslim League in the Province.

In the middle of all this, and shortly after the Muslim League had given up its non-violent non-cooperative campaign, to be exact on the 20th of February, 1947, Mr. Attlee announced the scheme for Partition. Here, perhaps I had better say a word or two with regard to the Cabinet Mission Plan, which had been developed during the summer of 1946, and on which eventually agreement had been reached between the Indian National Congress and the Muslim League. It had to be abandoned because of the differences that arose in regard to it which could not be reconciled.

In the early summer of 1946, Prime Minister Attlee had sent three of his Cabinet colleagues: Lord Pethick Lawrence, who was then Secretary of State for India; Mr. Alexander, who was First Lord of the Admiralty; and Sir Stafford Cripps, who, I believe, was then either Lord President of the Council or Lord Privy Seal, to India to make an effort to bring about a settlement between the Congress and the League on the basis of which Indian independence could be worked out.

They worked hard and eventually produced a plan on which agreement was reached. Briefly, the plan was that India should be divided into three autonomous zones: the A Zone to be the whole of the northwest, that is to say, including what is now West Pakistan plus the rest of the Punjab; the Zone B, the whole of the northeast, including what is now East Pakistan plus the whole of Assam and the rest of Bengal. These areas had a majority of Muslims, and the remaining, the bulk of the subcontinent, would constitute the C Zone. A, B and C would start off as a federation, with the Central Government in charge of defence, foreign affairs, communications, i.e., railways, telegraph, post office, telephones; finance for these purposes, currency, and connected subjects; the remaining subjects to be with the A, B and C Zones whose governments would be autonomous, subject to a certain degree of control in a state of emergency or to prevent a breakdown.

This was to be experimental for ten years. At the end of the ten years, A or B or both, if they were dissatisfied with the arrangement, could legislate themselves out of the federation and become independent.

Assam, which was a separate administrative province, was included in B but, taken by itself, it had not a Muslim majority in its population, though as part of Zone B, it would become part of a Muslim majority Zone. On the principle on which A and B were given the right of legislating themselves out of the federation later, the scheme provided that Assam, at the end of ten years, if it had found that B had chosen to go out of the federation, could legislate itself out of B if it wanted to go with C, that is to say with the rest of India.

Shortly after the plan was announced and everybody had breathed a sigh of relief that an agreement had been reached which would preserve the political unity of India, while safeguarding the Muslim position, Mr. Nehru, who, in the meantime, had been elected President of the Congress, made a public announcement and re-iterated it, putting his own interpretation on certain paragraphs of the plan including those relating to Assam. He contended that the paragraphs relating to Assam in the plan gave Assam not only a choice at the end of the years to legislate itself out of Zone B in case Zone B was to legislate itself out of the federation, but that here and now, at the very start, Assam had that choice and could exercise it. That tore up the whole plan. Lord Wovell, who was then Viceroy, made an effort with Messrs. Gandhi and Nehru, to restore the plan, but could not make any headway. Later Mr. Attlee sent for both Mr. Jinnah and Mr. Nehru to London and they went over, I believe, towards the end of 1946. Conversations were held but the differences could not be resolved.

Now events were moving so fast that the British Government felt that a solution of the Indian political and constitutional problem should be reached, announced and put into effect at an early date. So on the 20th of February, Mr. Attlee announced the scheme of Partition. Again, briefly, it was proposed that His Majesty's Government would transfer authority in India into the hands of the Provincial Governments, and that the Legislatures in the Punjab and Bengal would decide whether each would remain one administrative unit, as it then was, or whether it would insist upon partition in terms of contiguous majority areas of Muslims and non-Muslims.

At that time there was, I believe, a Muslim League, or, at least a majority Muslim Government in power in Bengal, but the Khizr Hayat Government was in power in the Punjab, and it was neither a Muslim League Government, nor even a government with a Muslim majority in the Legislature.

I felt worried as I studied Mr. Attlee's announcement and I spent the whole day considering in my mind what was likely to happen. I was then a judge of the Federal Court of India, but as a Muslim I was concerned with the likely developments. Before I became a judge, I had been a Member of the Central Government for a number of years and I apprehended that in the Punjab the position was going to be very difficult. Khizr Hayat and Mr. Jinnah already had a trial of strength and Mr. Jinnah had not succeeded in shaking Khizr

Hayat's position in the Punjab. With Mr. Attlee's announcement, a radical change had occurred in the situation.

After a restless night, I addressed a purely personal letter, to Khizr Hayat Khan, who was and is a good friend of mine, urging very strongly upon him the necessity of his resignation, thus at least opening the way for the Muslim League to take over in the Punjab. As soon as he received my letter, he telephoned to me indicating that he was inclined to agree with me, but urged me to go up to Lahore as he wanted to consult with me and other friends before taking a final decision. I went up next morning and he carried out consultations with his closest personal friends and also with his colleagues, Muslims and non-Muslims, in the Party. In the course of the day he decided that he would resign. He called on the Governor, Sir Evans Jenkins, after dinner and handed in his resignation. Thus his Party went out of office, and the way was clear for the Governor, if he would, to call upon the Muslim League to form a Government.

Thereby the principal hurdle in the way of the Muslim League in the Punjab was removed. By taking this step Sir Khizr Hayat Khan rendered a singular service to the cause of the Muslim League and to the cause of Pakistan.

**Question:** *Mr. Ambassador, I wonder if you would like to comment on what appears to be the continuity of two lines of Muslim political life in the Punjab, the first being the school of Muhammed Shafi, which perhaps later was translated into the Muslim League, and the school of Fazle Hussain and later Khizr Hayat Khan and Sikander Hayat Khan, which worked for a coalition in the Punjab. Do you see any long-term continuities in terms of the strength of political outlook of these Punjab Muslims?*

**Khan**: I would put it this way: What you have described as the Muslim League school of politics was perhaps the training ground in the theory and doctrine of politics and of political ideologies and what was needed by the Muslims not only in the larger political field, but also in the cultural field, in the field of education, etc. Sir Muhammed Shafi was almost a pioneer in the earliest stages and rendered great service throughout, but when the time came for practical activity and a certain amount of authority was transferred into the hands of the people through the Legislatures, Sir Fazle Hussain took the lead and he translated those principles and those ambitions into practice. In the practical political field, he felt that the most effective way of doing that would be through a party which would be devoted to the interests of the underdog. As the Muslims, though a majority in the population of the Punjab, were comparatively the weaker in the Legislature party, it would help the Muslims and it would help the rural interests among the Hindus and Sikhs if they could work together for the uplift of the rural and backward sections of the population. Very broadly speaking, the Unionist Party was the rural party as against the main Hindu's Party, which was the urban party. In the Punjab, Muslim interests throughout continued to be identified largely with rural interests. Gradually the practical considerations overrode theory and doctrine. Sir Muhammed Shafi fairly early reconciled himself to Sir Fazle Hussain's leadership on the practical side and himself continued to occupy a respected position as a senior leader, politician and statesman, but confined himself to the leadership of the Muslim League. There was actually no conflict between the two. The principal workers on both sides, behind them, were largely the same.

**Question:** *I wonder if I might ask, Mr. Ambassador, whether or not you see, as many people have been writing on the Punjab, a development of cooperation between the so-called official bloc, that is, British rulers and civil servants in the Punjab, and any wing of the Unionist Party as against other parties?*

**Khan**: There was no alliance, whether open or secret, of that kind at all. As a matter of fact, it was contrary to British policy to enter into any alliance of that kind. On the other hand, it was well known that naturally the British, as those in whose hands the overall authority still rested, were, in the first place, on the merits of the question, anxious to foster the welfare of the backward classes, mainly the rural classes. Also, as the rural elements were, as everywhere, the more conservative elements, except where an ideological revolution had overtaken them. In the Punjab fortunately there was no dominant landholding class. It had always been known as the "Peasant Province." Quite a large proportion of cultivable land was owned by the actual cultivators. There were very few large estates, not more than two or three, say a score in the Province. Official sympathy thus inclined towards the rural classes and they found it easier to work in co-operation with them, because the greater part of what was known as "nation-building work" of the administration affected them directly, e.g., rural schools, rural communications, extension of medical aid and facilities into rural areas, etc. That became the sheet anchor of Sir Fazle Hussain's policy and constituted his real strength. His policy proved very successful and it made Sir Fazle Hussain, as it were, the builder of the Punjab.  In that respect, Sir Fazle Hussain never made any distinction between Hindus and Muslims.  Both in the Province, and later in the Government of India, his first concern was to Indianize the services as far as possible; his second was that the Muslims should not be left behind, and that they should have a fair share of representation.  The provision of better facilities for training and education helped them greatly in that respect.

So long as he was in the Government, he was able to work in cooperation with the official bloc in the Legislature as well as with the Governor and the services.  They were happy to work with him for he was a go-ahead man, was working for the good of the country, and was able to keep a Party together in the Legislature which gave him a majority, and which brought strength also to what was known as the "reserved half" of government.  Though the "executive members" could not be turned out by vote of the Legislature, it is unpleasant to be voted down each time, and with the support he had in the Legislature, Sir Fazle Hussain was able to lend support to them too.  Judged by the results it was a wise policy in that stage of political and constitutional development of the country.

**Question:**  *I wonder if I could now turn your thoughts to Sir Muhammad Iqbal, the poet-philosopher, who is credited with giving the first major ideological impetus to Pakistan, both personal and theoretical considerations, if you like.*

**Khan**: Sir Muhammad was a poet, a philosopher and during a certain part of his career, had also been a teacher.  He later went to England and Germany where he studied philosophy as well as law and came back a barrister.  For a number of years, he practised law at the Lahore High Court Bar till his demise in 1938.

He furnished the Muslim younger generation with an ideology which also embraced the concept of Pakistan.  He was not too keenly interested in the day to day practical politics.  He was elected to the Punjab Legislature but never took much interest in its work. He was tremendously bored by the various procedural stages through which everything had to pass and by the long, sometimes very wearying debates that went on and on.  He was apt to get tired very quickly and leave.  I doubt whether he took part in more than one-quarter to one-third of the divisions.  By the time the matter under debate was to be voted on, Sir Muhammad Iqbal had gotten tired of the whole business and gone home to contemplation.  But even if he had paid more attention, I doubt whether he would have made much of a mark in the Legislature. That was not his milieu; his milieu was philosophy, poetry and ideology, and he did a tremendous job in sparking the ideology for the younger generation and the younger generation is still very devoted to him. His memory will live very much longer than the memory of the political leaders of his day, though on the practical side they accomplished a great deal more than did Sir Muhammad Iqbal, for he did not attempt much on that side; he left the day to day drudgery completely to them. He confined himself to putting forth his ideas through philosophical discourses and even more through his poetry, which caught on very quickly, not only in the Punjab, but to some degree in Afghanistan and to a much larger degree in Iran. The greater part of his poetical work during his later years was in Persian. He could be understood and was appreciated in the whole region where Persian was understood.

I had the honour of being a fellow townsman of Sir Muhammad Iqbal; he belonged to Sialkot as I do. I was also his pupil in the Government College at Lahore from 1909 to 1911, where he taught both English and Philosophy. I was not a student of Philosophy, but he taught us English poetry and he did it extremely well. Later when I was called to the Bar, I became his colleague at the Bar, though a Junior one, and had opportunities of working in closer association with him and appreciating more deeply his great qualities.

Apart from his teaching and his ideology he possessed many great qualities. He was content with very little. His nature was very simple, in some things almost childlike. He had not a trace of jealousy in his disposition, and he had little personal ambition. He possessed an endearing and ennobling personality and I am very happy that over several years I was vouchsafed the privilege of being associated with him in various capacities.

**Question**: *With the subsequent concern on the part of many students of Pakistan for the nature of the Islamic Republic of Pakistan, I wonder, and in reference to your comments about poetry as a vehicle for political expression and religious renaissance, I wonder if you might comment, at least very briefly, on The Reconstruction of Religious Thought in Islam as a magnum opus which may or may not have had a great effect on what the Muslims were feeling in terms of the Indian predicament in which they found themselves.*

**Khan**: It certainly has had considerable effect, but I believe I am right in thinking that it has had more effect in Islamic circles outside of Pakistan - and even amongst Western thinkers - than inside Pakistan. At the time when Iqbal delivered and later published those lectures, he was too much ahead of his time, so far as, what subsequently became, Pakistan was concerned. They made little impress contemporaneously and even later, the younger generation found it easier to get to the inner reality of his thought through his poetry. *The Reconstruction of Religious Thought in Islam* was printed in English and was a purely philosophical dissertation; it did not catch their imagination so easily; it did not fire them to the same degree.

I believe Sir Muhammad Iqbal's own endeavour also, certainly later, was to illuminate and fire the thought and imagination rather than to supply philosophical explanations of Islamic cultural, religious and other values. He would fix upon one central theme or idea and express it in a turn of phrase, which can be done much more easily in poetry than in prose, and that would illumine like a flash something for which people had been groping, and when they came upon it they were greatly enthused by it. That is one reason why his poetry has left a much deeper impress upon people's minds than his philosophical dissertations, like *The Reconstruction of Religious Thought in Islamic*.

**Question**: *I wonder then if you would comment on whether or not he falls within a tradition in the history of Islam in India. May he be considered a typical or a modern culmination of a particular school of thought, or is he the artist who seizes upon a predicament of people in a particular age quite apart from Shah Wali Ullah, for example, or any of the other forerunners of Muslim philosophical thought?*

**Khan**: He no doubt learned a lot and gathered a lot from divines and thinkers like the much revered Shah Wali Ullah and the great Jalaluddin Rumi and he held his own immediate teacher, the late Shamsul Ulema Maulvi Mir Hasan, in great reverence. But so far as his thought is concerned, it had a quality of its own. For example, his thinking exhibited a great deal of German influence; it was not derived altogether from Muslim sources, but wherever it was derived from, he gave it a Muslim colour and clothed it in Muslim values. He was influenced by German thinkers, but not perhaps always in the direction of their own philosophy. He often warned against their

## REMINISCENCES OF SIR MUHAMMAD ZAFRULLA KHAN

tendencies and his appreciation was also outspoken. He seemed to admire Nietzsche's thought and philosophy, particularly in regard to the endurance of pain and challenging and welcoming danger.

**Question**: *I am interested in whether or not Iqbal's thought and the rise of Muslim nationalism was part of an overall Muslim renaissance in the subcontinent and whether we could find any other evidence of it, say, in art, or perhaps in Chughtai, or some other Muslim thinkers, writers and representatives of their community.*

**Khan**: It definitely was a part of Muslim renaissance, for there was already a ferment in Muslim life and thought in all spheres at that time. Iqbal certainly influenced it in Pakistan and in the two neighbouring countries to a large degree. You have mentioned art and Chughtai. Chughtai is an eminent artist and a Muslim, but my impression is - it may not be worth anything at all - that though the art of a Muslim is bound to be influenced by his being a Muslim - it is part of his being - the process has not manifested itself noticeably in reverse, if I might so put it. The art of any particular artist, has not in turn influenced Muslim values or Muslim outlook on life. Of all the great faiths Islam has managed to keep its values intact, uninfluenced by what, after all, are adventitious and uncertain elements in a faith rather than the essence of the faith.

Perhaps that can be illustrated best with reference to Muslim services and Muslim places of worship. True, mosques in different Muslim countries have very different characters and some of them, for instance, in Egypt, and elsewhere are representations of types of architecture and decoration. To Islam that is entirely irrelevant. What is necessary, on the other hand, is that the architecture or motif should not be such as to divert the worshipper's attention. They should be as simple as possible. In Muslim worship there is nothing external, that is, outside the prayers and exhortation, no music, incense, vestments or other elements, to appeal to the emotions. Emotion is not excluded from life in Islam; Islam permits, and even seeks to make use of, emotion in its proper place, but it does not permit people to be carried away by emotion nor does it permit emotion to distort the essence. It seeks to arrive at the reality more through the exercise of reason and contemplation than through emotion.

In Islam mysticism has expressed itself emotionally; but then those who have concentrated on the study of Islam have not been inclined to attach much importance to it. Mysticism has had a

REMINISCENCES OF SIR MUHAMMAD ZAFRULLA KHAN **19**

tendency to degenerate into what has been described as pseudo-mysticism which has been roundly castigated by Iqbal. It is only pseudo-mysticism that is carried away in the current of emotion. True mysticism bases itself on contemplation. But perhaps we are going rather far afield from our subject.

**Question**: *May we now turn to the path of your political career from the time you were elected to the Punjab Legislature in 1926.*

**Khan**: During the period that we have dealt with so far, I was a minor figure on the scene, an apprentice, a pupil gradually taking up, as it were, the position of a lieutenant, of Sir Fazle Hussain, especially from the time I was elected to the Punjab Legislature.

The Montagu-Chelmsford Scheme of Reforms under which those legislatures had been set up had provided that at the end of ten years, after the working of the system of dyarchy had been in operation long enough to be evaluated, the position would be reviewed by a Royal Commission, who would report on the working of the whole system and make recommendations as to what should be the next stage. But as political thought in India was getting impatient for the next stage of constitutional advance, it was expected on all hands that the appointment of the Royal Commission would be announced during the fall of 1927.

During the 1927 summer session of the Punjab Legislative Council, held at Simla, the Muslim members of the Unionist Party decided to send someone to England who should get in touch with leading British statesmen and Members of Parliament and explain to them the Muslim position with regard to the next stage of constitutional advance. At the suggestion of Sir Fazle Hussain their choice fell on me, and I was asked to proceed to England for that purpose. I arrived in England towards the end of September. The Assembly of the League of Nations was then in session in Geneva and Sir Fazle Hussain himself had proceeded as leader of the Indian Delegation to Geneva, before I set out on my journey to London. I stopped on the way in Geneva, spent a day with him and with the Maharaja of Kapurthala, who was a member of the Delegation. A very pleasant day it was. I then went on to London where I began to make contact with British statesmen and prominent Members of Parliament.

I had spent two or three months in London in 1924, so that my contacts were not entirely new. I had met several people then and it was comparatively easy for me to get in touch with them and through them with others. I was still in England when the appointment of the Royal Commission was announced, which later got known as the Simon Commission.

It would perhaps be useful to explain that on safeguards, so far as the constitution was concerned, the Muslims at that time insisted upon two particular features being retained: one, that in Provinces in which they were a minority, they should have weightage in representation in the Legislature so that they could make an effective contribution, whether in support of the Party in power or in the opposition, as the case might be. And, secondly, that the system of separate electorates, that is to say, the system under which seats in the Legislatures were reserved for each community and were filled by members elected by that particular community should be continued.

I do not know whether I was able to achieve very much, but I know that it was extremely good training for me, to meet all those prominent people in British public life and to put the Muslim case to them. They all listened: some were interested, asked questions and criticised; and some, I have no doubt, were bored. The Royal Commission came out to India at the end of 1927 and again in 1928. The 1927 visit was an exploratory one, to get a bird's eye view of conditions and problems. But the personnel of the Commission had aroused a great wave of not only disappointment but resentment in India. All sections in India had hoped that the Commission would be composed of both British and Indian members, but it turned out to be an entirely British Commission, and the membership was very, very conservative indeed. The Chairman was Sir John (later Lord) Simon, who was then a liberal in politics and subsequently became a conservative, but who was by temperament a very, very conservative type of man. Very able, indeed one of the ablest English men of his time, but a very cold personality with a very sharp intellect, with no hint of warmth for any cause or individual. Major Attlee, as he was then called and who subsequently became Prime Minister, was a member, and so was Mr. Hartshorn of the Labour Party. There were three or four other completely colourless members. The Commission thus, in effect, was a one-man commission, for Sir John Simon was, intellectually, head and shoulders above the rest of them. It was suspected by Indians that all this was done deliberately so that the report should be a one-man report.

It looked at one time as though the Commission would be completely boycotted in India, and to a large degree it was. The absence of Indian representation on the Commission was fatal but an attempt was made to soften the blow by arranging that when the Commission arrived in India on its second visit, it would have associated with it, a committee elected by the Central Assembly and during its visit to each Province also a provincial committee elected by the Provincial Legislature. That did not, however, meet the wishes of the people.

The Central Assembly set up a committee; and so, in due course, did the Punjab Legislative Council. Sir Sikandar Hayat Khan and I were both members of the Provincial Committee, which was composed of seven members. We chose Sir Sikandar Hayat Khan as our Chairman.

We sat with the Commission when it visited the Punjab. We took part in all the proceedings, the examination of witnesses, etc. but we wrote our own report as did the Central Committee and each of the other Provincial Commission. In any case, again, it was an excellent piece of training to be associated with these eminent people that came from England, and those who were members of the Central Committee and of our own committee.

I might mention that a move had been made behind the scenes, which was attributed to Sir Fazle Hussain who was himself at that time an Executive Councillor and not a Minister - I never checked up on it - that the Provincial Committee that was to be elected should contain the three Indian Ministers, but this attracted little support and no Minister was elected to the committee.

The Unionist Party had always followed the line that while the objective was the same everywhere - to march forward to complete responsibility and independence as quickly as possible - there were two distinct methods which could be pursued to achieve that purpose: one, to attack and fight from the outside; and the other, to push forward through criticism, persuasion and co-operation. The Unionist Party while recognizing that both were necessary and, indeed, were complementary to each other, had chosen the latter.

The Commission made its report in due course, and it became a "best-seller," especially the first volume, which was descriptive of the conditions and institutions and of their historical background and development. It was an excellent piece of work. But the recommendations were very disappointing; they did not find support anywhere. So that the Commission's Report was, in that sense, stillborn. It is still a valuable document for the constitutional historian, but beyond that it did not have any effect at all. The feeling of disappointment and frustration was so deep and widespread in India that the British Government soon announced that a Roundtable Conference would be called in London to deal with the Constitutional problem. The announcement made no mention of the Commission's report. It was completely by-passed and became a dead letter.

In the fall of 1930, the first Roundtable Conference was convened. It met in St. James's Palace. It opened with great pageantry. There was the British section, in which all parties were represented. There was a whole galaxy of Princes, representing the Princely order of India. Then there were representatives of the various communities and interests of India and Burma.

We had some very eminent members among the Muslim representatives. There was, of course, His Highness, the late Aga Khan, who was not only leading the Muslims but was generally acknowledged to be, if not the leader of the whole Indian continent, the most eminent member of it. Everybody treated him with great deference. He did not make many speeches but his counsel was invaluable for us and he provided the opportunity of contacts which were extremely useful and indeed essential.

Then there were Sir Muhammed Shafi, Mr. Jinnah, Sir Syed Sultan Ahmed from Bihar, the Nawab of Chhatari from the United Provinces, and Maulana Mohammad Ali and I was one of the junior members.

At the very beginning, one question was got out of the way. The Burmese representatives put forward a demand that they wished Burma to be separated from India and to have its own constitutional framework and make its own way towards independence. That was conceded. So that, from then onwards, the Burmese section did not sit with the Indians; they had their separate discussions.

The concept of an All India Federation, including the British Indian Provinces and the Princely States, was put forward and was generally accepted; but, of course, a whole lot of problems had to be cleared up and resolved.

Mr. Ramsey MacDonald was then Prime Minister, at the head of a Labour administration. Between the first Roundtable Conference and the second Roundtable Conference, in 1931, an economic blizzard struck Britain and the pound sterling had to go off gold. Mr. Ramsey MacDonald found himself under the necessity of forming a coalition government and thus the Conservatives came into the government. During the first Roundtable Conference, Mr. Wedgewood Benn, subsequently, Slansgate, was the Secretary of State for India. By the time the second Roundtable Conference convened, that office had passed to Sir Samuel Hoare, subsequently Lord Templewood. From then onwards, Sir Samuel Hoare became the principal architect of the scheme that emerged from the three Roundtable Conferences, first in the shape of the Government White Paper and then in the Report of the Joint Select Committee of both Houses of Parliament.

The second Roundtable Conference had this great distinction, that between the two conferences, Lord Irwin, later Lord Halifax, who was then Viceroy, had been able to persuade the Congress, who had boycotted the first Roundtable Conference to participate in the second, and the Congress chose to send only a single delegate in the person of Mr. Gandhi, who was indeed a host in himself, universally respected, not only in India but also in England and in other parts of the world. It was, however, realized only during the actual working of the conference that, however respected and able an individual might be, it is a mistake for a strong and powerful party to be represented only by one individual in a conference. True, no decision was taken by counting of heads, and, therefore, it did not matter very much that a single individual who was backed by all the prestige and weight of his party represented it; but there was a psychological factor involved. When a question was being discussed, one person, whatever contribution he had to make, could make it in one intervention or two or three, and if the representatives of the other parties and interests did not see eye-to-eye with him, and their numbers were large and if they spoke only once each, his view was smothered under the avalanche of opposition.

Another development which took place during the second Roundtable Conference was the attempt by Mrs. Sarojni Naidu to bring the Muslims and Mr. Gandhi together so that, if possible, an understanding might be reached between them with regard to what was known as the communal problem, and a common stand could be made in support of whatever might be agreed upon as the immediate objective.

**Question**: *Mr. Ambassador, before we launch back into the many conferences which preceded the Government of India Act, 1935, I wonder if you might say a few words about the Delhi Conspiracy case from March 1931 to June 1932.*

**Khan**: I was Senior Crown Counsel in the Delhi Conspiracy case. In those days another very important conspiracy case was in progress, which was known as the Meerut Conspiracy case. There was some connection between the two cases, but they were not so interconnected that they could be tried together. In the Delhi conspiracy case, about a dozen or so young men were charged with having conspired together to manufacture large quantities of explosives for the purpose of blowing up cantonments and government establishments and institutions, for the purpose of creating terror in the country with the objective of pushing forward the independence movement. Thus, a group of terrorists were being tried for various specific offenses, in addition to the main conspiracy in the course of which those offenses were committed. For instance, one of them had, one bright afternoon, attempted to murder a police officer in the Chandi Chowk of Delhi who had spotted him as a wanted offender and was chasing him. This young man had turned around and discharged his pistol into the poor police official's bowels, but the man had miraculously escaped death. Other offenses, like dacoities and robberies, for the purpose of procuring funds for their activities, had been committed by members of the group.

The case came up for trial in Delhi before a tribunal, set up under the Ordinance. The tribunal was comprised of three judges: one European, Mr. White, who was a Sessions Judge from the United Provinces, and two Indians: one of them, Mr. Amir Ali, a retired Sessions Judge; and the other, Mr. Kanwar Sen, who at the time had been the Principal of the University Law College in Lahore, where I had served with him as part-time lecturer. Later, he had become Chief Justice in Jammu and Kashmir and had retired from that position.

The principal evidence in the case, which tied up the various scattered portions of it together, was that of the principal approver. There were two or three approvers, i.e., King's witnesses in the case. I was very much struck by the principal approver. That young man had a terrific memory; not only did he remain unshaken under cross-examination in respect of the main incidents of the story that he told at the trial, but even when I had questioned him before the trial, testing out various portions of his story, I had been surprised that he remembered the details so well. I was quite convinced that no part of his story was manufactured by him or was taught him by the police. As a matter of fact, he was too intelligent a man to have lent himself to any such attempt or procedure.

The trial proceeded very slowly indeed. My examination of the principal approver occupied seventeen days, and the cross-examination took nine months. That, I think, must be a record in trials, even of that kind. Part of the explanation is that the accused were up to every kind of trick. Some of them were graduates, some undergraduates, of universities; they were all educated people - and they not only knew the outlines of criminal procedure themselves - but had available defence counsel, who were paid for by government, but were chosen by them. Their principal counsel was Dr. Kitchlew from Amritsar. He was a barrister-at-law and as he himself was a very prominent worker in the Indian National Congress, he had the confidence of these people. He was assisted by some juniors. Part of the delay was caused by the fact that the accused would, on occasion, when they did not want the trial to proceed, refuse to come to court, and even if one of them refused to come to court on some paltry excuse or the other - he was not feeling very well, or he was suffering from a headache or something like that - under the normal procedure which applied, the trial could not proceed; the trial could only proceed in the presence of the accused and their counsel.

When it was found that the obstruction was not in good faith, amending ordinances had to be passed by the Central Government to permit the trial to proceed when the absence of any accused was not due to some good cause. Nevertheless the trial was so prolonged that it became a mockery of justice. All the Tribunal could do was to see that the trial should be fair, and that no prejudice should be occasioned to the accused. In this it received every assistance from me.

Before the commencement of the trial and after I had studied part of the evidence that was to be read at the trial and of the documentation in the case, I had advised that it would be wise on the part of the government not to proceed with the trial as planned, namely, as a conspiracy trial before a Special Tribunal, but that individual accused persons should be proceeded against in the ordinary courts of the country in respect of the specific offenses that they had committed, and that the conspiracy charges should be dropped.

For instance, Dhanvantri, who was charged with having attempted to murder a police officer, could have been tried in an ordinary court on that charge. The case against him was absolutely clear. The Crown would have produced two or three substantial witnesses, there was practically no defence, and a substantial sentence would have been a certainty.

It is possible that against two or three of the accused specific charges may not have been established to the satisfaction of the court, but that would have happened in any case.

I, myself, was of the opinion that if I was still in charge of the case on behalf of the Crown when charges were to be framed, I would not press the charges against two or three of the accused. With regard to one of them, a situation developed which would illustrate the spirit in which I approached the discharge of my duties in the case. This young man, a Maratha from Maharashtra - his name was Gajenand Sada Shiv Potdar - was found to be suffering from a mastoid and was released on bail for three months. His attendance at the trial was dispensed with. After three months he came back, his health having improved, and he was taken into custody again. After two or three weeks I began to notice that he was not looking very well. He became restless and took little interest in the proceedings. He would sit in the dock on the floor and read a book or would lie down and go to sleep. He was perhaps not very keenly interested in the proceedings in any case. He was one of those people against whom I was not going to press the charge because fairly early in the course of the conspiracy he had dissociated himself from the others, and there was not enough evidence to connect him actively with the conspiracy. Then the problem of his health arose and I felt the youngster was in a difficult position.

I suggested to Dr. Kitchlew, the senior defence Counsel, that he should put in a bail application. He was a bit reluctant, but yielded to my persuasion and put in a bail application. The Tribunal, of course, called on me, whether I had anything to say. I submitted that the application was based on the ground that the young fellow's health was again deteriorating, and that the Tribunal should ask for a report from the jail doctor. The jail doctor's report was full of technicalities and was not easy to follow. Each paragraph seemed to contradict the previous paragraph and the only clear thing was that since his return to custody the young man had been losing weight.

When the report came up and the Tribunal again asked me what I had to say, I submitted that the health of the accused had improved somewhat while he had been away on bail, and now since he had come back into custody, he had been losing weight. That was all we could gather with certainty from the report. We knew he had been suffering from mastoid and there was no evidence that he had been cured of it - there had been no operation. As matters stood, I, on behalf of the Crown, was not prepared to take the responsibility of keeping him in further custody. That left the Tribunal no choice but to admit him to bail.

That, incidentally, happened to be my last day in the case. Sir Fazle Hussain, who was a member of the Governor General's Executive Council, in charge of the Department of Education, Health and Lands, had asked for four months' leave and, no doubt on his advice, the Viceroy had written to me to ask whether I would care to officiate for him during that period. I was then only 39 years of age and considered that this was both a great opportunity for service and a challenge and also a great compliment, and I accepted the offer. I was leaving that evening, and was deeply moved when I received a message from this young fellow from jail, that if by that evening he was released on bail he would come to the railway station to see me off.

At the end of the proceedings on that day, an incident occurred, which was somewhat unusual and which gratified me. The President of the Tribunal made the usual complimentary reference to my not being available any further in the case, and Dr. Kitchlew also made complimentary reference, and then two of the accused stood up in the dock and they wanted to say something. I thought they wanted to seize this opportunity to pitch into me now that I was going to be in the Government of India and they knew that whatever they said would get the widest publicity.

But they associated themselves with what had been said by the President of the Tribunal and by their counsel and added that they were no judges of the legal ability of the Crown Counsel, but wanted to put on record that he had conducted the case on behalf of the Crown like a gentleman. In the annals of criminal jurisprudence, it must be rather unusual, that people whom I was making an honest effort to get put behind prison bars for terms of years should have formed that estimate of the manner in which I was conducting the case on behalf of the Crown.

It was during the pendency of that case that I was able to go to the second Roundtable Conference in the fall of 1931. I had an able junior who acted in my place while I was away. He had assisted me throughout the case and continued to assist my successor till the case came to an end, but he had very little to do in my absence, for I found when I came back and resumed my duties in the case that the first approver, whom I had left in the dock under cross-examination, was still under cross-examination.

Eventually, the Tribunal was dissolved and the accused were sent to the ordinary courts for trial on charges of specific offenses that they had committed.

I happened to be lunching with the then Viceroy, Lord Willingdon, a very gracious personality. He told me, "Oh, my dear, we have taken your advice. We have dissolved the Tribunal, and the accused are now, I understand, being tried under the normal procedure before the normal courts." I replied, "If Your Excellency's government had taken my advice at the time when I gave it, the whole thing would have been settled a couple years earlier, at very much less expense."

Two incidents arising out of the trial may be mentioned. I went over to the accused, who were in the dock and were preparing to go back to jail, and shook hands with each of them. When I shook hands with Dhanvantri, he kept my hand between his for a few seconds, and said, "May I ask you a favour?" I said, "Certainly." He said, "After all this business is over, I will probably have to serve a jail sentence anyhow, but when I am out again will you promise that you will come and meet me?" I said, "Yes, I certainly will." Happening to be up in Srinagar, two or three years later, I learned that his elder brother was Secretary of the Municipal Committee of Srinagar and I got in touch with him. I inquired of him where Dhanvantri was and he told me that he was serving his sentence in jail. Some years later, when I made some further inquiry, I discovered to my regret that he had died. He had served out his sentence and had been released from jail but did not survive for long. So, I was not able to keep my promise.

H.S. Vatsayana, who was an M.Sc. and Gold Medallist in Industrial Chemistry, was the scientist of the party. He came to see me years later, when, after having been for a number of years

REMINISCENCES OF SIR MUHAMMAD ZAFRULLA KHAN       **29**

Minister in the Central Government of India I was judge of the Federal court, which is now the Supreme Court of India. He sent in his card and I recalled the name but thought it must be a different person. But when the caller was shown in, he turned out to be one of the accused in the conspiracy case. We both smiled at each other and I greeted him, and I said, "We meet after many years under very different circumstances." He said, "That is so, and I have come to you with rather an unusual request." "What is your request?" He said, "I have applied for a job in the technical side of All India Radio, and I want to give your name as a reference. Would you be prepared to answer a reference that might be made by All India Radio regarding me?" I said, "I am surprised you should wish to go into government service. Look what you were charged with in that case and how much you hated the British Government, and now you want to become an employee of the British Government." He laughed at that and said, "Well, you see, those were days of youth, and one is apt to be carried away by emotion. One is much more idealistic and all that, and impatient for results. It is different now. There are various ways of working for independence; co-operation is one of them. So will you answer any reference in regard to me?" I said, "Yes, if the reference is made." Eventually a reference was made to me and I was able to say that I had known him as an accused person in a certain case, that he was a very able young man, and that I understood that his thinking was more positive and more constructive now. I do not know whether he got the job, but he seemed to think that he was likely to get it.

**Question**: *I wonder if you would like to mention any of the details on how you happened to be appointed the Crown Counsel in the Delhi Conspiracy Case.*

**Khan:** Shortly after my return from the first Roundtable Conference, I was in Delhi, and the late Sir Fazle Hussain mentioned the case to me in a few words, saying there was likely to be a prosecution of this kind, and that his colleague in the Home Department, Sir James Crarer, had asked him to suggest a couple of names of members of the bar who might be prepared to take up the case on behalf of the Crown. Sir Fazle Hussain told me that he had mentioned my name and that it was possible that I might receive a request to that effect, in which case it would be for me to consider whether it suited me to take it on or not.

**30**     REMINISCENCES OF SIR MUHAMMAD ZAFRULLA KHAN

Some time later I was attending a meeting of the Punjab Legislative Council at Lahore when Sir Donald Boyd, who was then a member of the Provincial Government, asked to see me and conveyed the Central Government's request to me. I agreed to take on the case. That was how the appointment came about.

**Question**: *May we now turn to a reconsideration of the interruption in the Delhi Conspiracy Case, or in broader terms, the second Roundtable Conference and the negotiations which went on at that time?*

**Khan**: The second Roundtable Conference which was convened during the fall of 1931, again in London, had this advantage, that the Viceroy, Lord Irwin, who subsequently succeeded his father to the viscountcy of Halifax and became Lord Halifax, had, in the meantime, succeeded in persuading the Congress that it should be represented at the Roundtable Conference. He negotiated with Mr. Gandhi, and the agreement to which they came is known as the Gandhi-Irwin Pact.

In pursuance of this agreement, Mr. Gandhi procured from the Congress the mandate of being the sole representative of the Congress in the second Roundtable Conference, and when the conference opened Mr. Gandhi was also present in London and thus the representation of all parties in the conference was completed.

Great hopes and expectations were raised by the participation of Mr. Gandhi in the Roundtable Conference, both with regard to a settlement being reached between the two major communities - the Muslims and the Hindus - and also with regard to a settlement between India and Great Britain on independence or responsible self-government.

Mrs. Sarojini Naidu, who was anxious to bring about a settlement between Hindus and Muslims and who was equally respected in both communities and was a personal friend of Mr. Gandhi, started the effort to bring about a meeting between Mr. Gandhi and the Muslim delegation to the conference. Eventually, a meeting was arranged in the suite of His Highness, the Aga Khan, in the Ritz Hotel in Piccadilly.

Mr. Gandhi arrived and we all rose as a mark of respect and received him standing. We had been sitting informally anyhow. The Aga Khan and everybody else offered his seat to Mr. Gandhi, but with a smile he declined and said he would prefer to be seated on the

## REMINISCENCES OF SIR MUHAMMAD ZAFRULLA KHAN 31

floor. Despite our insistence that he should sit on a sofa or in an armchair, he persisted he would be much more comfortable on the floor.

So he sat on the floor and some of us also, out of deference to him, did the same. He had brought in an attractive mahogany case in his hand, which he was holding by its handle. It looked like a radio set, but obviously it could not have been one as there would be no purpose in Mr. Gandhi bringing a radio set with him.

After returning all greetings, he very deliberately opened this box and brought out of it an ingeniously-constructed spinning wheel, a much smaller one than the ones used in India, which could fold into a small case. He set it up with great deliberation and the whole performance drew everybody's attention. We began to hope that a settlement between the Hindus and the Muslims might emerge from the spinning wheel.

Then he started spinning on the wheel. After he had drawn out a string or two, he indicated that he was ready to talk. He explained that eager, and, indeed, anxious as he was to come to a settlement with his brethren, the Muslims, and to that end was prepared to accede to whatever they might wish for as safeguards in the future constitution of an independent India, he was acting under a disability. Before he had left India, he had made a promise to Dr. Ansari, who was the most prominent Muslim member of the Congress, that he would not come to any settlement on these questions in his absence. Therefore, before considering anything that may be proposed he would require Dr. Ansari's advice and assistance. He suggested that the Muslim delegation to the Roundtable Conference should make a request to the Secretary of State for India to invite Dr. Ansari to come to London as a delegate to the Roundtable Conference.

That raised a very difficult question. After a settlement had been reached between Lord Irwin and Mr. Gandhi that the Congress would be represented in the second Roundtable Conference, and it had been announced that the Congress had given a mandate to Mr. Gandhi to be their sole representative, efforts were made presumably on behalf of the Congress that Dr. Ansari - a prominent Congress leader and a very respected figure indeed - should also be invited as a Muslim representative.

To this there had been fierce opposition on the part of some leading Muslim delegates who had participated in the first

32    REMINISCENCES OF SIR MUHAMMAD ZAFRULLA KHAN

Roundtable Conference and some who were invited to the second. They had no objection to Dr. Ansari, or any other Muslim member of the Congress, being invited so long as it was understood that they would participate in the conference as representatives of the Congress and not as representatives-at-large of the Muslim community.

What these gentlemen who took objection to Dr. Ansari's being invited in that capacity feared was that this would blur the Muslim stand on certain important matters and they were not willing to run that risk.

In the end Dr. Ansari was not invited. Those who had opposed Dr. Ansari's being invited had made it plain through public statements that if Congress chose to be represented by 100 delegates, they could send 99 Congress Muslims as members of their delegation, to that they had no objection. But that no Muslim member of the Congress should be invited as a representative of the Muslim community.

So the difficulty with what might appear to be a very reasonable request, made very politely by Mr. Gandhi, was that it put the Muslims in a dilemma. After having opposed Dr. Ansari's being invited for them now to go to the Secretary of State with the request that he should be invited would, to say the very least, be very embarrassing.

This went on for about half an hour, with Mr. Gandhi insisting that he could not discuss these matters in the absence of Dr. Ansari - he had given him his word - and the Muslims re-iterating that it confronted them with a very embarrassing situation. At this stage I thought perhaps I might venture to participate in the discussion. I was still one of the junior members of the delegation and did not feel that I should put myself forward out of turn, but an idea struck me and I asked Mr. Gandhi's permission to let me put it forward. As he very graciously assented I suggested that we should carry on the discussion, and that if we saw that we were likely to arrive at an agreement, we could then, Mr. Gandhi, as well as ourselves, transmit a request to Dr. Ansari that he should kindly come over and join in the discussion, so that an agreement might be reached. I added, "I would venture to submit respectfully that an invitation from us, that is to say from Mr. Gandhi and ourselves together, would be a matter of greater satisfaction to Dr. Ansari than to be invited by the representative of what Mr. Gandhi has so often described as the Satanic government."

Mr. Gandhi smiled at this and indicated his willingness to proceed with the conversations. The conversations occupied two or three meetings. The upshot was this: Mr. Gandhi said that on what were in those days known as the "Fourteen Points of Mr. Jinnah," and Mr. Jinnah, of course, was participating in the discussions, he was ready to agree. In fact, he had not much objection to any of them, except one, and some of them he welcomed, and that therefore on those there was not much difficulty. But that one of them, namely, the continuation of the system of separate electorates in the legislative bodies in India - a certain number of seats being reserved for a particular community to be filled by people elected only by the voters of that community, he felt great difficulty. He thought this was a harmful system, it tended to keep the two sides apart, and led to other undesirable consequences. But that was not what stood in the way of his agreeing to it. If the Muslims thought that it was a safeguard that they needed, and insisted upon its retention though he thought it would not be a happy solution of that particular aspect of the problem, he would nevertheless agree, but there was his promise to Dr. Ansari, that he would not come to any decision particularly on this matter without consulting him.

What was to be done? Again, it was, after a good deal of discussion, that I asked Mr. Gandhi's permission to put one or two questions so that I could get the position clear in my own mind. He again nodded gracious consent, and I said, "Sir, supposing we send for Dr. Ansari and Dr. Ansari agrees to come, and as you have very kindly said, you, despite your own disinclination, urge upon Dr. Ansari that in the interests of an agreement, you were prepared to agree and that he should also agree, and that you would even plead with him to accept the proposal, and supposing he said, 'Sir, I am devoted to you, as you know very well, and if an occasion arose for me to lay down my life for you, I would do it very readily and would be very happy to do it, but this is not a question of any personal sacrifice. I honestly and sincerely believe that this system is harmful to India and is also harmful to the interests of the Muslims, of who I am one. this is a trust on behalf of the people of India including the Muslims, and I cannot betray that trust by agreeing to something which I honestly consider is harmful,' what would be your attitude?"

He said, "My attitude would be that I would then support his position." I continued, "Supposing in the meantime the Muslims in the Congress held a meeting and they cabled you, 'In the interests of an agreement, we urge that this should be accepted' would that affect your position, if Dr. Ansari still continued his opposition?" He said, "No. I would still be with Dr. Ansari." Finally, I said, "Sir, if the position were reversed, supposing Dr. Ansari, as a result of your pleading and our pleading also if it became necessary, was willing to agree as you are willing to agree, reluctantly but in the interests of agreement, but all the other Muslims in the Congress sent you an urgent message that this should not be accepted, what would be your position?" he smiled and said, "I would still be with Dr. Ansari."

So it became clear that the final decision rested not so much with Mr. Gandhi, but with Dr. Ansari, though Mr. Gandhi was prepared to use his influence and his powers of persuasion with Dr. Ansari to persuade him to agree.

We put this aside for the moment, and proceeded to discuss the remaining safeguards. Mr. Gandhi intimated that he had no objection to any of them. He was doubtful with regard to the feasibility of some of them but he was quite willing to go forward with them. This position was reached at the end of the second or third meeting, and we then asked Mr. Gandhi to tell us what was it that he would require of the Muslim Delegation in support of the common cause. He said he would send us his proposals later.

Three or four days later a sheet of notepaper arrived from him written out in pencil on both sides with no beginning or end indicating what the document was, but stating simply in its first part the Congress demand for complete independence, including control of the armed forces and finances, and elaborating some aspects of independence to make sure there would be no reservations. We considered that if our position could be reasonably safeguarded we would have no difficulty in supporting the demand as elaborated.

What we felt worried about was the concluding proposal that the Muslim delegation should oppose any special arrangements or safeguards being provided in the constitution for the depressed classes, who were then generally described as the scheduled castes. We discussed this among ourselves and decided that this would be a very inconsistent position for us to take up. It was true that the Muslims were, as compared with the Hindus, in a very much weaker position in industry, commerce, education, training and everything

## REMINISCENCES OF SIR MUHAMMAD ZAFRULLA KHAN

else, but, as compared with the scheduled castes, we were more numerous, we were better educated, we enjoyed a better standard of living, we had some share in commerce, and if we had found it necessary to insist upon a set of safeguards for ourselves, then how could we justifiably take up a stand along with Mr. Gandhi as representing the Congress, that no safeguards were necessary for a community which was in a very much weaker position than ourselves.

So after a good deal of discussion, backwards and forwards, we decided to inform Mr. Gandhi that in case our demands were conceded, we would be very glad to take the position that any arrangement with regard to the scheduled castes was an internal matter for the Hindu community, because Mr. Gandhi had insisted that any special arrangements provided for the scheduled castes would disrupt Hindu society. We were prepared to adopt the position that they were a part of Hindu society, and that, therefore, it was a domestic matter for Hindu society to decide among themselves, and that whatever they agreed upon between themselves, we would accept, but that we could not take up the position that in our view no safeguards were needed for the depressed classes. After all, they had put themselves forward as a distinct and separate entity for the purpose of political representation and allied matters. How could we take up the position that they must be treated as part of Hindu society, and that no separate consideration should be given to their case?

It was on this that the conversations broke up. Mr. Gandhi was irrevocably opposed to any special arrangement for the scheduled castes. It will be recalled that subsequently, when the so-called "communal award" was published in July or August of 1932, he started what was called, "a fast unto death" in protest. Then the leaders of the scheduled castes and the Hindu leaders, who were all very fearful that Mahatma Gandhi would carry his fast right through to the bitter end, got together at Poona, where he was fasting, and a settlement was reached between them. That was accepted by all concerned, and that was how the matter was settled.

Mr. Gandhi's feeling on that matter was extremely strong and thus no settlement could be reached between us, not because he was opposed to any of our demands - at least he professed he was willing to accept them and would plead for their acceptance by the Congress - but because he could not reconcile himself to special arrangements by which separate representation and other safeguards would be provided for the scheduled castes.

**Question**: *Mr. Ambassador, I note that you were elected President of the All India Muslim League. Would you like to go into the details of that particular event?*

**Khan**: There is nothing much to it. The All India Muslim League was not a very active or forceful organization in those years. They held their annual sessions, elected a President, who continued as President for one year, and I was elected in December of 1931, as President of the League. The session was held in Delhi. I proceeded to Delhi and delivered my address, and presided over the Session. A number of resolutions were adopted.

I cannot now recall details for the topics with which I dealt in my address, but I am sure I touched on the set of safeguards that we were working for in the Roundtable Conferences. During the remaining five or six months that I continued as President, that is till June of 1932, when I joined the Government of India, and could not continue my connection with any political party and thus had to resign the presidentship, I carried on the effort to bring the two Muslim organizations - the All Parties Muslim Conference and the All India Muslim League - together. There was no justification for two separate Muslim organizations which were pursuing the same ends and objectives. There was nothing on which they differed, so far as their objectives were concerned; only some of the personalities were more prominent in one organization than in the other, even though the personalities were more or less common to both. I had hopes that I would be able to put an end to this duality in our political representation, but my appointment to the Governor-General's Executive Council put an end to that effort.

In the end, the League survived and the All Parties Muslim Conference sort of lost itself in the sands, but there was no amalgamation of the two. The League was then revived and revivified by Mr. Jinnah and became a very active political instrument under his leadership.

**Question**: *Mr. Ambassador, I would now like to ask you a little about the Viceroy's Executive Council and how you came to be a member of it, how it actually worked, what the personalities were like, how much of the business of the government of India was transacted there, how did the Viceroy use it, and so on.*

**Khan**: At this stage, perhaps I had better confine myself to my officiating period in the Viceroy's Executive Council in 1932, from June to October.

At that time, the Muslim member of the Viceroy's Executive Council was Sir Fazle Hussain. The Council was composed of eight members: three Indians, three Europeans, the Commander-in-Chief, who was always a member of Council in those days, and the Viceroy himself. Out of the three Indians, one used to be a Muslim. This had happened gradually. The first Indian was appointed in 1909. Up to then no Indian had been appointed a member of Council since the time of Warren Hastings, when the Council had been constituted in 1772. The first Indian appointed was the late Lord Sinha.

Later, when the number of Indian members was increased to three, the first Muslim, Sir Ali Imam, was appointed to the Executive Council. He was from Bihar and he was succeeded by Sir Muhammad Shafi from the Punjab. Sir Muhammad Shafi was succeeded by Sir Muhammad Habibullah from Madras, who was succeeded by Sir Fazle Hussain, again from the Punjab. Sir Fazle Hussain was appointed in April, 1930, and held office until April, 1935. His health had not been very good, even when he was Minister and later Revenue Member in the Punjab. He had developed some affliction of the throat. It was not cancer and he did not die of it, but it was a troublesome complaint which caused difficulty in breathing and sometimes put his temperature up when he had to take to bed. He carried on despite this serious handicap.

In the summer of 1932, however, he felt that he must have some respite if he was to carry on at all. So he decided to take four months' leave, which was permissible to members of the Governor-General's Executive Council. The then Viceroy, Lord Willingdon, had known me, as we had worked together on the Consultative Committee which had been set up between the second and third Roundtable Conference in Delhi to carry on the work of the Roundtable Conference and of which the Viceroy was Chairman. That Committee came to an end after two or three sittings, as no progress could be made on account of the fact that as the communal award had not yet been announced, the Muslims did not know what their position would be in the new constitution and, therefore, they could not come to final decisions on several aspects of the matters that were to be discussed.

It was not the Viceroy's choice that I should officiate for Sir Fazle Hussain. I am sure it was Sir Fazle Hussain's insistence that if he was to get any benefit from his leave, he should have somebody holding his place in his absence in whom he could place confidence, that the Viceroy was persuaded to nominate me.

The news of the appointment was as much a surprise to me as it was to the greater number of those who were interested in these matters. Though I had been a member of the Punjab Legislative Council since 1926 and had been to England to present the Muslim point of view to British statesmen and politicians, and had taken part in the first and second Roundtable Conferences, I was still so young that the appointment was looked upon as a departure from the normal practice.

I was extremely gratified that it should have been considered that I was fit to carry such a heavy responsibility. I took it up, as it were, in a state of fear and trembling, but very prayerfully determined, that with God's grace, I should not be found wanting.

The headquarters of the Government of India had moved up to Simla. I left Delhi in the evening and went up to Lahore by train. Sir Fazle Hussain had come down to Lahore from Simla on his way to Abbottabad where he was to spend his leave, and I met him in Lahore. I asked him whether he had any instructions for me, on policy or on particular questions or problems. He told me it was all up to me and that I would have to sink or swim on my own. He mentioned one matter on which he had not been able to persuade the Viceroy to agree with him, and thought I might make an effort. Sir Frank Noyce had been Secretary of the Ministry and had just been appointed Member of the Viceroy's Council in charge of Industry and Labour and thus the post of Secretary had fallen vacant. Sir Fazle Hussain had prevailed upon a somewhat reluctant Viceroy to agree to the appointment of Sir Girja Shankar Bajpai in place of Sir Frank Noyce. But Sir Girja Shankar suffered from high blood pressure, and the Viceroy, in a sort of rear-guard action, had made it a condition that Sir Girja Shankar should produce a clean bill of health. He had proceeded on leave to Vienna for treatment and also to obtain the necessary testimonial on his health.

In the meantime, Mr. Reed, who was the next senior officer in the Ministry, had been appointed officiating Secretary. The next officer in seniority was Mr. Ram Chandra from the Punjab. Sir Fazle Hussain said that he had tried, that when Bajpai became Secretary,

## REMINISCENCES OF SIR MUHAMMAD ZAFRULLA KHAN

Ram Chandra should become Joint Secretary, and that would have meant either sending Reed back to his province (he belonged to the UP cadre of the Indian Civil Service) or superseding him. The Viceroy had not agreed.

It was part of Sir Fazle Hussain's policy that wherever possible he would promote Indianization of the superior posts so that Indians could get more and more experience in view of the greater responsibility that they would later have to carry. It was as part of this effort that he was anxious that Ram Chandra rather than Reed should be Joint Secretary.

Incidentally, I was able to arrange that. The Viceroy was not too unhappy over the arrangement I proposed and he agreed.

That night I left for Kalka by train, and next morning from Kalka, I travelled by car up to Simla. I was accompanied by Khan Bahadur Nadir Shah, who was Sir Fazle Hussain's very experienced personal assistant. He was a Parsi gentleman, and was a good friend of mine - I had known him quite intimately during the period he had been working with Sir Fazle Hussain.

Nadir Shah and I were in the car together, and after we settled down in the car and it began to climb the winding hill road - it was about 65 miles to Simla - I asked Nadir Shah to tell me how official business was transacted. He explained the mechanics to me - how files came in and how they were disposed of, down even to the detail that any orders I wrote or dictated, needed only to be initialled by me adding the date and the month. I still remember his saying, "Your full signature is required only on very formal documents like dispatches, etc. and on your monthly salary bill. So long as you can do that, everything will be all right." Afterwards, when anybody asked me, "What do you think are the qualifications necessary for a Member of Council?" I used to say that it seemed that the qualifications necessary were that one should remember the date and the month and should be able to sign one's salary bill with one's full name!

In Simla, of course, I occupied the official residence of Sir Fazle Hussain. It was called the Retreat and was situated in a very favourable position, on the Mall, almost opposite to the principal hotel in Simla, the Cecil Hotel. It was a comfortable residence. All the Members' residences were attractive houses, nicely furnished. As soon as we arrived at the house, I asked Nadir Shah to ring up Mr. Ram Chandra and ask him to come down to the residence. Mr. Ram

Chandra was well known to me. He had done his M.A. from the Government College at Lahore and had been appointed temporary Assistant Professor of mathematics. I was then in my intermediate class, and mathematics was one of my subjects. So I had the honour of sitting at his feet for a few weeks, till he was awarded the State Scholarship and proceeded to England for higher studies. While in England he was selected for the ICS and was now Joint Secretary in the Department. The offices where this particular ministry was located were not very far, a five-minutes' walk from the house. He came along and we greeted each other and I said, "Mr. Ram Chandra, you taught me a little of mathematics and now you have to teach me the arithmetic of this place." So he gave me some further information on the mechanics of the department.

Presently, there was a telephone call from Mr. Reed to Nadir Shah asking him when should he call and when should the other officers in the department call. I might mention that a Member of the Governor-General's Executive Council was, so to speak, one of the galaxy of stars around the Viceroy. The Viceroy was the luminary of the political heaven of India, and he and the six Members of Council and the Commander-in-Chief exercised, subject only to the Control of the Secretary of State for India in London, absolute authority over the whole vast domain, which included not only what are today India and Pakistan but also Burma. Everybody looked up to the Members and the old traditions still applied in full force though there were now three Indian Members. The same deference and respect was shown to them as to the English members. Having been suddenly called to that position, I felt I had to safeguard myself against any tendency towards inflation of my ego.

So I asked Nadir Shah to tell Mr. Reed that he was not required to call nor were the officers required to call, that I would be in my room in Gorton Castle next morning at 10 O'clock, and that I would be grateful if Mr. Reed would meet me in my room, and then take me round to each officer to whom I would introduce myself, and that I would follow that procedure through with the Assistant Secretaries, the Superintendents Assistants, and the clerks. This meant greeting and shaking hands with a few hundred people, but I was determined to carry it through.

Nadir Shah protested, "Well, Sir, if these are your orders, I will tell Mr. Reed that, but it is not done! Officers call on the Member and that is the end of the business. Others, if they have any official business can ask for leave to come up, and they come up on business, but it is unthinkable that the Member should himself call on the officers, and not only on the officers, but also the non-Gazetted officers and the clerks and everybody."

I said, "I suppose it is a matter within my own discretion, is it not?" "Yes, Sir." "Well then, that is my decision." That was my first break with tradition.

The next one was another small matter, but it will give some idea of how insulated and rigid the whole system was. Simla is a hill station clinging to the mountain side and its roads are narrow, winding and, in certain points, precipitous. Only the Viceroy, the Commander-in-Chief and the Governor of the Punjab (Simla was also the summer headquarters of the Punjab Government) and perhaps one or two other high officials were permitted to use cars, and the cars had to proceed very slowly for the roads were not only narrow but there were no footpaths for pedestrians and people walked along the roads; in fact the roads were mainly for walking. The only other means of transportation were riding a pony or being pulled along in a rickshaw. Visitors who come for a short stay in Simla hired rickshaws like taxis. Those who were permanent residents for the season generally had their own private rickshaws with a set of four, and sometimes six men to pull and push the rickshaw. Those in front pulled and those behind pushed. They were a fairly comfortable means of transport and trained rickshaw coolies, as they were called, could take one fairly fast from one place to another, especially if they were going down a gentle incline where they could proceed at a fairly fast pace. Rickshaw coolies propelling private rickshaws wore uniforms, suttees on the shins, breeches, and long jackets down to the knees with a broad belt around the waist, and across the breast-piece the initial of the owner. Turbans covered their heads. Mine, I remember, wore wine coloured jackets with a bright yellow Z across the breast. Everybody told me it looked like a streak of lightning against that background, especially when the rickshaw was proceeding at a fast pace and the bodies of the coolies swing up and down.

When I was not in a hurry and the distance was not long, I preferred to walk. There again I was told I was breaking tradition; no Member of Council was supposed to walk, but if he chose to walk the rickshaw must follow immediately behind him, as a sort of insignia of the member. I did not choose to conform.

I remember one day when I was walking along from my house to the office, Sir Launcelot Graham, who was then Law Secretary and later became Governor of Sind, was passing on a pony. He greeted me and said, "You are breaking a tradition." I asked, "Which one, Sir Launcelot?" He replied, "Why, you are walking and your rickshaw is not following you." I enquired, "What do you think God has provided me with a pair of legs for?" He passed on with a smile.

In regard to the discharge of my duties, looking back now over more than 30 years of public life, I may say that I wielded a firmer pen during those four months than I did later at any time. It may have been due to an inner determination that I would always make my view clear and would set it forth as cogently and strongly as the occasion demanded.

My portfolio included a bewildering variety of subjects, the principal ones being Education, Health, Lands, Archaeology, Indians overseas (for instance, Indians in South Africa); and various Surveys of India. As a matter of fact, all miscellaneous subjects were shoved into what was called E.H.L. I was told that at one time the Department used to be called H.E.L., which occasionally raised a laugh at the expense of the Minister, so the nomenclature was re-arranged and the Department was described as Education, Health and Lands, making the abbreviation E.H.L. instead of H.E.L.

The most interesting part of my work during those four months was that the major dispatches of the Government of India on the proposed constitutional reforms which were then under the consideration of His Majesty's Government in London went through the Council during my four months' tenure of office. The recom-mendations of the Government of India on the communal award had already been made, but they had not yet been approved by His Majesty's Government. Within a few days of my taking over charge, the comments of the Secretary of State for India on the communal award were received, and were circulated to the Members. When I saw what they were, I was very disturbed and felt that my tenure of office was not likely to last for four months and might come to an end within a week or so. I was determined that if the changes that the Secretary of State had proposed were insisted upon by his Majesty's Government and were adhered to, I would not continue in the Council, and would resign. Sir Fazle Hussain had been a Member of Council when the original proposals had gone through, and now they were to be modified much to the prejudice of the

Muslims. I was not prepared to assume responsibility for the suggested modifications as Member of Council.

I asked for an interview with the Viceroy and told him that I was not prepared to accept the modifications proposed by the Secretary of State, and that they created a very difficult situation for me. If the original proposals of the Government of India were not approved by His Majesty's Government, I would have to go. I also sent an immediate verbal message to Sir Fazle Hussain at Abbottabad explaining the situation to him and adding that I would fight as hard as I knew how but that if I did not succeed, I would resign.

The Viceroy was very sympathetic and kind. Lord Willingdon was a very understanding man and it was India's great good fortune that at that juncture in its history, he was the man at the top. He told me he would speak to the Home Member - Sir Harry Haig - and to Sir Philip Chetwood, the Commander-in-Chief and he was sure they would take the view that we cannot afford any disturbance of what was discussed at great length in Council. "Ours was a compromise proposal, the only one that would work, and except for a minor change here or there, which could be justified on the merits, we would refuse to accept any modification. I shall stand by the old proposals. That would make three of us, and, of course, if you are of that opinion, that will make four. That would mean an even division, even if all the others should be unwilling to support the old proposals and should push for major changes, which I doubt, I would then use my casting vote and we would go back to the Secretary of State and I am sure he would give way. I should not take too dim a view of the situation if I were you."

That was comforting, and a meeting was called for that very evening. The Viceroy managed that meeting with consummate skill. It was his habit not to start on the agenda immediately on meeting. As he walked into the Cabinet room he would welcome each of us and put us at our ease. If any of us had been away he would chat with him for a minute and ask some personal question, or address an observation to one or the other round the table. He was on a first-name basis with everybody which is more an American rather than a British habit, especially in high office. He addressed everybody either by their personal name or as "My dear," so that one felt completely at home with him.

Well, when we had all arrived and the first greetings were over, he turned to his private secretary, Sir Eric Mieville, who

## 44    REMINISCENCES OF SIR MUHAMMAD ZAFRULLA KHAN

subsequently became assistant private secretary to the King at Buckingham Palace, and enquired what the business for the day was. Mieville explained that the business was the Secretary of State's telegram on the communal award. "Oh," he said, "Yes, yes. Well, now, my dears, as you know, this is a very troublesome business, and I think we would better start with an understanding, if we are to get through this evening's business within reasonable time, and that is that we should agree that unless the Secretary of State should have given some very good reason for any change that he proposes, we shall adhere to our original recommendations. Is that all right?" It was all right, and we proceeded.

I might say here that later when I went to the third Roundtable Conference in England, I learned that it was not the Secretary of State who had proposed the modifications: the modifications had been proposed at the insistence of the Prime Minister, Mr. Ramsay MacDonald. I had been surprised that Sir Samuel Hoare, a good friend who understood the Muslim case very well should have made these suggestions.

The suggestions were that in the Provinces in which the Muslims were in a minority, the Muslim representation may be increased by one seat here and two seats there, which would be of no benefit to the Muslims because they would still remain a minority. In the two major provinces, i.e., the Punjab and Bengal where the Muslims were a majority in the population, it was proposed that Muslim representation should be reduced by two or three seats. The result would be that in the Punjab we would lose our majority of one or two seats that the Government of India had recommended and in Bengal we would go even below 48 percent that had been recommended.

After getting agreement on principle the Viceroy asked, "Well, now, what does he propose with regard to Madras?" In Madras the Secretary of State had proposed two extra seats for the Muslims, but no reason had been given for the change. The Viceroy asked me, "Do you want these two extra seats for the Muslims in Madras?" I said I did not want these extra seats, provided, no reduction was made in the number of our seats elsewhere.

We all agreed on that. Of the four women's seats in Madras, one was proposed to be earmarked for Muslim women. We all agreed on that. The Viceroy then took up the case of each Muslim minority Province where any extra seat or seats were proposed for the Muslims and obtained from me an intimation that I did not want the extra seat or seats. Thus by the time we got to Bengal and the Punjab the Council was committed to the position that the Muslims would not have any extra seats in the Muslim minority provinces, which implied that their representation in the Muslim majority provinces would not be reduced. In the case of the Punjab, no difficulty was raised and the Council agreed that the original recommendation should be adhered to.

On Bengal, there was a good deal of discussion. In Bengal in the old Legislative Council, we had only 28 percent of the total number of seats, and that was because in the Bengal legislature quite a large proportion of the seats had been allotted to special interests. The European representation was 10 percent and it had to come out both of the Hindu and Muslim seats. Then there was the university representation, industry representation, representation for commerce, etc. in which the Muslim share was almost nil. Under the Lucknow Pact, the Muslims had been given 40 percent of the general seats. Thus with 40 percent only of the general seats, and failing to get more than a seat or two of the special seats, they ended up with 28 percent of the total house in a province in which they were a majority in the population. This position has to be corrected.

Now that the principle was accepted that, as far as possible, communities were to be represented according to their population strength - some weightage to the minorities - Muslim representation had to be substantially increased and the change appeared very big.

The Bengali Member of Council was Sir B.L. Milter. He was the Law Minister and a good personal friend of mine. We continued good friends right to the end of our association, not only in Council but also later when he became Attorney General and I went to the Supreme Court. Naturally, he put forward the Hindu case for Bengal and I put forward the Muslim case. The upshot was that the original recommendation, from which both Sir Fazle Hussain and Sir. B.L. Milter had dissented was adhered to, subject to Sir B.L. Milter's dissent on behalf of the Hindus and my dissent on behalf of the Muslims who, though a majority in Bengal, were to get only 48 percent representation.

Thus the original proposals were sent back and His Majesty's Government agreed to them. This apportionment of seats in Provincial Legislatures became known as the Communal Award.

This is an illustration of the type of despatches that were passing from the Government of India to the Secretary of State. Of course, they were not all so... controversial. I remember the very first day I arrived in Simla there was a Council meeting and the item on the agenda was the "Military Despatch," which had been prepared by the Commander-in-Chief's staff. The Commander-in-Chief was Sir Philip Chetwood and his Chief of Staff was General Wigram, who was rated very highly in military circles.

The time was short and I knew little of the subject-matter of the Despatch. I read it with care and made a pencil-mark in the margin where I felt an improvement was possible. In the Cabinet meeting the Despatch was taken paragraph by paragraph and, barring an explanatory observation by Sir Philip or General Wigram, there was scarcely a comment. The Despatch dealt with a highly specialized subject. Presently we came to a paragraph opposite which I had made a mark and on which I had something to say. Having joined the Council only that day I was the junior-most Member and did not know how my comment might be received. I made my comment with some diffidence but felt encouraged by the fact that Sir Philip Chetwood was looking at me with interest and General Wigram who sat behind, was smiling and nodding his head in assent. Then I saw him whisper something into Sir Philip's ear, and the Commander-in-Chief said, "That is quite acceptable to us. We think this is an improvement."

As the discussion proceeded other Members made an occasional comment, but I was the one who made more comments than anybody else round the table. I began to fear my senior colleagues might think I was being officious. But every time, the same thing happened. The Commander-in-Chief and General Wigram readily accepted my suggestions. I felt greatly encouraged. From that day onwards, even after his retirement, Sir Philip (later Lord Chetwood) was a very good friend. From my point of view, all this was very educative; it widened my horizon. This was my first practical experience in public affairs. I found myself among people who had been steeped in these matters for years and I learned from them. In my own Department, all my officers were happy with me. They were very cooperative. I do not recall any serious differences with any of them.

On the 8th of August, Mr. (later Sir) Girja Shankar Bajpai came back from Vienna having already submitted a clean bill of health. I mentioned this to the Viceroy and recorded an Order appointing Bajpai Secretary of the Department. I was also able to adjust matters between Reed and Ram Chandra. Reed was appointed Joint

## REMINISCENCES OF SIR MUHAMMAD ZAFRULLA KHAN

Secretary till Sir Fazle Hussain's return from leave, he was then to go on leave and on return from leave would revert to his Province. Ram Chandra was to go on leave till Reed left on leave and would then become Joint Secretary. The Viceroy approved.

A slight difference arose between General McGaw, who was Director-General of the IMS and me. The post of Deputy Health Commissioner of India fell vacant and a Colonel Russell from Madras was recommended for appointment. Papers were put up to me with that recommendation and I noticed that at one place Sir Fazle Hussain had noted that it was time that there should be Indian representation at the Headquarters of the Indian Medical Department in the Government of India. I thought I had better carry the matter a little further and I asked General McGaw to come over.

He came in and I asked him whether something could be done in that direction. He told me that for the moment nothing could be done, as there was this vacancy and Colonel Russell was the best qualified man for it. I told him I would be glad to support his recommendation but could we say that when the next vacancy arose he would be prepared to consider a duly-qualified, senior Indian officer for appointment? He said he could not bind the hands of his successor. I said, "Very good, General, I will do the binding. Thank you, good morning," and he went out.

I then sent for the Deputy Secretary, Mr. Hydari, who dealt with these matters when they came up from the IMS side. He was the son of Sir Akbar Hydari, the Prime Minister of Hyderabad, and both of them were good friends of mine.

We put our heads together and we selected three Indian officers of the I.M.S. who possessed the necessary qualifications and would soon attain the necessary seniority. One of them, Major Ganapati, was the son-in-law of Sir Hari Singh Gour, who was a well-known lawyer in the Central Provinces and had been a member of the Roundtable Conference. Major Ganapati eventually succeeded Colonel Russell in this post.

Having fortified myself with these names, the next time I went up to the Viceroy, I broached the matter with him. When I mentioned Colonel Russell's name, he said, "Oh, my dear, I hope you approve of him, I knew him when I was Governor of Madras and I think he is an excellent officer."

I told him I was prepared to recommend Colonel Russell, but that I wanted to mention in my recommendation the names of two or three Indian officers in the Indian Medical Service, who were Majors but would soon be Colonels, and that when the occasion arose one of them should be considered for appointment at the Headquarters of the I.M.S. He agreed and I recorded an order adding, "H.E. approves" and that was the end of the matter.

I was later told by Hydari that when the file went back to General McGaw, he was very upset and he went to Mr. Hydari and said, "I want to request an interview with the Viceroy. I want to protest against the Order of the Minister." The Deputy Secretary told him that he would put up his request to see the Viceroy and that he was sure I would not stop him from seeing the Viceroy, but that the Viceroy having given his approval was not likely to change his mind.

I suppose General McGaw was chagrined, but he did not show it to me. When he left India he was appointed Medical Adviser to the Secretary of State in the India Office. He wrote a book on his experience in the IMS in India. He inscribed a copy for me and gave it to me during one of my visits to England.

Mr. Hydari continued to climb the official ladder, became Joint Secretary and then Secretary and, after independence, was appointed Governor of Assam. He died of heart failure while holding that office. He was a very capable officer.

Outside the department, on one occasion, I came into conflict with Sir Allan Parsons, who was officiating as Finance Minister in place of Sir George Shuster, who was away on leave. Parsons was known in his Department as "the Sultan," meaning he was very autocratic. A file went to Finance from our side with Reed's note. Parsons wrote a rather severe note on it and it came back to us. Reed came to me with almost tears in his eyes, showed me the noting and asked whether I could do something to help. I asked him to leave the file with me. I took it home and dictated a rather strong note, making out a defence for poor Reed as well as I could. I think I was able to make out a plausible case. I sent this along to Parsons with a covering letter suggesting that he should write a fresh note omitting the offending paragraph in which case my enclosed note need not go on the file, but that if he could not see his way to accepting my suggestion my note would go on record. Within an hour I received a letter from him stating that he had taken his note

# REMINISCENCES OF SIR MUHAMMAD ZAFRULLA KHAN

off the file and substituted a new one omitting the particular paragraph.

These matters were bureaucratic routine and illustrate how there was no joint responsibility, as understood in a Cabinet. The Legislature could discuss, criticise, obstruct, pass resolutions and amend or reject official measures but it could not vote ministers out of office. The whole system had become unrealistic and anachronistic. In the Cabinet, Lord Willingdon very often obtained unanimous decisions. In one case out of ten, a vote was taken and majority decision was reached. His method of work was that the Member within whose portfolio the item under discussion was included, gave a brief account of it and made his presentation. Anybody who felt impelled asked a question or made a comment; and a friendly discussion took place. In most cases, an understanding was soon reached and the matter was disposed of accordingly. Failing this a vote had to be taken.

Lord Linlithgrow's method was more formal and rigid. He was a very able man. The Archbishop of Canterbury, later Lord Lang, once remarked to me, "You know, Linlithgow with twice the ability of Willingdon is not half as successful a Viceroy." He lacked the human touch. He wanted everything regulated along the prescribed lines. As soon as he had taken over, he intimated that Members should attend Council meetings in cutaway suits. We conformed, but soon we were overtaken by the war and then we rebelled.

Sir James Grigg, who had succeeded Sir George Shuster as Finance Member, and loathed all ceremonial, had a word with me and we let Sir Gilbert Laithwaite know that we were too busy to spend time over changes of clothes in preparation for and on return from Cabinet meetings. We heard no more about it.

His method was that as soon as we were seated, he would announce the first item on the agenda and ask for comments round the table in strict order of seniority. Each Member formulated his view and became committed to it, so that differences arose, discussion was prolonged, and the Viceroy's desire to obtain unanimity was defeated. Counting of votes became the rule. If only he had been informal and let people talk across the table, it might have been much easier. Lord Willingdon had the knack of putting everybody at ease within the first few minutes. I remember my very first interview with him - I was not yet a Member of Council and I had gone to see him over something or other in connection with the

**50**      REMINISCENCES OF SIR MUHAMMAD ZAFRULLA KHAN

troubles that were going on in Kashmir, in the early 1930s. As I entered the room he got up from his chair, shook hands with me and said, "How are you, my dear? Come, let's sit down here," and we sat down on the fender seat, which was rather broad, and afforded plenty of room. He made one feel one was welcome, and that the Viceroy was prepared to talk to you and listen to you. I could not imagine Lord Linlithgow doing it ever. He nominated me to represent India at the Dominions Ministers Conference in London, called by Prime Minister Chamberlain early in the war. When I came back I was invited to dinner with the Viceroy and Lady Linlithgow. There was nobody else, not even an ADC. It was the most intimate meal we ever had together and I told him what had passed in England, and I deliberately mentioned that we had been honoured by being invited to the Palace for dinner, by the King, in black tie suits not in white tie dress. The Viceroy himself used to insist upon not merely white tie, but full-dress uniforms, even during the war at his official, formal dinners. He raised his eyebrows and mumbled, "Mmm!" meaning that the King had been lacking in due ceremonial. In England they knew they might be bombed out of existence any night and they could not be bothered with ceremonial.

□ □ □ □ □

# INTERVIEW - MAY 12, 1962

**Question**: *I wonder if we might start, Sir, with the Third Roundtable Conference in 1932.*

**Khan**: The Third Roundtable Conference was a much more business-like affair than the First and the Second Roundtable Conferences. During the first two conferences, the discussion was mostly on general principles. In the Third Roundtable Conference we got down to making concrete proposals, on various aspects of the future constitution. Also, the membership was much more limited. There were only five or six Muslim delegates from British India, and I was consequently called upon to take a leading part on behalf of the Muslim delegation in the Third Roundtable Conference.

His Highness the Aga Khan was, of course, our leader and he was a pillar of strength. But he had intimated at the First Roundtable Conference that he would not take part in debates and make speeches. His standing and prestige were, however, of very great help. When any occasion arose for conversations or negotiations

## REMINISCENCES OF SIR MUHAMMAD ZAFRULLA KHAN     51

behind the scene, with the Prime Minister or the Secretary of State, his help was invaluable. But in the cut and thrust of debate, those of us who represented Muslim interests, had to do our share, and looking back upon it, it seems that I took the leading part.

The main committee of the Conference which sat throughout, was known as the Federal Structure Committee, and as its name indicated, it concentrated on preparing a blueprint of the proposed Federal structure. The discussions in the Third Roundtable Conference, served as the basis of the proposals put out by His Majesty's Government in the shape of a White Paper.

One of the difficult questions, for instance, that we had to deal with was that on behalf of the Punjab Hindus it was urged that a distinction should be made between the Punjab and the other provinces with respect to the transfer of responsibility for law and order.

This was part of a bigger issue. The Muslim position had been that in the federal set up, the minimum unavoidable should be committed to the centre and that everything else should be transferred to the autonomous provinces. The reason for that was obvious. Complete provincial autonomy in respect of matters which were declared provincial subjects - was one of the safeguards on which the Muslims had been insistent. The Muslims would be in a majority in the Punjab, Bengal, the Northwest Frontier Province, as it was then called, and Sind, and this would, to some degree, furnish them with a safeguard vis-a-vis the Federal Centre and the other provinces where there would be a fixed, unalterable majority of Hindus. To have taken away law and order from the Muslim key province of the Punjab would have meant stultifying provincial autonomy in that province.

The main attack proceeded from the Hindu representative from the Punjab, Pundit Nanak Chand, a lawyer from Lahore. Our personal relations were friendly. He put forth the suggestion not because he entertained any hope of its being accepted but only to be able to say when he went back that he had very valiantly upheld the non-Muslim cause in the Punjab.

He delivered a long, passionate denunciation of the Unionist Party in the Punjab Legislature, which was composed of Muslims, Hindus, and Sikhs. It was not a communal party and it had been organized under the leadership of Sir Fazle Hussain. A majority of its members were Muslims. Pundit Nanak Chand, in the course of

## REMINISCENCES OF SIR MUHAMMAD ZAFRULLA KHAN

his declamation against the irresponsible Muslim elements in the Punjab Legislature appealed to the Chairman, Lord Sankey, "My Lord, you are a judge. You will be surprised to know that one of their members was tried seven times for murder! Seven murders to his credit, My Lord."

I was more amused than irritated for I knew the facts. So when he paused for breath, I interjected a very gentle question: "Was this gentleman who is being referred to a Hindu or a Muslim?" "Never mind what he was, he sat on your side," and the Pundit continued on his course. In fact the person he had referred to was a Hindu member from Rohtak.

Lord Sankey was irritated by this harangue on a question which had been settled in principle and was not likely to be re-opened. What he was afraid of was a counterblast from the Muslims the next day. The Committee sat late that day to let Mr. Nanak Chand finish.

When we got down to the cloakroom below and were getting our coats and hats, Nanak Chand asked, "Zafrulla, will you answer me tomorrow?" and I said, "Nanak Chand, I am afraid I will not gratify you in that respect." He enquired, "Why not?" I said with a laugh, "My dear Nanak Chand, if I were to answer you, then what would be the difference between you and me?"

Next day when my turn came I made my comments on the merits of whatever was under discussion and wound up with, "My Lord, yesterday we heard a long speech urging that an exception should be made in the case of the Punjab with respect to the transfer of law and order to popular control. All I wish to say on that is that if any such distinction is attempted, it will wreck the whole scheme altogether. Thank you, Lord Chairman."

Lord Sankey must have felt greatly relieved and said at once, "I entirely agree." That was the end of that particular suggestion.

The Third Roundtable Conference did very useful work in giving concrete shape to proposals on which the White Paper could be based.

Mahatma Gandhi, who had been present at the Second Roundtable Conference, had gone back and started his non-cooperation or passive resistance movement, and the Congress and the Government were again at loggerheads. The Congress was thus not represented in the Third Roundtable Conference.

REMINISCENCES OF SIR MUHAMMAD ZAFRULLA KHAN    **53**

The Third Roundtable Conference was, in due course, followed by the Joint Select Committee of both Houses of Parliament on Indian reforms. His Majesty's Government issued a White Paper on Indian constitutional proposals, summarizing the results reached through the Three Roundtable Conferences. They presented the White Paper to Parliament, and they invited both Houses to set up a Joint Select Committee to study the proposals, take evidence, and to make their report. On the basis of their report a bill was drafted, which subsequently became the Government of India Act of 1935.

The Joint Select Committee was, of course, composed only of members of both Houses of Parliament, but an Indian delegation was also invited to sit with the Committee while it was taking evidence and to take part in the examination of witnesses. The participation of Indian delegates in the work of the Committee finished at the end of the public sittings. They took no part in the discussions in the Select Committee.

The Select Committee was a very representative one. it included all the available ex-Viceroys, Lord Hardinge of Penshurst, Lord Reading and Lord Halifax. Between them they brought to the deliberations of the Committee a fund of experience and knowledge of Indian affairs and conditions which could not be surpassed by any other three men. Then there were men like the late Marquis of Salisbury, father of the present Marquis, Austen Chamberlain, the elder brother of Neville Chamberlain, who subsequently became Prime Minister, the Archbishop of Canterbury, Dr. Cosmo Lang and many outstanding and eminent members of both Houses. Sir Samuel Hoare, later Lord Templewood, was still Secretary of State for India, and defended the proposals contained in the White Paper.

The Indian delegation included Sir Tej Bahadur Sapru, Mr. Jayakar, Sir Hari Singh Gour, and many other eminent Indians. The Muslim delegation was a comparatively small one. I think there were only four or five of us. Sitting with eminent statesmen from Britain, occupied with this very grave and important project, observing their methods and the working of their minds was a privilege and a very valuable experience.

Of the witnesses, some came as groups and some as individuals, but the most outstanding one who came to give evidence was, Mr. Winston Churchill. He came as an individual, in his own right, but he was a host in himself. He was then out in the cold, as it were; he was not in office and he fought India's advance towards immediate dominion status every inch of the way. He was examined by the Committee for four days, and though, of course, the Indian side differed with him on every point, yet everybody admired the way he stuck to his point of view and the great skill, dexterity and ability with which he tried to uphold it. When he finished his evidence, everybody around the table, Indians as well as British, gave him an ovation - the cheering went on for some time.

Amusing incidents also occurred. One of the members reminded Mr. Churchill that in his original presentation he had urged that a good deal of weight should be attached to the views and opinions of the men on the spot, who had experience of running the administration in India, which, of course, was a valid point. The member pointed out to him that Sir John Thompson, who had been a distinguished civil servant in India and had been Chief Commissioner of Delhi, had expressed his strong support of the White Paper proposals.

Churchill affected ignorance of who the man was and added, "If you mean somebody of that name who has become vice-chairman of some organization, set up for the express purpose of boosting these proposals on which the Committee is engaged, surely, surely, I cannot be expected to attach much importance to the views of a person who is openly advocating one particular point of view."

On this the Archbishop of Canterbury interposed, "Surely, My Lord Chairman, Mr. Churchill does not mean that the Committee should not attach any weight to the views of anybody who advocates one particular line of approach on these questions?," implying by that token Mr. Churchill's own views should not receive any consideration on the part of the Committee.

But Churchill wriggled out of it. He said, "My Lord Chairman, I must explain what I mean. Of course, the Committee must pay attention to everything that is submitted to it. What I said was that I could not be expected to attach much importance to such views." One morning Sir Samuel Hoare asked me whether I intended to put any questions to Mr. Churchill. I said, "Sir, I dare not." He smiled and said, "Well, I don't know that you dare not, but let me tell you that most of the questions addressed to Mr. Churchill have been on general principles whether India should be accorded dominion status or not. Now Churchill is the cleverest debater in the House of Commons and it is very difficult to pin him down. You will have seen that he has been reminded of some of his own speeches where he has advocated 'dominion status for India,' and he has just waived that aside maintaining that status is one thing and function is another. India, he says, already has dominion status. India was a signatory to the Treaty of Versailles; India is a member of the League of Nations. That is dominion status. But function is quite a different matter and India, he says, is not yet ready for it."

Sir Samuel suggested that if I decided to ask any questions of Mr. Churchill, I should not ask him questions on generalities but should try to draw his attention to specific aspects of the Indian problem, e.g., what progress had already been made in the exercise of responsibility, a criterion which he himself had put forward as determining whether a substantial advance should now be made towards self-government.

That was a very helpful suggestion, and I tried to take advantage of it when my turn came. When Mr. Churchill was confronted with something on which he had to make an admission, he had no hesitation in doing so but as the questions proceeded and he became wise to their trend he began like a parliamentarian, to be less definite in his answers so that nothing could be built on them.

On one such occasion I put the question to him a second time; the answer was still not quite precise. So I said to him, "Mr. Churchill, you see, I am under a disadvantage. English is not my mother tongue and I have twice failed to make my meaning clear. Will you permit me to make a third attempt?" He assented politely and I put the question to him hedged round with "ifs" and "provideds," so that he should be brought to face the point that I was trying to make. He finally answered it. And we carried on like that until the end. I examined him for about an hour the first day, the committee then adjourned and I continued my examination for another hour the next morning. I took care to show him all the respect and deference to which he was undoubtedly entitled as an eminent statesman. I am sure Mr. Churchill appreciated that and when I finished he addressed the chairman and said, "My Lord Chairman, may I be permitted to say that I have not noticed that Mr. Zafrulla Khan suffers any disadvantage from any lack of knowledge of the English language," which I thought was extremely gracious of him.

When his evidence was concluded on the fourth day, he got up and came over to me, shook me by the hand, and with a twinkle and a smile, said, "You have given me the two most difficult hours before this committee." That made us friends. Later when I visited England during the war when he was Prime Minister, I called on him and he was extremely kind to me. On each occasion he gave me the latest volume of his speeches as Prime Minister and inscribed it for me.

This association of ours with the Joint Select Committee went on during the spring and early summer of 1933. It was interrupted by the usual English summer recess, during August and September, and we got together again in the autumn. During the interval, instead of going back to India, I accepted the invitation of the Royal Institute of International Affairs to be a member of the Indian delegation to the Commonwealth Relations Conference which was being held at Hart House, University of Toronto, Canada.

That again was a valuable experience. These Commonwealth Relations conferences were initiated by Chatham House, the home of the Royal Institute of International Affairs, located in St. James's Square in London, and a whole series of them have been held in various parts of the Commonwealth. This was my first experience of them. It was also my first visit to America. We crossed the Atlantic from Liverpool to Montreal in one of the Duchesses. They were such unsteady boats that they used to be called "the drunken Duchesses." Our voyage was uneventful, and I particularly enjoyed the run between Quebec and Montreal, the greater part of which was through French Canada. The view of Quebec itself was very lovely and impressive and something quite new for us. The air seemed different in that part of the world. I found the Canadians a very kindly, hospitable and gracious people, both French and those of British origin.

The Indian delegation was composed of Mr. (later Sir) Ramaswami Mudaliar, the late Mir Maqbool Mahmud, and myself. We had a young secretary, Mr. Yudhishtar Raj Wadheva. He was then studying for the bar in London, and I thought it would be a good experience for him to come along with us and work as secretary of the Indian Delegation. He did very well in that capacity.

I took advantage of the few days that were still available before the conference to pay brief visits to New York, and to Chicago, where I had an engagement to address the World Fellowship of Faiths in the Morrison Hotel. This was my first experience of the United States, which was struggling to emerge from the Depression with the help of President Roosevelt's New Deal and it left me somewhat confused and bewildered. I conceived an extremely good impression of the people whom I met. My feeling was that they were much more forthcoming than Europeans, and especially than the British; there seemed to be no limit to their hospitality or to their kindness. My reception in Chicago was overwhelming! A group of youngsters who came in with my friend who received me at the station accompanied me to my hotel room and sprawled all over, on the chairs, on the bed, on the table. The Century Exposition was on in Chicago - and they wanted to take me immediately to the Exposition, and succeeded in doing so. I still have a somewhat shy and retiring disposition, and it was a bit of a strain to jump at once to the level of intimacy that they seemed to expect and took for granted.

Out of that first batch, I made friends with two or three, and that friendship I was able to keep up over a period of several years. One of them, and his whole family - and now that the second generation has grown up, also their children - are still very good friends. Whenever I got to Chicago they insist that I must stay with them. I have often stayed with the parents, and the junior members of the family come over and we have a reunion. Their name is Powells. I keep on telling Michael Powells, Jr. that I saw him first when he was only three years old; he is now 22, so he has grown up in the consciousness that I am a friend of the family.

To go back to Toronto. The discussions were very educative. One of the topics in one of the panels was, "Is the Crown Divisible?" For instance, could the Crown be at war as the Crown of one Dominion and be neutral as the Crown of another Dominion? We did not come to any conclusion; we thought this was a difficult problem to push to a precise conclusion. Then the Second World War decided it. Eire was still a Dominion and remained neutral during the war. There was a German Minister at Dublin, while the rest of the Commonwealth was at war with Germany.

We were put up in colleges of the University, as it was vacation time and the accommodations were available. We found ourselves comfortably lodged, the rooms were spacious and were fitted with every modern convenience. Each set for two undergraduates comprised a bedroom and study, neat, clean, airy, well lighted and centrally heated. The only embarrassment we encountered was that the showers had no door or curtain in front. This was soon remedied.

One evening one of the young undergraduates who was in charge of our section came up and told me that I was wanted on the telephone. So I walked down and picked up the receiver, the voice at the other end said, "This is Howard speaking." I asked, "Which of the three?" The gentleman at the other end said, "It is surprising that you should remember. As a matter of fact, this is Walter Howard speaking." I said, "I remember very well your father and mother visiting England in 1912, and they stayed in the same house in London where I was staying. Your mother talked often about the children as you were the same age that I was. I remember that you and I started a correspondence but when I went back to India, somehow our correspondence petered out. The moment you said 'Howard,' I guessed it could only be one of you. But how did you get to know I was here?"

He said, "As a matter of fact, mother rang up from Brantford" - it was their home, not far from Toronto - "she had noticed your name as a delegate to the conference, and asked me to find out if it was the same young man whom she had met 21 years earlier in London." I said, "It is the same one, and returning from Chicago only three days ago, I passed through Brantford. If I had known that your father and mother were there I certainly would have stopped and paid my respects to them." He said, "Father died some years back, but mother still lives there. She remembers very well meeting you there and how you talked; she of us, and you of your own mother, and how close you were to each other, and she wanted to convey her very kind regards. If there should be any opportunity, she would be very glad to meet you."

I asked him to come up immediately and we had a talk. I have since met him every time I have been in Canada, or almost. Unfortunately, I could not meet Mrs. Howard, though she was alive during two of my subsequent visits to Toronto. Somehow a meeting could not be arranged.

At the Conference we had Lord Robert Cecil, younger brother of the Marquis of Salisbury with us, who was a great advocate of the League of Nations and the idea of international co-operation and of the settlement of international disputes through peaceful methods. We had a very representative delegation from Canada and there were delegations from all the Commonwealth countries. We were entertained very hospitably in different homes in Toronto.

One visit that I remember particularly, which was most enjoyable, was to the Donald Farms, outside Toronto, owned by Mrs. Dunlap. She took great pride in her excellent breed of cattle. She

## REMINISCENCES OF SIR MUHAMMAD ZAFRULLA KHAN 59

entertained us at an afternoon party in the grounds of Donald Farms, which were kept in spick-and-span condition; the lawns were as smooth as velvet, a very rich green. A police or military band was in attendance. After tea we were asked if we would like to visit the barns. We went down, and when we approached the building I thought this must be the manager's residence; their were wire gauze windows, with flowerpots on the window wills. We went in and found it was the cow house. The cows were provided with every comfort. There was an arrangement even for music, brought by radio, and we were told the cows were so accustomed to the music that one of them resented being moved from her stall near a loudspeaker to a more distant stall, so much so that it affected even the quantity of milk she would yield. So she had to be brought back to her original position.

A valuable calf of a particular breed, which had been purchased somewhere in the Middlewest was brought to the farm by airplane, and was lowered down by a parachute arrangement and landed safely.

Mrs. Dunlap was a very gracious woman. She had set up this luxury farm in memory of her husband. He was a qualified lawyer and had either not set up in practice at all, or could not make much headway at the law, and he took on the job of teaching. Some people who had formed a corporation for the purpose of prospecting for silver, approached him and asked him to draw up the legal documents. They told him they had not much money and could not pay him a fee, but that they would allot him some paid up shares. If they struck silver, he would be well off, and if not, he would lose nothing. He agreed to draw up the documents on that basis and see them through registration, etc.

In the end they did not strike silver but they struck gold. The shares rose in value and he found himself very rich but unfortunately he developed TB and died of it at an early age. He had wished to set up a farm and live the life of a farmer in the open air. So his widow - they had one son, Moffat, who succeeded to the farms later - bought and established this farm in memory of her husband.

The log cabin in which Mr. and Mrs. Dunlap had started life had been taken down and had been reconstructed inside one of the principal rooms of the farmhouse, which was a veritable mansion.

When I went back again to Toronto in 1942 I met Mrs. Dunlap in the house of Mrs. Starr. I had met Mr. Starr during my first visit;

## 60       REMINISCENCES OF SIR MUHAMMAD ZAFRULLA KHAN

he was an eminent surgeon. By the time I went back in 1942, Mr. Starr had died, but Mrs. Starr was still very active. Every time I have been to Toronto I have met her again and also her sister, Mrs. Ross, whose husband was at one time Lieutenant Governor of Ontario. When I mentioned to Mrs. Dunlap all that we had seen on the farm, her face beamed with delight, and she said, "That you should remember all that after nine years!" I said, "Mrs. Dunlap, to us who come from foreign countries, these things are like windows through which we have looked at things, and they press themselves on our memories, and when we go back they remain with us."

**Question**: *While you were in Canada, did you talk with various delegations and individuals in support of Indian Dominion status?*

**Khan**: By that time, it had ceased to be a very live issue. It was taken for granted on all sides that India would, as the result of the discussions that were taking place in London, be set up as a responsible Dominion. Nobody questioned that position. We were treated exactly the same as if India were already a Dominion and we represented a Dominion in that conference.

In addition to those whom I have already referred to, I also met Philip Noel Baker, who subsequently became a Cabinet Minister and also won the Nobel Prize for Peace. He was truly a man of peace and steadfast on principle and an admirable personality. I have always considered it a great privilege that I met him then, and I feel greatly honoured that he considers that I am a friend of his. The last time we met was last year, when he was here in connection with some conference up in Vermont in support of peace.

Another British Delegate was Mr. Donald Sommerwell, later he became Solicitor General, and then Attorney-General, and then a Lord Justice of Appeal. Meeting with him was of great interest on account of our common professional experiences and interests. His wife who accompanied him was a very gracious personality.

I went back from the conference to continue our participation in the sittings of the Joint Select Committee, and when the Joint Select Committee finished the examination of witnesses, our delegation returned to India.

In the early summer of 1934, I began to think that it might be useful if I went back to England for the summer months. The Joint Select Committee was still sitting; it had still to make its report. I felt that if I could keep in touch with the principal members, I would

REMINISCENCES OF SIR MUHAMMAD ZAFRULLA KHAN 61

know what aspects of the constitutional problem they were discussing and I might be able to assist in conversations behind the scenes with regard to matters in which we were interested.

So I consulted Sir Fazle Hussain whether he thought this might be useful. During the First, Second and Third Roundtable Conferences and the sittings of the Joint Select Committee, delegates were anxious to proceed to England. It was considered a compliment to be chosen to take part in the discussions, and this was made easy as passages and living expenses in London were looked after. I felt that if anything in which we were interested as Muslims now went wrong, there might be a feeling that while everyone rushed to England as an invited member, with expenses paid, we had been guilty of neglect during the crucial stage.

Sir Fazle Hussain said, "It would be good if you can manage it. I hesitate to suggest it to you because you have been to England four times and it might have affected your practice. It might be too much to ask you to do it again." I assured him that my previous visits had not affected my practice prejudicially; it was that I had to concentrate on my work and practice in the remaining months of the year, but somehow, though the number of my cases I could deal with had not increased, my fees had risen, and I had suffered no financial loss. On the contrary each year had been better than the previous year, so that I had no anxiety on that score.

He said, "Well, in that case, if you were to go, I would be very happy. Do keep me in touch with things."

That journey became memorable from one other point of view also. It was my first journey to England by air. We started from Delhi by the Indian Transcontinental Airways, on the board of which I was one of the Directors representing Imperial Airways. Imperial Airways was the predecessor of what is today called the BOAC. They had a certain interest in the Indian Transcontinental Airways which entitled them to nominate two directors and one of them had to be an Indian. They nominated one of their own people, Mr. Pinhorn, and I think it was at the suggestion of Sir Eric Mieville, who had been Private Secretary to Lord Willingdon and who had known me fairly intimately, when I was a member of the Governor General's Executive Council in 1932, that I was nominated as their second director.

Starting from Delhi we made a stop at Jodhpur, but while landing at Jodhpur, the pilot made a slight miscalculation. The

**62** REMINISCENCES OF SIR MUHAMMAD ZAFRULLA KHAN

result was that the bottom of the aircraft was damaged, though we felt only a bump, a noticeable one but nothing to frighten any of us. The landing otherwise was safe, but the aircraft was in no condition to carry on. So we had to stop for the night in Jodhpur instead of proceeding to Karachi according to schedule.

Next morning, one of the lumbering Helena-type aircraft, which we were to board from Karachi, came up from Karachi to pick us up from Jodhpur. Things were so primitive in those days that there was no arrangement in Jodhpur for refuelling, except that ladders were put to the top of the aircraft and porters had to carry two-gallon tins, two of them each time up those ladders, and pour the gasoline into the aircraft. The aircraft seemed to be insatiable; it took hours to refuel it. We could not leave until sometime in the afternoon, and by the time we arrived in Karachi it was evening, and we were taken to the Killarney Hotel; it has since been re-christened the Palace Hotel. We dined there and got a couple of hours' sleep, and were taken again to the airport. We left at 2 a.m. to make up for the lost time. But the cruising speed of this aircraft was only about 75 miles an hour so progress was slow. We stopped at Jiwani, Gwadar, Sharjah and Bahrain. After we left Bahrain and were hoping that the next stop would be Basra, the pilot, Traverse Humphreys, came through and said, "We cannot make Basra because I am being pushed back rather than going ahead because we have got very strong headwinds. We are just above Kuwait and I propose to land here."

We made the landing and we stopped the night inside the walled village which is what Kuwait was then. The Jam of Jawanagar's nephew, who was travelling with us and was going to Switzerland for treatment as he had incipient TB, and I, being the two Indian passengers, were put up for the night in the home of the family who had the agency for petrol for Kuwait. They were very good to us. Their name was Chanim.

We were very tired, having had a long and fatiguing day and were anxious to get as much sleep as we could. The poor nephew of the Jam Sahib was altogether spent. I suggested he should lie down but he was anxious not to do anything which our hosts might think was not quite gracious. They expected that we should receive the neighbours who were calling on us while dinner was being prepared. The calls went on until midnight, and then the dimmer was ready, and we ate, and had a few hours' sleep.

The next morning we started quite early and made Basra by 8 O'clock, where we stopped for a wash and breakfast.

Our next stop was Baghdad, which proved to be the hottest place I have ever encountered. I mean, on that day it certainly was. I consumed six long glasses of orange squash with plenty of ice but it had no effect on my raging thirst.

The next stop was Rutba Wells, where we stopped for lunch, right in the middle of the desert. I had not seen such a cluster of flies anywhere in my life as I saw in Rutba Wells. I was surprised that right in the middle of the desert with nothing else visible, there should be so many flies that the veranda of the place was absolutely black, as though it were paved with flies. Luckily, the rooms had wire gauze doors with automatic springs, which kept the flies out. We took off after lunch and we had to land for refuelling again at one of the pipeline stations; there was no name to the place, only a letter and a number.

For dinner we stopped at Gaza where we experienced the first cool breeze on that searing day, and by midnight we got to Cairo. The next morning we took a flying boat and crossed the Mediterranean. We stopped in Crete alongside a small British Naval boat which was moored there, and were served tea and biscuits. In the evening we got to Brindisi. From Brindisi to Paris, we had to travel by train because Mussolini would not allow Imperial Airways to fly over Italy. On the days on which aircraft was expected to land in Brindisi, a sleeping coach was reserved by Imperial Airways for their passengers. The passengers were taken to a hotel in Brindisi, and after dinner boarded the train and spent two nights and one day on the train. It proceeded along the Adriatic Coast, and then through Switzerland and on the third morning arrived in Paris. We were taken to a hotel for breakfast and on to Le Bourget, which was then the only airport, and there we got into a comfortable aircraft of Imperial Airways. It so happened that Lord and Lady Willingdon, who had been on leave from India in the middle of their tenure of the Viceroyalty, and had been vacationing for a fortnight in the South of France, joined the aircraft there and presently we landed at Croydon, which was the airport for London.

Sir Samuel Hoare, Secretary of State for India, together with members of his council and other high officials, was at the airport to receive the Viceroy and Vicerine. I paid my respects to Sir Samuel Hoare and he asked me whether it was my first trip from India by air, and I said it was. He had been Secretary of State for Air and was interested in the development of air communications. He asked what my impressions were. I asked, "Do you want to have a frank expression of my views?" and he said, "Of course." "Well, from Delhi we flew over the Rajputana desert with not a blade of grass or green leaf to be seen and after Jodhpur, over the Sind Desert, again the same thing. Karachi was a well-populated town, and then we flew over the Persian Gulf with bare hills on one side and sand dunes on the other, a few date gardens in Basra, and then along the water, a little bit of greenery, up to Baghdad, and then from Baghdad to Rutba Wells, again the desert, Rutba Wells to Gaza, again the desert, Cairo, of course provided a delightful view at midnight from the air, all the lights and the river. We began to fly the next morning over the Mediterranean, presently we were over the Greek islands, so lovely down below. Then we journeyed through Italy as if through an orchard. I had seen these places before, but had not passed over them so rapidly. The thought that came to my mind was how much more blessed, in the things that make life worth living, are you people in contrast with us who have almost nothing. This was followed very insistently by the reflection, why cannot you settle down to enjoying these things and sharing them together beneficently rather than boil up as you did in the First World War, from 1914 to 1918? And now you are on the brink of war again with Hitler having blatantly proclaimed his programme in Mein Kampf."

Sir Samuel asked, "Zafrulla, do you really think we are heading for war?" "I am absolutely certain, and I will tell you the sort of picture that has come to my mind of the situation in Europe." "Indeed." "Well, what is that picture?" "The picture is that you are all in a showboat, floating merrily along on the river, with music and dance and all manner of amusement. You are utterly unconscious that there is a waterfall down below and that you are going to crash into it." He was very much struck by that. This was May, 1934. He said, "I do not think the calamity is so imminent and that it is unavoidable. On the other hand, we think the danger is not so real." "It is a matter of feeling. I have told you my feeling."

He asked me how long I was going to stay and I told him the purpose of my visit. He said, "I am very glad you have come. Come to India Office tomorrow, and we will plan something." So I met him in India Office next day, and he said, "Zafrulla, if you will keep in touch with me, I will keep you briefed on what is happening in the Committee, and surely you can be of great assistance. All members of the Committee appreciate your collaboration, which you gave to them when you were sitting with them, and of course many of them know you through the Roundtable Conferences." I kept in touch with him and from time to time he told me how I could help. For instance, he told me to talk to Lord Hardinge who was feeling very doubtful with regard to the viability of Sind as a separate province, and to Lord Derby who he thought was not quite firm on the transfer of law and order to the provinces, and Lord Zetland who was very upset with the apportionment of seats in Bengal under the Communal Award.

I met those three and several others, and the experience was different with each. Lord Hardinge was another very gracious personality. He had been a diplomat. He had been British Ambassador to France before he was appointed Viceroy of India. He was the first Viceroy who started using the expression, "Our Indian fellow citizens" which delighted us and made us conscious that we were fellow citizens with the British and that our relationship was not merely that of the governors and the governed.

In his time the capital was transferred from Calcutta to Delhi, and the partition of Bengal, which had been carried out by Lord Curzon and had been very unpopular, was cancelled. He had been a very popular Viceroy and was still active in politics.

He always addressed Indians with the same title of respect in one of the vernaculars. When I went to see him, he addressed me as Janab, which made me feel very embarrassed that an ex-Viceroy should call me Janab, which is an expression indicating great respect. When I raised the question of Sind with him, he said, "Now, just answer me one thing. Are you satisfied that Sind will be viable?" I said, "Frankly, Lord Hardinge, I have not made a study of the question from the financial or the economic point of view, but I feel very strongly that with its resources, especially large tracts of arable land, of good quality, and all these schemes of barrages for irrigation, it should do very well." He said, "Very good then. Janab Zafrulla Khan, your assurance satisfies me. I am quite prepared to rely on your word." This was very flattering. Probably he did not express any further doubts on this question in the Committee. Maybe having already expressed his doubts he did not intend to take the matter any further anyhow. But it was very nice of him to put the matter the way he did.

Lord Derby I knew very well also, but I suggested to His Highness, the Aga Khan, that if he would kindly ask Lord Derby to luncheon as they were good friends, both being racing gentlemen, and would ask me to meet him at lunch, I thought that would be a good atmosphere in which to discuss the transfer of law and order with him. This was arranged and at the end of the discussion, he said with a laugh, "It does not matter whether I am satisfied or not, but I can make one promise to you, that I will not raise the matter again in the Committee." I said, "Lord Derby, that is not enough," at which he laughed again and said, "You are a hard bargainer, what is it that you want?" I said, "I want you to advocate the transfer of law and order." He looked at the Aga Khan and then looked back at me, and said, "All right. I am prepared to say that I am satisfied with the proposed transfer."

With Lord Zetland, I could not make much progress in argument. It was true that whereas under what was known as the Lucknow Pact, the Muslims had secured a representation in the Bengal Legislature, which, in effect, gave them only 28 percent of the total house - 40 percent of general constituencies - and the Communal Award gave them 48.4 or 48.8, and therefore the difference looked very great. Lord Zetland went on pressing that point; I went on pressing that the injustice from which the Muslims had already suffered - being a majority and having only 28 percent representation - was so great that any fair correction of it was bound to appear large. In the end he said, "Look, Zafrulla, you cannot convince me that this is a fair apportionment, and it looks as if I cannot convince you. But let me tell you this, I have done all I could in the Committee, and the Committee are determined to uphold the decision that has been reached, so that should be comfort enough for you."

Again, the way these gentlemen in high positions - Lord Zetland later became Secretary of State for India - treated one was very gratifying. After all, who was I? So far as the Committee was concerned, I was an outsider, occupying no particular position, not even in a representative capacity; a private individual. Yet, they received me kindly, they were willing to discuss these things with me, which showed they had confidence in me. In that way the trip proved very much worthwhile.

One day, in July, when I was with Sir Samuel Hoare at the India Office, he asked me, "Well, now, Zafrulla, what is your program?" and I said, "Sir Samuel, I understand that during the recess you are going

## REMINISCENCES OF SIR MUHAMMAD ZAFRULLA KHAN

to Switzerland to do some skating, and I also intend to go on a trip - I had Scandinavia in mind - but I shall come back and plan to continue what I am doing as the Joint Select Committee will be sitting through October and part of November, and then I shall go back to India."

He said, "Well, that is interesting, but that was not the point of my question. You have been for four months a member of the Viceroy's Executive Council, would you care to go back to public life in that capacity? As you know, Sir Fazle Hussain is vacating office in April next year, and the Viceroy is here and he and I have had word together, and both of us will be very happy if you will agree to go on the Viceroy's Council." I said, "Sir, I am free to confess to you quite frankly that at my age and with my standing I consider it a great compliment to be invited to take a seat on the Viceroy's Council, but there are two or three considerations which I wish you to take into account before you make up your mind."

"What are they?" "In the first place, since the Council began to have Indian members there have been four Muslim members of Council. The first one was Sir Ali Imam from Behar; the second was Sir Muhammed Shafi from the Punjab; the third was Sir Muhammed Habibullah from Madras; and the fourth is Sir Fazle Hussain, again from the Punjab. Thus Punjab has had two terms, and Behar and Madras, which are minority provinces have had a term each, but Bengal which is a majority province and the United Provinces, which though a minority Province from our point of view has many eminent and prominent Muslims, and also Bombay have not had a look in. The Muslims there might expect that this time the choice should fall upon one of them." He said, "Well, it is good of you to put it that way, but your work has been on behalf of the Muslims of India and it has been mostly in London, so that in a sense you are the representative of the Muslims of the whole of India. We do not think it open to objection that somebody from the Punjab should succeed somebody from the Punjab."

He was kind enough to add, "We take the best man from wherever we can find him." It was not my own estimate of myself but that is the way he chose to put it.

I said, "Sir, on this question of representation of Muslims, I must warn you that I belong to a particular religious movement in Islam which is not very popular with the general run of Muslims on account of differences of doctrine. When I was appointed to officiate for Sir Fazle Hussain in 1932 a certain amount of opposition was expressed in the press and in the public to my appointment on that account and, I very much fear that on this occasion the expression may be a little more vigorous, and I think that is something you ought to consider."

"Well, I must say, I am surprised to hear that, that the Muslims should be so unmindful of the great service that you have done to the Muslim cause. But if they are likely to adopt that attitude, that is not something that should operate with the Viceroy and me, to deprive them of the services of the best Muslim that we can find for them to uphold their interests." I said, "Sir, it is very kind of you to say so."

He said, "I hope you have no more objections." I said, "Sir, these are not objections; these are considerations that you must pay attention to. There is still one more, if you will permit me to mention it." "What?" "On the selection of the individual, I would like you to consider at least two names: the Nawab of Chatari, Sir Said Ahmad Khan, who has been Home Member in the United Provinces, and has officiated as Governor of the United Provinces. He has a distinguished career and is an eminent Muslim, and I am sure Sir Malcolm Hailey, would wish to press his claims."

The Secretary of State asked, "Who is the second?" I said, "The second is Sir Sikandar Hayat Khan, who is almost in the same position in the Punjab. He has been Revenue Member and he has officiated as Governor, and his claims should be considered also." He smiled and said, "Zafrulla, do you think that either of them would be a good choice?" I said, "Sir, it is not a question which can fairly be put to me. It is for you to determine."

He said, "They have both been here, as you know, and I know both of them and I respect both of them very highly, but I think the Viceroy's choice and mine in this case is the best one." Again I said, "That is very kind of you," and he asked, "Then may I tell the Viceroy that you agree?" I said, "Sir, I have already said that I consider it a great compliment to me, and I am very grateful if you feel that way." He said, "All right, then. I will let the Viceroy know. We shall later, as you are coming back here, discuss the details."

Now, this was July, 1934, and the appointment was to take effect in April, 1935. So I said to Sir Samuel Hoare, "Very good, Sir, we can discuss details then, but there is one matter I want to mention now. It is usual to make these announcements in the beginning of the

# REMINISCENCES OF SIR MUHAMMAD ZAFRULLA KHAN

year. Now, I am a practising lawyer and I propose to practise right to the last day before I take charge of the office. It might be embarrassing for me to have the announcement made too early."

He said, "Very well, I shall keep that in mind. We can discuss it when we meet again."

A week later I was due to call on the Viceroy, a matter of courtesy. We had been colleagues in his Council and both he and Lady Willingdon had been extremely gracious to me. Lord Willingdon had brought to the Viceroyalty a great deal of humanity. He met people at an equal level, made them feel at ease, and showed them every courtesy. He was a man of very liberal ideas. Without any change in the constitution, his running of that very high and exalted office became much more liberal than it had been during any earlier regime. All of us respected him very highly.

When I went to call on him I knew that the Secretary of State and he had decided that I should succeed Sir Fazle Hussain, but perhaps he did not yet know that the Secretary of State had mentioned the matter to me. In the course of our conversation he said, "Oh, my dear, would you do me a favour?" I said, "Yes, Sir, anything you ask." He said, "I know you are making tons of money at the Bar, but I think I may claim I have some right to ask you to do something for me." Now this was a very gracious way of putting it. I knew at once what he had in mind, and with regard to "the tons of money," I also knew what he was referring to. He had on one occasion, after I had officiated at his Council, asked me whether I would be interested in the Chief Justiceship of the Lahore High Court, and I had said, I would consider it an honour if I were called upon to take it on but that it was due both to the office and to me that I would not run after it.

He was very struck by that and had said, "Well, my dear, I look at it this way. You have been doing a lot these last few years for your people and you have never asked me for anything, but I have been on the lookout to see whether I can do something for you before I leave. Now, if you are interested in this, perhaps you would not mind speaking to Emerson about it." Sir Herbert Emerson was then Governor of the Punjab.

I said, "Sir, I do not see why you should feel that you are under any obligation to do something for me. Whatever little I have been able to do has been a public service in the interest of India, and I do not know that for that I deserve any compensation or reward. It is a compensation in itself. I am glad that the opportunity has been afforded to me to do something. After all, what does one desire in life? A reasonable competence and the respect of one's fellow men. I do not think I am being unduly vain if I say that to a reasonable degree I possess both. So I hope you will put this idea out of your mind that there is any reason why you should wish to do something for me."

He mentioned this to the Aga Khan when His Highness arrived in India and was staying with him. He told him, "I have been Governor of Bombay for five years, Governor of Madras for six years; I have now for four years been Viceroy; and this is the one Indian whom I wanted to do something for and he said, 'No, there is no necessity.' Everybody else who has worked with me or done something has always wished that something should be done for them." The Aga Khan told me this with great pride.

Well that was why he thought I was making tons of money at the Bar. I had a reasonable practice but nobody made tons of money at the Bar in Lahore; the fees were not very high, and in any case I was not making tons of money.

He continues, "You know Fazle is to complete his term of office next April, I will be in India only a year after that and whoever succeeds me and however able he might be, he will not have the same experience of India as I have had." As I have said, he had been Governor of Bombay, Governor of Madras, and then he had gone as Governor-General to Canada, and come back to India as Governor-General. "And I want to leave the very best Council that I can get together for my successor, and I want the best man available to succeed Fazle."

I interrupted him here, and said, "I am rather disappointed." He looked at me with a puzzled expression and said, "Why are you disappointed?" I said, "Well, Sir, I worked with you in an officiating capacity for four months on your Council, and I had the notion that you were reasonably satisfied with my work." "Of course I was. I was delighted with it." I said, "Well, then I had hoped that when the time came for you to select a successor to Sir Fazle, you would also consider me." At this his face cleared up and he said, "You are a naughty man. Of course I mean you." I said, "Sir, I do not see that the definition fits me. You said you want to get the very best man you can find, and I do not consider that I am the very best man." He said, "Oh, now, come off it. Will it be all right with you?" I said, "Not only would it be all right with me, but I am extremely grateful." I did not let on that the Secretary of State had already mentioned it to me; I wanted him to have the pleasure of thinking that he had made the offer to me himself. This was his very kind and gracious way of doing it.

When I met the Secretary of State again in early October, he said to me, "Zafrulla, you were perfectly right in one thing, and that is that there has been an awful hullabaloo in India, not over your appointment, because they do not know it yet, but over the prospect of your appointment. I have received numberless telegrams and letters of protest, and I told Croft to put them in the wastepaper basket, so do not worry about that. But the Viceroy is anxious that we should put these people out of their agony by making the official announcement, and I am afraid I must request you to agree to an early announcement being made. I regret I am unable to comply with your wish that we should hold it up until next year." I agreed and he rang for Croft and told him to send a telegram to the Viceroy that he had mentioned the matter to me and that the announcement might be made on Wednesday of the following week.

Then he mentioned another matter to me. He said, "There is another matter which both the Viceroy and I wish you to consider. You know that Sir Fazle Hussain holds the portfolio of Education, Health and Lands and several miscellaneous subjects and whoever succeeds him will take over his portfolio. You have done that before and I know it will be easy for you. But both the Viceroy and I think that you ought to take over the portfolio of Commerce and Railways from Sir Joseph Bhore which we consider a much more important one." I said, "Sir, this is very kind of you. I would personally prefer Education, Health, Lands because it is an area in which I am more familiar with the ropes." He smiled and said, "You are a young man. You should not be afraid of hard work. True, this other portfolio involves a good many problems: there is the Trade Agreement with Britain and there is the trade agreement with Japan and on the railway side there are many problems." The railways, incidentally, were the biggest financial asset of the Government of India. In those days, the railway budget, which was presented to the Assembly by the Railway Member, was bigger than the whole of the rest of the budget of the Government of India. That was always a matter of some difficulty with the Finance Member. The Secretary of State continued: "But one difference it will make to you is a technical one. Sir Joseph Bhore completes his term of office three or four weeks after Sir Fazle Hussain does. I am prepared to suggest to the Viceroy that you should take over from Fazle Hussain when he completes his term of office the portfolio of Education, Health and Lands for three or four weeks - till Sir Joseph Bhore retires - and then you switch over to his portfolio, and whoever is to succeed Sir Joseph Bhore will take over Education, Health and Lands from you."

I said, "No, Sir, I would not suggest such a complicated arrangement. I am quite willing to wait to take over from Sir Joseph Bhore direct, when he completes his term." He said, "This will mean two things. For three or four weeks there will be no Muslim Member of Council, which is not too long an interval, but it would make you junior in status and in protocol to whoever takes over from Sir Fazle Hussain. You are entitled to come in first."

I said, "Sir, these things do not worry me at all." What happened was that Sir Joseph Bhore's successor, in the non-Muslim vacancy turned out to be Sir Jagdish Prashad, a member of the Indian Civil Service from the United Provinces, a perfect gentleman, with whom I never had the slightest difference of opinion. While he and I were together on the Council I had, as it were, two votes in the Council. He was a member of the Civil Service and had a lot of administrative experience, but he told me that till he came up to Simla, to take charge of his portfolio, he had never travelled up to Simla before. Simla was the headquarters of the Government of India; the summer headquarters of the Government of the United Provinces was at Nainital, and he used to go there for the summer. On every matter of policy he would consult with me; we would put our heads together, and whatever we decided both of us did together. It was a very happy companionship. Though he was three or four weeks my senior and, therefore, at meetings of Council etc., he sat above me, we were such good friends that I felt that I held both portfolios. I did not interfere with anything in his portfolio, naturally, but we were in constant touch and it turned out to be a very happy arrangement.

So that was settled in London, but by the time I got back to India I found trouble had been brewing.

□ □ □ □ □

# INTERVIEW - MAY 19, 1962

**Khan**: The Secretary of State asked me how long I was staying in England, and I told him until the middle or end of November. He said he would give directions that I should see documents and dispatches concerning the Ottawa Trade Agreement, and other important matters comprised in the portfolio that I was to take over. He added that when I went back to India, he would let the Viceroy know that papers relating to all those subjects should be sent to me at Lahore, so that when I took over the portfolio in the following April or May I should to some degree be familiar with the problems with which I would have to deal.

When I got back to India, a serious difficulty arose. Shortly after my return to Lahore, I received a message from Sir Eric Mieville, the Private Secretary to Lord Willingdon, that the Viceroy wished to see me and would I go down to Delhi at some convenient time and let him know when I could be expected. I went down and saw the Viceroy and he told me that some of his colleagues were a little worried over the distribution of portfolios and would I be prepared to discuss the matter with them. I asked the Viceroy what was proposed, and the proposal broadly was that a portfolio of communications comprising railways, telegraphs, post office, etc. should be constituted, which would be held by one of the European Members. The idea was that Sir Frank Noyce should take it over, and that I should keep Commerce.

I told the Viceroy that my initial reaction was not favourable to any such change, but I told him that I would be happy to discuss the matter with anyone he wished. He said I had better see Sir James Grigg first, the Finance Member, and later meet Sir Josephy Bhore and Sir Frank Noyce, and perhaps also Sir N.N. Sarkar. He was the Law member, and was anxious to have something more besides law as he said law did not occupy him all the time.

I had not met Sir James Grigg before, though I had heard about him. The Viceroy, when suggesting to me that I might go down and see him, had said, "Oh, my dear, I am sure you will get along all right with him, but never mind his language. His language is not always that of a gentleman, but he does not mean any harm by that." Then he had called Sir Eric Mieville and said, "Eric, will you ring up Grigg and ask him whether Zafrulla might go down and see him immediately?" Sir Eric brought back a message that Sir James was at his residence and was ready to receive me. So I went down to his residence. I thought the best thing was to make a direct approach, and I said, "Sir James, we have not met before." He said, "No, I do not recall having met you before." I said, "Well, you know nothing at all about me, and all that you can even now guess is that I choose to wear a beard in the Twentieth Century but that is my personal affair. What is it about me that you do not like?"

He said, "I am glad to see that you talk quite frankly. I will tell you with the same frankness what is the trouble that I feel about you." "I would be glad to hear it." "I am told that you are Fazle Hussain's political protege. Fazle Hussain is a communalist, Railways are our most valuable asset, and frankly I do not want to see the railways committed to the care of a person who is a communalist and whose main preoccupation will be to appoint as many Muslims as he can to the railways and perhaps in the end ruin the whole business."

I said, "I am very glad to hear what your objection is. In the first place, it is true that Sir Fazle Hussain has been a very kind, generous, gracious, considerate friend, and in a sense you may say that I am both his political pupil and his protege. I absolutely repudiate the charge that he is a communalist; that he fights for getting better conditions for Muslims both for the purpose of getting more Muslims properly trained and also for their proper representation in the services does not mean that he is a communalist. As a matter of fact, one of the problems in this country is that the development in many directions is ill-balanced and it bodes ill for the future of the country as a whole that one section, and quite a large one, though a minority in the total population, should lag behind the other in many fields. But we will not enter into a discussion over that just now.

"But let me tell you something about Sir Fazle Hussain. As you probably know, I officiated for him in 1932 when he went on sick leave, and when I took charge of the portfolio I asked him whether he wished to give me any directions, and he said to me, 'I cannot be standing over your shoulder all the time. You sink or swim on your own. You go ahead and do what you think is right.' So if when he was going on leave he would not tell me anything about his own portfolio which I was to hold in his absence, do not have any fear that he will try to run my portfolio for me when I am Minister. What is more, I am not a person who lets somebody else do things for him,

REMINISCENCES OF SIR MUHAMMAD ZAFRULLA KHAN 75

however much he might think he could do them better. I will be the Minister in charge and I assure you that I will be the person who will run the portfolio, for good or for ill. You might like it or you might not, but I can give you that assurance.

"Now, let's go on to my possible attempt to ruin what is the government's largest asset. On that, what is your real worry? Tell me that." He said, "Appointments." I said, "Good. All initial appointments to the officer's grade are made as the result of a competitive examination held by the Public Service Commission. The Minister in charge has nothing to do with that. The Government has recently, mainly as a result of Sir Fazle Hussain's efforts, to which I was also able to contribute when I was officiating for him in 1932, adopted a resolution that to all senior services under the Government of India a recruitment of 25 percent Muslims shall be made. If 25 percent are not available, as a result of the competitive examination, then enough shall be selected from candidates who have qualified at that examination to make up the 25 percent by nomination. That is the Government's decision. I shall see that that decision is carried out on the Railways as elsewhere. Anything wrong with that?"

"I have no objection to that. Naturally, the Government having made that decision, whether it is good or bad, it has to be carried out." I said, "I know I shall be under constant pressure from the Muslim side to do more. It will be equally my duty to resist that pressure. I must carry out Government's decision, and I shall neither go beyond it by devious methods nor permit anybody to evade it, so far as I can prevent it. Is that satisfactory?"

He said, "Oh, yes. That is quite above-board, that is quite satisfactory. I am with you on that."

I continued, "In the lower gazetted service, appointments are made on some proportionate ratio of communities in the different railways, by the heads of those railways called Agents. The Minister cannot interfere in those. So I do not come in with regard to those appointments. To the clerical staff I do not even know how appointments are made. The Minister cannot interfere with those from the top, they are too far below. In any case there is no question there of ruining your best financial asset, because the only qualification that I can see which is needed by the clerical staff of the railways is that they should be able to speak and write bad English.

I can assure you that the Muslims can speak and write as bad English as the non-Muslims."

He laughed at that and said, "No, no. Look, the real danger is that in transfers and in promotions hanky-panky might come in." I said, "Well, then, in transfers and promotions, do you think that I would have been selected by the Secretary of State and the Viceroy to be a Member of the Cabinet, if they thought I was the kind of man who, if the appointment of Chief Engineer on the Assam-Bengal Railways fell vacant, would insist with the Railway Board - because it is on the recommendation of the Railway Board that these appointments are made and the Minister, unless he notices something gravely wrong, okays what they recommend - that a friend of mine who happens to be an assistant engineer on the Northwestern Railway should be appointed Chief Engineer? Do not you think that anybody who had not that much sense of proportion would have been selected by Sir Samuel Hoare? He selected me on his own personal knowledge, and you can disagree, but he has known me intimately for some years and you have seen me only today."

We discussed other things and parted on a friendly note. When I met the Viceroy later he asked me how we had gone along. I told him what had transpired. He laughed and said, "I wish I had been behind a screen listening." I said, "As a matter of fact, Sir James Grigg was not nearly so formidable as I had been led to expect. He was quite reasonable. He had his apprehensions; he put them to me; I tried to meet them. I think we shall get along all right. As I have not the slightest intention of doing the kind of thing that he apprehends, I have not any fear at all that we will not understand each other quite well."

The meeting with my other colleagues was a different affair. I say "colleagues," not only because they were going to be my future colleagues, but I had been their colleague when I was an officiating Member.

I went at the appointed time to Sir Joseph Bhore's room in the Secretariat Building in Delhi, and met Sir Joseph Bhore and Sir Frank Noyce. Sir Frank Noyce did not take much part in the discussion; it was Sir Joseph Bhore who talked. I was a little amused to see that several volumes of the Assembly Debates were on the table in front of him, with slips at various places, as if for reference.

They greeted me kindly, and I sat down and said, "The Viceroy suggested that I should come and meet you and here I am. I will be

## REMINISCENCES OF SIR MUHAMMAD ZAFRULLA KHAN

glad to be told whatever you want to tell me." The gist of what I was told was that during the debates in the Assembly, Government had given an assurance to the European Group, who for some years had been pressing for a separate portfolio of communications - railways, telegraphs, post office, etc. - that such a portfolio would be set up at an early date. As they had committed themselves to it, the Viceroy thought that this was a convenient time, when Sir Joseph Bhore would be handling over charge, to split the portfolio of Commerce and Railways and put Railways with communications and make Commerce a complete portfolio by itself. That was what was proposed to the Viceroy and he appeared to have agreed to it.

After the explanation was made, Sir Joseph Bhore and Sir Frank Noyce, both looked at me, and I held my peace. Then Sir Joseph Bhore, a little embarrassed, said, "Well, you see, that is what the Viceroy asked us to explain to you." A second time, but more briefly, he explained the situation over again, and still I did not say anything. I looked steadily at him and said nothing. He repeated, "Well, you see, the Viceroy was anxious that we should explain this to you."

I then said, "Sir Joseph, I appreciate that. The Viceroy told me himself that you would explain the situation to me and I am very grateful to you that you have done so. Did the Viceroy tell you what to do after you had explained it to me?" He said, "Uh, well, uh, no. What do you mean?"

I said, "You have explained it. Thank you very much."

So he was rather nonplussed. What he expected, of course, was to get my views on it, did I agree or did not I agree. I was intensely annoyed at the trick they had sought to play on me behind my back, but I did not wish to give expression to my annoyance. In the end he said, "Well, he did not say anymore, but I am sure Sir Frank Noyce and I would be glad to know your reaction to it." Sir Frank Noyce, who was much more intimate with me than Sir Joseph Bhore had been, said, "Zafrulla, I want to make it quite clear that all I am anxious to know is, is there going to be a change or not? You see, I propose to proceed on leave next year and before I go on leave, I would like to know what would I be in charge of when I come back. Both of us would be glad to know what your reactions are to the proposed change."

I said, "Sir Joseph, this commitment that you say has been made to the European Group, what was the date of it?" So he tried to look into the volumes in front of him and said, "I can soon find out the exact date. Is that of particular interest to you?" I said, "Yes, it is. It was on the 3rd of October that in London the Secretary of State proposed, I had not asked for it, that I should take over the portfolio of Commerce and Railways, and he said it was the desire both of the Viceroy and himself that I should do so. Now, you made this commitment before this was said to me or after. If you made it before, then so far as I am concerned, it is wiped out by the offer of the Viceroy and the Secretary of State to me in London on the 3rd of October that I should take over Commerce and Railways. I do not say it is wiped out forever, but you cannot make these changes just now because I was made this offer, and accepted it. If anything arises later we shall see."

"If the commitment was made after that date, you had no business to make it after this offer had been made to me and I had accepted it, without making any reference to me."

They looked at each other and after reminding Sir Joseph Bhore that the Secretary of State had told me, and the Viceroy had confirmed that until I took over charge important papers concerning trade agreements and other questions that were pending in the portfolio would be sent to me for my information, and receiving an assurance from him that I would be kept fully informed, I left. I might add that Sir Joseph Bhore carried out that undertaking by not sending me a single line from that date until the date that I took over charge!

I met the Viceroy again in the evening. He asked me what had happened an I reported the conversation to him.

I went back to Lahore and wrote a letter to Sir Samuel Hoare telling him what had transpired in Delhi and added that I did not wish to cause any embarrassment to him or to the Viceroy or to the gentlemen who would have been my colleagues if I had taken over charge. The simplest way out was for me to withdraw from my acceptance of the office of Member of the Viceroy's Council and that the Secretary of State and the Viceroy were free to choose anybody else they liked.

I received a brief reply from Sir Samuel Hoare saying he had received my letter, and appreciated the position. He had written to the Viceroy and he was quite sure that everything would be all right.

## REMINISCENCES OF SIR MUHAMMAD ZAFRULLA KHAN

I received another invitation from the Viceroy to go down to Delhi. The Viceroy, as usual, met me very graciously, and he said, "Oh, my dear, Sammy Hoare has sent me a stinker! But, of course, if you are not agreeable to the change, there is no reason why the change should be made, and you will take over the portfolio as it is."

And on that occasion I told him that what had upset me was not merely this change that had been proposed behind my back. As soon as I had returned to India, I began to see in the papers, particularly in the Hindu press, a regular campaign against my being - "a mere youngster" - given the most important portfolio and certainly the biggest portfolio in the Government which carried so much patronage, etc. All sorts of charges, communalism and this and the other were preferred against me. I had been a member of the government for four months. Had I shown any tendency towards communalism? I continued the tradition of Sir Fazle Hussain to carry Indianization as far as possible, and the only people, who, it so happened, benefited from that were non-Muslim officers who were promoted. There was not a single Muslim who had benefited under the Indianization policy. That was all right with me. Nobody can charge me with communalism in what I did during those four months. The Hindu press is dead set against me that I should not have these portfolios. If I were to agree to that it would be thought this fellow is only running after office. He does not care whether he is given a proper portfolio or not, whether it is important or unimportant; so long as he gets a seat in the Cabinet and gets a salary and the prestige, nothing else matters to him. That is position I was not prepared to accept, and that is why I wrote to the Secretary of State that he was free to make a fresh choice.

He said, "So far as I am concerned, I can assure you that there was nothing in it. Those people, after all, they sit in the Assembly and have to face the criticism. It is true they had asked my assent to this arrangement and I thought they would make sure that it would go through. Anyhow nothing will now be done till after you have joined the Cabinet."

In May the question was brought up again in Cabinet. But now I was a member of the Cabinet, I could argue on an equal basis with my colleagues. The matter was discussed back and forth, and then Sir Philip Chetwood, the Commander-in-Chief, who, as I have already said, had become a very good friend during my first association with him in 1932, said to the Viceroy, "Sir, you have heard the views of your colleagues on this matter, and I propose that you take the whole matter in advisement, reflect over it and come to your decision. Let us here and now agree that all of us will accept whatever you decide.

I knew what the Viceroy's decision was going to be, so I was perfectly happy over it. I said, "Very good. I agree," and the others said, "Very well, we agree." The next morning, a paper was circulated that the Viceroy, after having considered the matter, had decided that no change should take place in the portfolios till after his successor had time to look round and it would be for him to make proposals to his colleagues.

But it was proposed, as I had already suggested myself to the Viceroy, that Sir N.N. Sarkar, who was Law Member, should take over the amendment and consolidation of Company Law and Insurance Law, which were two big matters pending within my portfolio. That would keep him occupied fairly heavily.

**Question**: *But how were the other disputes resolved within the Viceroy's Council?*

**Khan**: If you mean with regard to this change of portfolio, what had actually happened was that the Viceroy had sent for me and had said, now that Sir Frank Noyce was about to proceed on leave, he was anxious that this matter should be settled one way or the other before he left for England, and therefore it was proposed to put it on the agenda of the next Council meeting. He asked me what my reactions would be. I told him that my reactions would still be the same as they were before I had joined the Cabinet, but that I was willing to suggest a compromise and if it appealed to him, he could perhaps take action accordingly.

Lord Willingdon was always willing to consider any adjustment of a question which could be carried through by mutual agreement rather than by a decision one way or the other in favour or against something. He was eager to know what I had in mind. I proposed that things should continue as they were while he was Viceroy - he had another year to go - and that his successor, after he had taken over charge and had made himself familiar with everything could make any proposal as head of government, which was always open to the Viceroy to do with regard to redistribution of portfolios and that I would have no objection at all.

## REMINISCENCES OF SIR MUHAMMAD ZAFRULLA KHAN

One specific matter that I did propose was that as Sir N.N. Sarkar had said, which was perfectly true, that he had not enough to do, I was quite willing that he should take over the amendment and codification of Company Law and Insurance Law. These matters had been pending for some time; they were now ripe for action, they were both rather controversial subjects and I had not the time to devote as much attention as was necessary to them, I would be very glad if he would take them over, and I would assist him as much as I could as Minister in charge. That was the arrangement that was put through by the Viceroy.

**Question**: *I wonder, Sir, if you might now like to talk a little about religion, how it has influenced you, how it has influenced your political life, how you came to it and so on.*

**Khan**: That is both a solemn and a wide topic. It is wide in the sense that to my way of thinking, and I believe to the way of thinking of most Muslims, religion comprehends every aspect of one's life. With me it began very early, as it should with everybody. I was particularly fortunate that my mother was such a very outstanding personality in our household.

She had no book learning; indeed, she was not even competently literate, if I might so put it. She had been born at a time when our part of the country, the Punjab, was under Sikh rule, and in rural areas such arrangements for education and cultural advancement as had existed during the earlier period of Mogul rule had by that time faded out. So that all that she had acquired by way of what might be called literacy was that she could barely read the Qur'an, which has the same script as Urdu, but without comprehending its meaning because she did not know any Arabic at all. She could just pronounce the text correctly, which is often the case with people who are not educated, but are anxious that they should at least be able to recite the Qur'an.

But she was a deeply religious woman, and her religious experiences started early in life. Many of them were connected with the loss of her first three children, before I was born. I will not go into too much detail about them, because I would then be talking for days. I have written a biographical sketch of her in Urdu which I have called "My Mother." It is not very long, about 150 pages, and I have set out most of these things briefly in it.

By the time I began to perceive anything at all, I began to perceive that both my father and mother were deeply religious persons. The picture of my father that comes most often to my mind is that in the afternoon, when he returned from his business in court and we were all waiting for him to join us at tea, he would first wash and engage in prayer in the corner where a prayer carpet had been spread for him. He would be at prayer much longer than I was accustomed to see other people at prayer. Sometimes we were impatient that he should finish and join us, but he seemed to be utterly unconscious of anything outside of what he was engaged in.

My mother, while she was careful of her duties in that respect, enjoyed deeply spiritual experiences through her dreams and visions and, was the recipient occasionally, even of verbal revelation, which guided and influenced her life, showed her the right way at a time of crisis and gave her the courage to follow it. Her life and her experiences were a constant lesson for us. We had not to look for much outside.

I shall mention one or two of her experiences as illustrations. Long after my father's death - as a matter of fact, it was in 1935 when I was a Member of the Viceroy's Council and we had moved up to Simla only two or three weeks earlier. We were at The Retreat, which was my official residence. I received a telegram from Hyderabad, Deccan, that one of my very close and dear friends, who was like a brother to me and like a son to my mother - she was very fond of him - who had journeyed down to Hyderabad on some business of his own, was very seriously ill. I told mother and asked her to pray for his recovery. That night I left for Delhi and I was in Delhi just for a day on some business there and was back at Simla the following day.

While I was in Delhi, I received a telegram redirected from Simla that my friend had died the previous night. When I got back to Simla, my mother came down immediately when she knew that I had arrived and asked, "What is the news about Inamullah?" - that was my friend's name. I said, "The news that was feared has arrived." She was caught in the grip of emotion, but she controlled it, and asked, "When did it happen?" I said, "I received the telegram yesterday in Delhi redirected from Simla, and it said the previous night, so it happened the night before last." She said, "At what time?" I said, "The time was not mentioned in the telegram. We shall know the time when the man whom we despatched immediately on the news of his illness to Hyderabad comes back." She said, "It was about 3 O'clock." I asked, "Had you any indication?" She said, "Yes. I had been saying my pre-dawn prayers and had been praying for his recovery and when I finished, I lay down in my bed but instead of snatching another period of sleep before the dawn prayers I thought to myself that I would keep awake and go on praying for his recovery even in bed. Suddenly, I heard, as if somebody was standing next to my bed, voice, 'His current has been cut off at the source.' I got up immediately and went and roused your wife and said, 'Inamullah has died,' and she said, 'Mother, have you had an indication?' and I said, 'Yes, I have just had this experience.'"

Sure enough, when the man whom we had sent to Hyderabad came back and gave us the details of the last hours of our friend, he told us he had died at about 3 a.m.

I might mention one event that happened when I was only 17 years old. We were then in Sialkot, where my father was practising as a lawyer. It was the year of King Edward VII's death. There was no news yet of the King's illness or anything of the kind and mother had a curious dream. She saw that she had gone for a drive into the cantonments at Sialkot and passing near the Church of England cathedral she noticed that a stone was missing from the spire of the church, from near the top, and that there was an unsightly vacuum. She said to a cousin of mine, who was with her in the carriage, "Sharifa" - this was the cousin's name - "look there is a stone missing almost from the centre of the tower and the vacant space looks very unsightly." My cousin replied, "But, Aunt, do not you see the masons are having another stone made ready and it will soon be fitted in so that nobody will notice any difference." When mother related her dream she said, "I wonder what this portends." Within a week or ten days, we heard the news of King Edward VII's death. He was, of course, the head of the Church of England.

I mention these two not as being too typical, but as showing the kind of experience that she used to have. There were others through which she was definitely guided along certain ways. It was through such guidance that she was led to join the Ahmadiyya Movement in advance of my father.

In those days the Movement attracted much more opposition than it does today. The Founder was alive and fierce controversy raged around him and his claims. Mother saw him in her dreams though she had never set eyes on him in real life. Subsequently, when she had the opportunity of seeing him she was able to recall all the details, the house, the place, and everything else was exactly as

## REMINISCENCES OF SIR MUHAMMAD ZAFRULLA KHAN

she had seen in her dreams. She had not known who he was or what his name was or what his claims were. My father knew, but she did not. She had heard only his courtesy title, the Mirza Sahib. When she saw him the third time, in her dream, she asked him who he was. She said, "People ask me, who is this personality that you have seen in your dreams, what shall I say?" He said, "If anybody asks, say you have seen Ahmad." His name was Ghulam Ahmad, and he was known as Ahmad also, but mother did not know that. When she mentioned this to father next morning, he said, "Ahmad is the name of the Holy Prophet of Islam also. Maybe you have seen him." She said, "No. I am convinced that it is a living personality through whom God is seeking to guide me."

Later, within a month or so, the Founder of the Movement visited Sialkot, and she asked my father whether she might go and meet him, and he said, "Yes, by all means. But do not come to any decision." As I have said this matter was very controversial and any home in which the husband took one side and the wife took the other, could become a place of controversy, and religious controversies can be very bitter. She said, "You are a learned person and you are making a study of these things, and you will come to a decision on the basis of your studies. I am almost unlettered, and certainly can lay no claim to learning; but God in His own way is seeking to guide me, and if I find it is the same person, then I am accountable to God if He is seeking to guide me and I hold back. I shall have to declare my acceptance of him. But if it is not the same person, you will carry on your studies and you can tell me what you think."

Father went away to his work in court, but he sent the carriage back to take mother to the house where the Founder of the Movement had put up on his arrival the previous night. I went with her. There had been hostile crowds at the railway station and in the streets through which his carriage was to pass and brickbats had been thrown at the carriage and there had been hostile demonstrations of every description.

Arrived at the house, mother met his wife, and told the lady who she was, and asked if she could have an interview of a few minutes' duration with the Mirza Sahib. A message was sent to him and he intimated he would presently pass through on his way to the afternoon service and he would be glad to stay for a few moments.

I had heard her dreams - I was only eleven and a half at that time, but I knew what the dreams were - and I was anxious to see, from the very first look that she might cast on him, what her reaction would be. I knew I would be able to judge whether it was the same person or not.

He came and sat down a few paces away. Mother was sitting on a wooden settee and he sat down next to his wife. I noticed afterwards that it was his habit to keep his face bent down as if he was in contemplation. When anybody wanted to join the Movement, he would often warn them, "This is a very grave matter. You should consider it further, take time to reflect whether you would be able to carry the responsibilities, because the way is hard and you might meet many difficulties."

Now, here was a woman whose husband he knew slightly, and he knew he had not yet become a member of the Movement. As soon as he sat down mother said, "Sir, I want to take the covenant." And he said, "Very good then. Repeat after me the words that I pronounce." He said those words, and she repeated those after him, and then he prayed, and he left for the prayer service. My mother stayed a little while with his wife, and then we came home.

When father came home he went at once to where she was and he enquired, "Did you go?" She said, "Yes, I went." He asked, "What did you find?" She said, "It is the same person." He said, "I hope you have made no decision." She put her hand over her heart and said, "I have taken the covenant." My father was very agitated and muttered, "That was not well done." He then called his personal servant and told him, "Make my bed in the next room," whereupon mother said, "Make his bed in the men's guest room." Father turned to her and asked, "Why?" She said, "Because I have seen and recognized God's light and you are still in the dark."

Now if anybody had told me, I never could have believed that mother could say anything of that kind to father, not because what she said was so grave and serious but because the two of them were truly two bodies and but one soul and it was unthinkable that any serious difference should rise between them. But when she felt it was a matter of her duty to God, nothing else could stand in the way.

At that father smiled and turned to the servant, and said, "You can go. I know she will win in the end." Sure enough, within a week, he too, and exactly in accord with a dream of hers, went and made his covenant. I was with him also at that time.

We were brought up in an atmosphere of that kind. Three years later on the 16th of September, 1907, when I was fourteen and a half, and I happened to be at Qadian, the headquarters of the Movement, which is now in India, with my father during the courts' annual vacation, I too decided - my father had never said anything to me on the subject, perhaps he thought I was too young to make any decision on these things - to take the covenant. The Founder was in the little mosque, which was part of his house - after the noon prayers or the afternoon prayers, and I asked permission to take the covenant. He graciously consented, and I formally became a member of the Movement.

I am so happy that I did it at that time because the Founder died on the 26th of May following, 1908. If I had not done it at that time, I would have regretted it always that I had not taken the covenant at his own blessed hands.

He was succeeded by the first Khalifa, who was elected. He was his principal disciple, but no connection or relation of the family. He died in March, 1914, and he was succeeded by the eldest son of the Founder, who was only 25, but was the most outstanding personality already in the Movement and was not considered disqualified for election because he was the son of the Founder, nor was he elected just because he was the son of the Founder, but because everybody realized, from the qualities that he possessed, that he was the fittest person to lead the Movement. He is the present head of the Movement. He has been in very weak health the last five or six years and is not able to take any very active part in administering the affairs of and guiding the Movement. But the Movement is now well along the course that had been marked out for it, and under the guidance of the Second Khalifa it has spread far and wide. It has now active branches in both East and West Africa, quite a sizable community in Indonesia - I mean, outside Pakistan and India where there is the largest concentration - and there are some even in Europe. Recently the Movement started an effort in Scandinavia and already in Denmark there are over 40 adult Danish Muslims who have joined the Movement. They have now decided to build a mosque in or near Copenhagen. The Movement has built mosques in London, in the Hague, in Hamburg, in Frankfurt, and I had the great and inestimable privilege of opening the last three: the one in the Hague, the one in Hamburg, and the one in Frankfurt. One is in the course of construction in Zurich. There are small communities in a dozen cities of the United States.

The Movement seeks to revive the true Islamic values. There are some doctrinal differences with the orthodox mass of Muslims, but it is not necessary to go into them here. The main value of the Movement lies in the fact in the case of Muslims and non-Muslims alike who have joined the Movement, the emphasis is on that our conduct should be in accord with the values inculcated by Islam, which are: universal brotherhood, upholding of peace and the service of one's fellow beings. For instance, after the early centuries of Islam, it was not always kept in mind that the Qur'an says expressly: You are the best people for you have been raised for the service of mankind. The service of mankind concept has slowly, during the centuries, been overloaded with nationalism and sectionalism, whereas it should be the chief characteristic of Muslims.

Again the very clear and emphatic verse of the Qur'an that God has created mankind and divided them into nations and tribes for the greater facility of human intercourse, but that the most honoured in the sight of God is one whose life is most righteous is not always kept in mind as furnishing the only standard for judging a person's worth. Neither family, nor rank, nor office, nor wealth can procure any privilege for anybody, and there should be no discrimination between mankind on any of these grounds. The badge of honour in the sight of God is righteousness. He alone can appraise it. A person would not be truly righteous if he should claim to be such, because that would be self-righteousness for none of us can know whether in the eyes of God he is righteous or not. It is this activating of the inner values so that they should appear in conduct and action, that is the chief aim of this Movement.

I do not claim that I can in any way be taken as a model member of the Movement or as a model Muslim, but one tries, one goes on striving, one hopes that one might travel a certain distance along that way.

Islam is a religion which inculcates the acceptance of life, not the rejection of it. Monasticism and asceticism are prohibited in Islam. The attitude of Islam in that respect is: you have to live in the world but not to be of the world and therefore you have to carry on in beneficent co-operation with each other. That is what I meant when I said that religion permeates all spheres of life so far as Islam is concerned. I try, like many others, that when we approach any problem, we should keep those values in mind which are of permanent beneficence rather than any immediate advantage. One often falls short of that, but we constantly remind ourselves and try to correct our faults and shortcomings. That perhaps may have influenced my career, but it is difficult to say.

An amusing incident may be mentioned. A friend of mine, who had been a judge of the Lahore High Court for many years, was Governor of the then Province of Sind. I was talking to him one evening in a social function, and asked him, "Have you good news of your son?" One of his sons was then a student in England. "Oh, yes." I said, "I am glad. In your next letter to him you might caution him to be a little more careful," and I told him about a dream I had had concerning the young man whom I did not know. I added, "It may not mean anything at all, but as it was a clear dream and it has left an impression on my mind, I thought I might mention it to you. I trust everything will be all right." He said, "All right, I shall write to him."

Two or three weeks later we met again at some function and he said, "A curious thing has happened. My son has written to me explaining something which is almost exactly what you had told me. I was so deeply affected that were it not for one thing, I would take the covenant at your hands." He did not mean the covenant of our Movement, but a covenant means to accept somebody as your spiritual guide or mentor. I knew what he meant and I smiled and said, "What is that one thing that stands in the way?" He said, "Your being a member of the particular Movement to which you belong." I said, "Does not it strike you that maybe that anything that has appealed to you on the basis of which you would be ready to take the covenant at my hands may be due to my being a member of the Movement?"

To me, the Movement has not only been a very great help; it is, as it were, my chief support in life. It constantly reminds me that the ultimate value to be aimed at, the ultimate objective to strive for is, in the words of the Qur'an, "to win the pleasure of God." That consciousness helps to enlighten one along the path, to indicate in the midst of difficulties the way that one ought to choose. Where one falls short, quickly the realization comes: "I should have taken greater care. Next time I shall be more careful." That kind of thing becomes a sort of living experience. I do not know whether I am making too much of a claim, but I think it is that kind of thing that all of us need a great deal more than we practise. It is open to all of us. One of the Jews in Medina accepted Islam and said to the

Prophet, "Sir, even before I became a Muslim I used to help people and spend a lot in charity, do you think that will find acceptance in the eyes of God?" And the Prophet said, "You have been guided to Islam on account of the very things and values that you used to follow. This is proof that God accepted what you were doing, so that your mind and heart have been opened to the recognition and acceptance of the light."

□ □ □ □ □

# INTERVIEW - JUNE 2, 1962

**Question**: *I wonder if we might now discuss the period between 1935 and 1941, in which you were in the Viceroy's Executive Council, and perhaps the most expedient way to handle this would be to discuss the internal periods, that is, on the basis of what portfolios you held: Commerce and Railways from 1935 to 1938, and then perhaps you would like to discuss the 1937 election in India, and then Commerce, Industry and Labour and Public Works in 1938 and 1939, and then at the onset of the war, Law and War Supply.*

**Khan**: To start with the period 1935 to 1938, I have already indicated that I had two very important portfolios committed to my care during that period, Railways and Commerce. To an outsider, Railways may not mean very much, but in the then situation in India, Railways was an extremely important portfolio. In the first place, the railway budget, which had to be presented by the Railway Minister to the Assembly, exceeded the whole budget of India, including the defence estimates. That would be some indication of how important that portfolio was.

When I took over charge, I found that, though my immediate predecessor, Sir Joseph Bhore, was an Indian, the spirit of railway administration was altogether too official, as if the railways were a government department to be run along the same lines as any other government department. There was too much red tape, and too little consideration of the human element. The passengers were treated as incidental to the running of the system. I could have to some degree understood that attitude while the portfolio had been in the charge of successive British ministers, but during five years Sir Joseph had been in charge, and he had not paid the slightest attention to the railways. He had been occupied most of the time

**90**  REMINISCENCES OF SIR MUHAMMAD ZAFRULLA KHAN

with the no doubt important questions that arose in the Commerce portfolio.

But there were certain discounting factors in the case of Sir Joseph Bhore. In the first place, he was an Indian Christian, and Indian Christians, especially those in high positions, somehow or other looked upon themselves, as if by the mere fact of becoming Christians they had become more European than India.

Then he was a member of the ICS, the Indian Civil Service, which some wag, on the model of the Holy Roman Empire, had described as neither Indian, nor civil, nor a service. So, I suppose, the welfare of the average Indian passenger on the railways did not concern him very much. I had to devote a good deal of attention to it. I had not been an official and from my childhood upwards I had a good deal of personal experience of railway travel. Within a couple of months of my taking over the portfolio, the six-monthly session of the Railway Conference Association took place at Simla. One of the agents of the different railways in India was chosen President for each year of the conference, and the conference was held alternately in Simla and in Delhi. The Railway Minister was the principal guest at the banquet which inaugurated the conference, as it were.

I attended the banquet but that was only a social occasion and I could not do much. But I told Sir Guthrie Russell, who was Chief Commissioner of Railways and head of the Railway Board which supervised the administration of the whole system from the top, that I would like to address the conference, but that only the officers participating in the conference should be present, and the stenographers and the secretariat staff should be excluded, as I wanted to talk to them at an intimate level.

That was arranged, and I addressed the Conference for about an hour. I told them I would like to speak to them of the spirit that I would wish should pervade the administration of the railways. If they found that they were doing what I was suggesting, that was all to the good. If they found that it had to be supplemented in any respect, I had no doubt they would do it. "I do want to say one thing which might appear rather strange to you, but it is nevertheless true. I do claim that I have more experience of the passengers' trials and difficulties with regard to railway travel in India than any of you have. I know many of you are Indians, but you became superior railway service officials when you were recruited into the railway service, and from the very first day of joining the railways, you were

## REMINISCENCES OF SIR MUHAMMAD ZAFRULLA KHAN 91

entitled to first class passes and many of you could arrange to travel in saloons, and you have no experience of what the ordinary passenger, particularly the third class passenger, suffers on the railways.

"Of course you realize that the railways are a common carrier, but they are not being administered like common carriers, not for the benefit and convenience of the freight or the passengers that they carry."

I could see from the faces of some of those who were present that they did not like the introduction; they did not know what was coming next.

Then I told them half a dozen of my own experiences which highlighted the lack of courtesy, the lack of attention, the lack of sympathy, the lack of helpfulness, which an average passenger experienced on our railways, more particularly the third class passenger who was generally illiterate, could not read the notices on the notice boards and did not know from which platform the train would leave. The average railway employees, even the booking clerks used the occasion when such a passenger wanted to purchase a ticket or asked for information to show their authority rather than to help the poor man by telling him the exact fare that was payable or by giving directions where he should go for his train.

Thereafter I began to find that on certain systems immediate attention was being paid to these things and an improvement began to be noticeable. Curiously enough, the Great Indian Peninsula Railway, which had a reputation for efficient running but also for an anti-Indian bias among its European officers was foremost in carrying out the suggestions that I had made. The Agent, Mr. Wilson, came down to see me and I found him an extremely sympathetic man. I began to see visible proof that every aspect of that to which I had drawn attention was being paid attention to, and there was a general air of improvement.

I made the question hour in the Assembly a means for stimulating railway effort to conform to what was desirable. I never tried to ward off a question. My staff would look into every question. My staff would look into every question put and would put up a draft answer to it; if a defect or shortcoming was discovered which was often the case, we confessed it and said we would pay attention to it.

Then came the railway budget the following February. In the general debate on the railway budget a good many of the complaints which had been voiced for so long were repeated. Some had already been remedied, at least partially, some were in the course of being remedied, some would be looked into and remedied. I gave firm assurances that they would be looked into, so that when I finished my reply to the debate the opposition joined in the cheers that followed.

I may say that I infused a new spirit, or if I did not infuse a new spirit, at least I stimulated the kind of spirit that should have inspired the administration of the railways.

We were able to carry out one or two significant innovations also. It was in my time that we inaugurated a service of air-conditioned coaches on some of the long distance trains. When I mentioned this in the Assembly there was great opposition from the Congress Party. "Pandering to the rich! Nobody will ride in these coaches. They will run empty," was the kind of thing shouted at me. It so happened that wherever they were progressively introduced every berth was booked weeks ahead; it became difficult to find accommodation in them. Some of the Congress Members of the Assembly were not above seeking the comfort and cleanliness which they provided.

Perhaps one instance might be mentioned as illustrating the contrast between the official outlook and the non-official outlook on these matters. Questions were put in the Assembly that on a particular train in South India, towards the latter part of the night the toilet rooms in the third and intermediate class carriages were in an unspeakably filthy condition and that something must be done to improve conditions. The official report sent up to me was that they were always in a state of cleanliness and that there was nothing wrong. This was not a case of a difference of view, but of difference on a question of fact.

So the next time I was on tour in South India, I had my saloon attached to this train during the latter part of the night, and I got out at every stop to go and look at some of these toilet rooms. I found that the truth, as often is the case in such cases, lay between the two statements, but that there was room for complaint.

When I got back to headquarters, I enquired from the railway board what could be done about it. I was told the train was an express train and stopped only for a few minutes at each scheduled stop, and that the staff employed for this purpose could clean out only two or three of these toilet rooms. Nothing more could be done.

I said thee was an obvious way of doing what was needed and the experts raised their eyebrows wondering how could I know an obvious way of doing the job that they did not know about.

I told them to schedule the cleaning out of these toilet rooms, for instance, the toilet rooms of the first three coaches next to the locomotive to be cleaned out at the first stop, the next three at the next stop and so on. In this way the whole train would be cleaned out two or three times during the latter part of the night, which was the time about which we were getting the complaints.

They said that was quite feasible, and wondered why it had not been done. It was a very small matter but it illustrates the prevailing bureaucratic attitude.

Occasionally the lighter side of things came out during a question hour which I always enjoyed. The day I was under fire, as it were, the greater part of the question hour in the Assembly was taken up with railway questions and commerce questions, and I was on drill all the time, standing up, sitting down and standing up again. Mr. Satyamurthi, who was the Deputy Leader of the Congress Party and was a very diligent worker - I might say a good friend, in spite of the fact that we were on opposite sides of the House - was particularly active during question hour and I appreciated the serious manner in which he carried out his duties. When we were in committee, I got full co-operation from him. His supplementary questions used to come like pistol shots. Before I had sat down after answering a question, I had to be up again on my legs answering his supplementaries. But some members put their questions merely to give expression to their sense of humour or to pull one's leg.

One prominent Congress member who had a bent in that direction was Sri Prakash - he was subsequently the first Indian High Commissioner to Pakistan after Partition and later became Governor of Madras - a nice man, personally quite friendly towards me. His father, Dr. Bhagwan Das, was a very revered member also. During my time, that was the only instance of a father and son being members of the Assembly at the same time.

On one occasion Sri Prakash put down a question: "Does government wish to encourage the use of bad English on the railways? If not, why is it that on many railway platforms a notice is stuck up: 'Do Not Spit. It Spreads Disease.'?" Mr. Frank d'Souza, who was my Director of Traffic, and used to bring up these questions to me, asked what draft answer should be put up. I told him no draft answer was needed. I would deal with the matter from the floor of the House.

So when the question was called, I stood up, and said, "Sir, Government has no desire to spread the use of bad English on the railways. With regard to the second part of the question, I have never seen any notice of that kind or any other kind stuck on any platform." The point, of course, was that notices are not stuck on platforms, they are stuck on walls. We met in the gallery afterwards and Sri Prakash said, "Touche!" He was rather proud of his English, being a Cambridge graduate.

On another occasion, the same member put down the question, "Is it not a fact that a second class ticket is double of an intermediate class ticket. If so, why is not intermediate class accommodation half of second class accommodation?" I answered, "Sir, it is not a fact that a second class ticket is twice an intermediate class ticket. They are exactly the same size. The second part of the question does not arise."

He objected: "Sir, the Honourable Minister is quibbling!" I continued: "Sir, one has got to be very careful with this particular Honourable Member in the use of English, he is so insistent upon the use of correct English."

Another abuse that was rampant on the railways was that the enormous number of railway staff, officers and others, were entitled to free railway passes for travel home and back, and when they travelled on duty. Sometimes it happened that all available sleeping accommodation in second class coaches was occupied by these railway pass holders and paying passengers had to manage as best they could, though the rule was that a railway employee could use his pass for occupying a sleeping berth only if it was not required for a paying passenger. Once an incident was related to me which showed that my pecking away at these things at the top was beginning to have some effect. Some railway employees, Indians, had occupied practically all the sleeping accommodations in one of these coaches, and at an intermediate stop a couple of passengers came in and found the sleeping berths all occupied.

They sat down at the ends of two berths, and one of them said to the other, "Never mind, I know some of these gentlemen are railway

REMINISCENCES OF SIR MUHAMMAD ZAFRULLA KHAN    **95**

employees and I shall write to Zafrulla about it. He is sure to look into the matter. Immediately two or three of them got up and pleaded, "Please do not do that. You can take these berths. We will sit. You can lie down."

I have said, the whole spirit had been that the railways were a government establishment and had to be run for the benefit of government and its employees which was completely wrong. I think I made some contribution towards that attitude being charged.

But much the more important portfolio of the two was the Commerce portfolio. It raised much more difficult and far reaching problems. The most difficult and important matter that I had to deal with fairly early was the Ottawa Trade Agreement. The Ottawa Conference, which was a conference of the whole Commonwealth and Empire, had instituted the system of inter-Commonwealth preference in customs duties, which is still operative to a certain extent and is, incidentally, creating a serious difficulty for Britain with regard to its entry into the Common Market.

It was considered that this system would stimulate inter-Commonwealth trade, and would do a lot of good. It did indeed strengthen the commercial bonds between different sections of the Commonwealth and also made it easier for Commonwealth members to get together and make adjustments and corrections which were needed, particularly with regard to the price levels of primary commodities, which are a very important factor in the economy of most of the Commonwealth countries. Britain was the one outstanding industrial partner and the rest of the Commonwealth comprised mostly producers of primary commodities.

The way the Ottawa system worked was by grant of reciprocal preferences. For instance, certain British products, particularly Lancashire textile products, enjoyed preferential rates of duty in India. They paid lower rate of duty than, for instance, Japanese products and products from other parts of the world. On the other hand, Indian primary products like cotton, spices, etc. enjoyed a lower rate of duty in the United Kingdom than, for instance, cotton from Egypt and spices from Indonesia, and thus secured a better share of the market in the United Kingdom.

The actual working of the Agreement over a period had shown that it needed adjustments in certain respects. There was opposition in the Assembly to it, more political than on the merits. That kind of opposition was a part of the constitutional pattern. The Assembly could put questions, pass resolutions, criticise and refuse to grant supplies. But ultimately it could be overridden in everything under the then Constitutional system. It could, however, make a lot of noise. It was a system under which the Legislature had the power of criticism without responsibility. But very often the criticism was very helpful. It helped us who were in charge of departments vis-a-vis Britain and we could make use of the criticism to make progress along certain lines.

In due course, the Ottawa Trade Agreement came under review in the Assembly, and the Assembly passed a resolution that the Trade Agreement needed revision in several respects and called upon the government to undertake a revision with the Board of Trade, and to explore possibilities of expanding India's trade with countries outside the Commonwealth and Empire.

As Commerce Minister I was entrusted with this task, and I had to go over to England in 1937 and twice in 1938 to hammer out a new trade agreement. The Coronation of King George VI was to take place in May 1937, to be followed by what in those days used to be called the Imperial Conference and is now called the Prime Ministers' Meeting. It was arranged that I should represent British India at the Coronation, while the Maharaja Gaekwar of Baroda would represent the Princes. After the Coronation I was to stay on, first to take part in the Imperial Conference and then to start negotiations with the Board of Trade for modification of the Ottawa Trade Agreement. Thus I had to stay in England for several months in 1937. I had with me a panel of non-official advisers on the Trade Agreement Negotiations. At my instance it was decided that the panel should be composed of persons who would examine everything from an independent point of view and give me useful advice.

This panel, which had six members, included three prominent Congress industrialists: Mr. G.D. Birla, Mr. Kusturbhai Lalbhai and Sir Parshotam Das Thakar Das. Representing agricultural interests we had the late Nawab Liaquat Ali Khan, who subsequently became the first Prime Minister of Pakistan, and Sir Datar Singh from the Punjab. The British commercial and industrial interests in India were represented by Sir Edward Benthal, who some time later became Railway Minister in India.

When invitations to serve on the panel were sent out Sir Parshotam Das Thakar Das came up from Bombay to see me and he told me that he had been deputed by G.D. Birla and Kusturbhai

Lalbhai to represent them also. He wanted to have a frank talk with me before any of them would signify their acceptance of the invitation to serve on the panel. He wanted to know whether the panel was only for show that Government were consulting non-official opinion also, or whether it would be consulted on everything and full advantage would be taken of the advice it gave. I was able to reassure him completely.

I must say we worked very happily together, and they were a great help. They gave me realistic advice and I was able to make full use of it.

Towards the end of 1938 I happened to be on tour in Bombay. Sir Parshotam Das Thakar Das gave a lunch in my honour in the Taj Mahal Hotel, to which he asked prominent people from the industrial and commercial sections in Bombay. Towards the end of the lunch he got up and related the whole of this story, how they were invited to serve on the panel, and his two colleagues had asked him to go and talk to me, and what assurances I had given them, and concluded, "I want to state publicly that he carried out those assurances one hundred percent. We worked very happily together."

The Board of Trade also set up a delegation to carry on discussions with us. Their delegation was led by Sir Frederick White, who had been the first President of the Indian Legislative Assembly. He was an extremely formal gentleman, and, I hope I am not being unfair to him, slightly pompous. I remember one occasion when we were discussing spices and we got to the item of carda-moms. He enquired in a very lofty tone, "What are cardamoms?" I put my hand in my vest pocket, brought out a couple of cardamoms, and placing them in the middle of my palm, said, "These." The effect on those round the table was exactly as if he had asked, "What is a white elephant?" and I had produced one, as it were, out of the air, and all this in the Committee Room of the Board of Trade in Whitehall. In fact, it was a coincidence that I had them in my pocket. Kasturbhai Lalbhai used to have cardamoms and betel nuts with him as he was in the habit of chewing them, and he had given me a few cardamoms the day before which I had put in my pocket.

We soon found that that method of negotiation was not getting us very far; it was too slow, too ponderous, too formal. So after a few days' experience of this procedure the Permanent Undersecretary of State of the Board of Trade, Mr. Brown and I, arranged that he and I would carry on the deal discussions; then he could consult his colleagues and his ministers, the President of the Board of Trade, who at that time was Colonel Oliver Stanley, son of the Earl of Derby, and I would consult my panel, and report to Government. We made good progress in that way.

Our main anxiety was not preferences on articles like spices and the like, it was to get a commitment from the United Kingdom to take much larger quantities of Indian cotton than they were taking at that time. They, on their side, were anxious to obtain more favourable preferences for Lancashire cotton textile goods, because Lancashire was beginning to feel the competition from Japan and India itself. That, ultimately became the crux of the matter.

Once Brown and I had agreed on the intake of Indian cotton by Lancashire and my panel and Government had approved of the arrangement, I thought we had fixed up that part of the business satisfactorily. But a difficulty arose in that Col. Oliver Stanley refused to sponsor the arrangement before the Cabinet.

I remember I had to go to Lord Derby, whom I had known fairly well during the Roundtable Conferences. During the early part of the First World War, Lord Derby had been Secretary of State for War, and had started a vigorous campaign for recruiting. I noticed that in the room in which I was waiting there was a cartoon on the mantelpiece, in which an old cockney woman was trying to put the fear of God into her child and was saying, "I will put Derby onto ye, if you don't behave!"

Lord Derby came in and after greeting me asked, "Zafrulla, what can I do for you?" and I replied, "Sir, I have come to put Derby onto Oliver." He laughed, and said, "Poor Oliver, what has he done? He is very ill just now, not at all well." I said, "It is not what he has done. It is what he refuses to do!" So I told him what the difficulty was, and he promised to speak to his son and do what he could to help. Ultimately it was the Prime Minister, Neville Chamberlain, who really helped. I got to know what happened in the Cabinet. Stanley would not sponsor the proposals, but they were put up to the Cabinet with the help of Wilson, who was the personal adviser of Neville Chamberlain, and had his office in 10 Downing Street, Sir Findlater Stewart, who was Permanent Undersecretary of State for India and was extremely helpful, had suggested I should see Wilson and had arranged a meeting.

After the Cabinet meeting I was told what had transpired. After Stanley had put forward his objections, the Prime Minister had

REMINISCENCES OF SIR MUHAMMAD ZAFRULLA KHAN    **99**

intervened and said, "I know Zafrulla, and if he says that this is the utmost they can do, you may be sure he cannot get anything more out of them. We have enough trouble outside the Commonwealth; I do not want to have more trouble inside, if I can help it. In this matter, we are the bigger partner, and we should be generous. I think we should accept these proposals."

That closed the first round of discussions. I think I had better finish with the Trade Agreement before we come back to the Coronation, and the Imperial Conference.

The next question was: What is it that Lancashire wants from us? For this we had to go back to England in 1938. We discussed things with the Lancashire Delegation, and we could not get to an agreement. We went back and asked them to send a delegation to India. Their delegation came to India, we had a series of talks and we could not come to any agreement. I had to go back to England a second time in 1938, and in the end we were able to fix things up.

An amusing incident occurred among my non-official advisers, not worth mentioning, perhaps, for its own sake, but significant as revealing a certain type of attitude which also affected the political future of India. On some particular aspect we had pushed the matter as far as it could go and, having arrived at a point which I considered satisfactory, I put it to the panel that we might agree. But Mr. Birla stood out and said no. So I asked Parshotam Das Thakar Das and Kusturbhai Lalbhai to try to convince him and bring him into line. We could have gone on without him but this was the first occasion when the non-official advisers were not unanimous in their support of what I proposed to do and I was anxious to maintain that unanimity. So they talked to him and in the end Birla came out with, "All right. I shall go along with this, provided you leave me the right to interpret this when the time comes for its implementation." I pointed out that we were engaged upon working out an agreement between two governments and that nobody outside the two governments would be concerned with its interpretation and implementation. Our effort was that the language should be so clear that both sides should understand quite clearly what the meaning was so that there should be no room for any misunderstanding. In any case the agreement would provide how any difference in interpretation and so forth would be settled. How could the interpretation of any part be left to him?

Mr. Birla observed, "But that is what Bapuji always says." "Bapuji" means revered father, and meant Mr. Gandhi. I asked, "What do you mean by that?" He said, "Inside the Congress, when there are differences over this formula or that formula, in the end he says, "All right, I shall accept your formula, provided you leave me to interpret it when the time comes."

I was compelled to retort, "You will forgive my saying so, but it does not sound to me to be quite honest, that if one does not agree one should reserve to oneself the right to get what one is aiming at through a specious interpretation. It almost amounts to cheating." Mr. Birla repeated, "But this is what he always says." I replied, "In the Congress you cannot help it. You have, in the end, got to accept whatever Gandhi says, either by accepting his phraseology or by leaving the interpretation to him. But that does not apply here.

Much later, whenever, for instance, over the Cabinet Mission Plan or over other agreements, a question on interpretation has arisen, I have known that this is one of the favourite devices of the leaders of the Congress Party. They will, if driven to it, accept a certain formula always reserving to themselves the right to interpret it in a different way when the time comes. That is what ultimately wrecked the Cabinet Mission Plan and made Partition inevitable.

My association with Brown, the Undersecretary of State for the Board of Trade, was rewarding. We were able to do business in one afternoon, which would have been taken a delegation perhaps a fortnight to settle. Once we had got each other's point of view, he would say, "Now, Zafrulla, perhaps I could persuade my minister to go as far as this, or the Lancashire interests to accept this or the other. Let me try, and we will meet tomorrow or the day after tomorrow." When we met, knowing how far each of us could go, we were soon able to reach agreement. There were only a few matters on which we needed more than two meetings.

When I went back the second time to England in 1938, and made a courtesy call on Colonel Oliver Stanley, he had been a member of the Roundtable Conferences and we used to meet constantly and knew each other well. When I called he started with, "Zafrulla, I have not yet made up my mind whether I will not resign over what happened last time when you were here." I rejoined, "Well, Oliver, that does not frighten me at all. In the first place, if you had wanted to resign, you would have done it long ago. But it does not make any difference to my efforts at getting an agreement whether you resign

## REMINISCENCES OF SIR MUHAMMAD ZAFRULLA KHAN          101

or you do not resign. If you resign I will be sorry that I will lose a personal friend from the Board of Trade, but I have got to carry out my instructions and try to do the best for my people. Equally, you have got to do the best for yours. So, let us carry on in a business spirit rather than on the question whether you will resign or not." He found that that did not carry him very far. Anyhow, we carried on, and again, unfortunately he fell ill, and this time he was not even present when the matter went up to the Cabinet. The then Minister of Health, Kingsley Wood, was put in charge of the matter. Brown told me that the proposition which we had jointly put up was accepted, and added, "But only a Minister can communicate a Cabinet decision to a Minister, so you will have to come along with me tomorrow to the Board of Health for Mr. Kingsley Wood to convey the decision to you."

We had been working on alternative proposals, one I had not been able to accept, the other I could. Both were sent up to the Cabinet and the Prime Minister had very kindly supported the one I could accept.

When Brown and I met the Minister, he said, "Mr. Minister, I have been commissioned to tell you that the Cabinet has decided..." and he began to read the Cabinet decision. This was what I had not been willing to accept. I looked at Brown and he got up and said, "You will forgive me, Mr. Minister, this was not the paper that was approved."

"Oh," he said, "I beg your pardon." Brown drew his attention to the relevant paper, which he then read out to me. It was not his case, the matter was complicated, and his mistake was understandable. I thanked him, and we withdrew.

The main feature of that agreement was that the main concession to the United Kingdom was on the part of the cotton textile mill owners in India, in the shape of reduced preferential customs duties on Lancashire goods, and the major benefit resulting from the agreement was the higher quantities of short staple Indian cotton that Lancashire bound itself to take. There were other features, but those were minor as compared with these. From that point of view, I think we were able to fix up a fairly good arrangement. Even Sir Homi Mody, who was President of the Bombay Millowners' Association and happened to be in England towards the end of our discussions expressed himself more than satisfied with the result. But when the agreement came up for approval to the Assembly it was all politics again. The Congress opposed because they were the opposition, though Sir Homi Mody, the President of the Bombay Millowners' Association, abstained on the vote, which in effect meant that he supported it. The Muslim League also abstained.

Thus the trade agreement did not obtain the approval of the Assembly, though Mr. Jinnah in his speech in the Assembly did say that the new agreement was miles better, tons better, than the previous one, and paid me a personal compliment. He was very nice about it, but, again, the voting was pure politics.

Government gave effect to the Agreement disregarding the vote of the House, and everybody was happy. Congress knew it was a good agreement and that it would work well for Indian interests. Working with the Board of Trade on it and meeting so many people in England added a good deal to my knowledge and experience of these matters.

The Viceroy, Lord Linlithgow, who was not given to paying compliments, shook me by the hand, and said, "A good job, well done!"

**Question**: *Why did Birla and the other Congress people go along with you in London? Why did not they oppose you there, since they knew the Congress would oppose you when you got your agreement back to India?*

**Khan**: As I have said, that was politics. They co-operated with me in London because they thought it was a good opportunity for them to be in on the whole business after I had given that assurance to Parshotam Das Thakar Das. He must have told them that his experience of me during the Roundtable Conferences had been that I meant what I said. They knew then that they could by co-operating with me put me in a good position to fight on behalf of India, and would thus succeed in safeguarding themselves against any harm to their interests and could help me push India's interests with regard to other matters besides the interests of the mill owners. Once they were satisfied on the commercial aspects of the new agreement it would not matter to them whether Congress then opposed it for political purposes or supported it. Congress opposed because they were the opposition, but I knew that they too thought it was a good agreement on its merits.

To get back to the Coronation; that was not politics in any sense at all. It was a very delightful experience during which the graciousness and hospitality of the Royal family were to the fore. Those of us who represented various countries were for three days - the Coronation Day and the two following days - not the guests of the British Government; we were the guests of the King, though, of course, we had to be put up in hotels. Buckingham Palace could not have accommodated all of us! We were bidden to lunch and dinner at the palace each day, so that we had an opportunity of meeting the members of the Royal family in an intimate atmosphere. The two Princesses were still quite small. The Queen (now Queen Mother) was, as everybody has known, a most gracious personality, putting everybody at their ease. It was a privilege to meet her. Of course, one met the King intimately also. He still suffered from his handicap, the impediment in his speech. I recall the occasion in St. Stephen's Hall, where the Empire Parliamentary Association gave a lunch in his honour. Normally when the King's health is drunk, the King does not respond to the toast but this was a very special occasion. His health was proposed by the Lord Chancellor and the Speaker of the House of Commons, and the King replied to the toast. He got up to make a speech, and for a minute or two he could not articulate his words. There he stood, a lone figure carrying the heavy burdens of the Empire on his shoulders, with this distinguished audience drawn from the four corners of the globe waiting for his words. Suddenly tremendous cheers broke out! He had not said a word and we all went on cheering I should think for a whole five minutes until our hands were almost sore. That expressed a much deeper appreciation of his position that anything he could have said. He must have felt greatly encouraged by the demonstration. Then he made his speech. It was a very moving occasion.

The coronation ceremony was a long affair. We had to be at the Palace at 8 O'clock in the morning, where the Prime Ministers' processions started. We were in horse-drawn carriages. First Mr. and Mrs. Baldwin followed by the coaches of the Prime Ministers of the Dominons, Canada, Australia, New Zealand and South Africa. Then came India. I was not accompanied by my wife and so Dr. Baw Maw who represented Burma, shared the coach with me. I was in the full uniform of a member of the Viceroy's Council: a white turban with a gold cap inside, full gold-laced coat, white Kersymere breeches and a sword stuck on my side. I had to sit up absolutely stiff, because otherwise the sword would get entangled somewhere or the still gold front of the uniform would be rumpled.

Dr. Baw Maw who was very fair, with a smooth, clean-shaven face, was in his Burmese national dress, a silk handkerchief tied over his head and a silk blouse and silk skirt. He lounged in the seat next to me. I was told that at one place where the coaches had to stop, owing to the traffic, somebody from the sidelines shouted to me, "Hey, Governor, do sit back and let's have a look at your lady!"

The Coronation was one of those exceptional occasions when the rigid British adherence to tradition had to some degree to be relaxed. Those who attended as guests were to go to a somewhat late lunch in the House of Lords. But those of us who had to be in the procession, including the King and Queen, were to go without lunch. For them a buffet was laid out in a temporary annex to the Abbey, enclosed by canvas marquees, where we had a couple of sandwiches each and a cup of coffee, and then we had to start back to the palace.

The Coronation was a longish affair but everything went with clockwork precision, according to the usual British efficient methods, particularly where royalty is concerned. Inside the Abbey I was seated in the line of the Prime Ministers, sixth or seventh from Mr. Baldwin. His Highness the Gaekwar of Baroda, being the representative of the Princely order of India was just above me in the line. He was in advanced age by that time, and had some difficulty in maintaining his pince nez over his nose during the proceedings and also keeping his hold over the beautiful book in which the whole procedure and the service were printed. The seats were narrow, because accommodation had to be found for a large number of people within a short space, and all through the service either his pince nez kept falling or his book kept falling, and I had to perform the almost impossible feat of bending down straight to recover each article and to restore it to him. I had to lower my whole body in a straight line and pick up the book, and by the time I had given it to him and had opened it for him at the page at which we had arrived, his pince nez had fallen down!

The service, the anointing of the King, the sacred ceremonial, the glittering company, the solemnity of the occasion, and the procession and the joyous crowds were a very memorable experience. I remember Dr. Baw Maw saying to me during the return journey to the palace, "If these people were to stage a coronation, say, every 10 or 15 years, the people would be kept happy; they would never put

REMINISCENCES OF SIR MUHAMMAD ZAFRULLA KHAN **105**

the government out of office. The British people love these pageants and shows."

The Coronation was followed by the Imperial Conference, which in a different way was also a great experience. Technically, India was represented by the Secretary of State, at that time the Marquis of Zetland, and by me. The Marquis of Zetland attended the opening meeting, and then told me, "Zafrulla, you can take care of this. If you find on any occasion that you need to consult with me, you are welcome to come over to the India Office and we will talk. If you want me to attend a meeting, I will come in, but you can talk on behalf of India," which was very kind of him, for it put me, as it were, on the same level with the Prime Ministers, India not being independent and having no Prime Minister at the time.

In the middle of the Imperial Conference, the changeover from Baldwin to Neville Chamberlain took place. Baldwin resigned and Neville Chamberlain became Prime Minister. We all welcomed Neville Chamberlain the day he took the Chair. He used to be present, of course, as Chancellor of the Exchequer when Baldwin was presiding. I added a few words to what the others had said. He may have felt perhaps that there was a greater ring of sincerity in what I had said. When we were passing out at the end of the meeting and shook hands with him, he said to me, "I am particularly grateful for what you said about me." It seems it was not merely a formal expression on his part, because later, as I have already said, he helped me a lot over the trade agreement.

We continued to meet in social functions during my visits in 1937 and 1938. A slightly amusing incident took place one day in 1938. I was staying at that time with Sir Firoz Khan Noon, who was our High Commissioner in London. He used to live at the top of Putney Hill. We used to come up in his car, drive up to St. James's Park and if the weather was not unfavourable, took a walk around the Park, and then I would go to the Board of Trade, if I had a meeting that morning, or we would carry on together to India House.

One day, we were walking through the Park, along the lake, and we saw the Prime Minister and Mrs. Chamberlain coming along. The High Commissioner, in an audible whisper, said, "The Prime Minister is coming." When we passed each other, we raised our hats to each other, and I heard Mrs. Chamberlain say to the Prime Minister, "That was Sir Zafrulla." He said, "Oh, yes I know. I know him very well," but no mention of the High Commissioner, who had pointed him out to me, thinking I did not know who the Prime Minister was and being quite sure the Prime Minister did not know who I was! Apparently the Prime Minister had a good memory for faces, and, as I have said, he was very helpful to me over the trade agreement.

The Chamberlain family was well known to be a Unitarian family, and once when I had called on him, I told him that his being a Unitarian brought us nearer to each other, because Islam was very strong on the unity of man, and the Unity of God. An observation like that sometimes helps people to understand each other better. Later, when it came to dealing with Hitler - it is difficult even now to say whether he was right or wrong in what he did - but I have always felt that he was misjudged. The people who jumped over their desks and seats in the House of Commons when he announced in the course of the sitting that he had received message which had just been handed to him from Hitler that Hitler had agreed to meet him in Munich, and shouted, "For heaven's sake, go sir! For God's sake, go!" were the very ones who afterwards turned against him. They were so anxious that what appeared to be an imminent outbreak of war should somehow be averted. England at that time was in no position to take on Germany as it then was. Later they thought he had done a very wrong thing.

Where I think the matter went wrong was that the interval of time thus gained was not put to the best use. Everybody should have been convinced by then that there was bound to be war with Hitler, and they should have prepared furiously for it.

It is a curious quirk of history, that Austen Chamberlain, the elder brother, who had been brought up, educated and trained for a public career, was in public affairs for a long time, became Foreign Secretary, never got to be Prime Minister, which must have been his ambition. Neville Chamberlain, who had been given a Business training and training in Municipal Affairs so that he would be the boss of Birmingham, ultimately achieved the Prime Ministership, though the ending was not very happy.

□ □ □ □ □

# INTERVIEW - JUNE 16, 1962

**Question**: *I thought today, Sir, we might ask you some questions about the 1937 elections.*

**Khan**: The 1937 elections were the provincial elections under the Government of India Act of 1936. The elections returned Congress majorities in seven out of the 11 provinces. Before the Congress consented to take office in those provinces, they raised the question of the special powers that were reserved to the Governors in the Government of India Act of 1935, by virtue of which the governors could intervene and, if necessary, overrule their Cabinets, for the preservation of law and order, for protecting the interests of the minorities, and for safeguarding the rights and privileges of the services.

The Congress leadership wanted a clarification from the authorities as to how those powers would be exercised. They were anxious to get an assurance that these powers would not be used for interference with the day to day provincial administration. A certain amount of negotiations took place and in the end, Congress was given the assurance they had asked for and they agreed to take office in the provinces in which they had secured majorities.

The result of these assurances was that in practice the special powers reserved to the governors were eliminated. A Governor, in view of the assurance given, might have felt that if he attempted to intervene, and failing persuasion, he overruled the Cabinet by exercising any of the special powers vested in him, it would be made an immediate issue and his ministry would complain that he had misused his powers in order to interfere with the ordinary administration of the province. It would be very difficult, in any specific case, to say whether a ministry's action was a legitimate exercise of normal administrative powers or whether it trenched upon the safeguards and assurances that were contained in the Act with regard to minorities and services. Thus, the Congress secured for itself a position in which they could go ahead, disregarding altogether the safeguards contained in the Act designed as a brake upon the powers of a majority, to ride roughshod over the interests of the minorities and the services.

One matter created serious trouble: That was that the Congress refused, in the provinces in which they were in the majority, to include Muslim ministers in the Cabinets unless they were or became members of the Congress Party. They began to emphasize the so-called parliamentary convention or doctrine that a Cabinet could work smoothly and properly only if it was representative of the majority party in the legislature and that they could not, therefore, include in a Cabinet elements from outside the party. They said they would be willing to give representation to Muslims in each of these provinces provided the person selected to be appointed as minister was either already a member of the Congress Party or would agree to become a member. The Muslim League took this as an assault on the Muslim league claim that the Muslim League alone represented political elements among the Muslims in India. That generated tension and the situation grew more and more serious with the rift widening all the time till when the Congress provincial ministries threw their hands in, over the issue of India's participation in the War. The day was called Deliverance Day by the Muslim League because they had been delivered from the tyranny of the Congress ministries.

In the remaining four provinces, where the Congress was not in the majority, normal governments had been formed, and they continued to function smoothly and no crisis arose. The system worked fairly well, until and during the war, till the question of the constitutional advance, especially with reference to the war effort, began to occupy the front of the stage again.

**Question**: *What do you feel about the possibilities in the UP particularly offered the coalition ministry having worked in 1937?*

**Khan**: It is very difficult to assess today what would have happened. One can only speculate. In all situations it is difficult to assess what would have happened if something else had been done in place of what was actually done. Today so many factors have overtaken the whole situation and over-spread it that it would be a purely academic exercise to attempt an assessment. Besides, I do not have ultimate knowledge of conditions in the United Provinces, so that my opinion would not be of any great value.

**Question**: *Shortly after this, at the outbreak of war, you became Minister of War and Supply?*

**Khan**: We set up the Ministry of War Supply, just before the outbreak of the war. It was one of those measures that were taken as a matter of precaution. We set up an organization of supply in which all the British territories, dominions, colonial areas and India, south and east of the Suez, took part. A representative conference was called, which split into committees. The Viceroy was President, and as Supply Minister I was Chairman. In consequence of our joint efforts, through this organization, which worked very well indeed, mobilizing all the resources of these areas in support of the war effort being made in the United Kingdom, we made a substantial contribution.

The major contribution was that of India. India was the largest area and certainly had vast resources awaiting development. This development was carried so far that, in consequence, India was able to build up before the war ended - although I gave up the portfolio in September 1941, when I went to the Federal Court - a credit, vis-a-vis the United Kingdom, over its war supplies which was utilized, first, to retire all the indebtedness of India to Britain, and then, to build up a credit in England of over 200 million pounds sterling, which at that time was quite a substantial figure, and gave India a strong position vis-a-vis England and in the sterling area.

In March of 1941, Sir Shah Sulaiman, who was the Muslim judge of the Federal Court of India, died. The Chief Justice was Sir Maurice Gwyer, a very distinguished personality. He was an intellectual, a member of the All Souls set at Oxford, one of those rare Britishers to whom a man's complexion mattered no more than the colour of his jacket, and a man of very deep humanitarian sympathies. I had known him very intimately as he was the principal draftsman of what became the Government of India Act of 1935, and we had had opportunities of meeting in England during the Roundtable Conferences and the sittings of the Joint Select Committee on the White Paper on Indian Constitutional reforms. It was a great privilege to work with him.

I learned afterwards that he told the Viceroy that if he had to recommend a Muslim to replace Sir Shah Sulaiman on the Court, he would not recommend anybody except me to fill the vacancy. The Viceroy told him that he could not spare me from the Cabinet. We were in the middle of the war and I was War Supply Minister and Law Minister. The Viceroy had also asked me to advise him on what advances in the constitutional sphere we could make without undertaking a revision of the Constitution; that is to say, within the letter of the old Constitution, how could the spirit be enlarged. From time to time I made suggestions to him. For instance, it was in consequence of my suggestions that the Viceroy's Council was enlarged and was almost entirely Indianised.

## 110 REMINISCENCES OF SIR MUHAMMAD ZAFRULLA KHAN

I was also, being the senior Indian minister, Leader of the House. The Viceroy told the Chief Justice that I was almost indispensable to him and that he could not spare me at that stage. I did not know that this was going on between the two. For the moment, they agreed to appoint Sir John Beaumont, Chief Justice of Bombay, as officiating Judge on the Supreme Court so that the Court could finish its work in the summer sittings.

But the matter could not be postponed for long, as the Court was entering upon its vacation in June, and the Chief Justice was anxious that the matter should be settled, so that he should know who would take the place of the late judge when the court reconvened after the judicial vacation.

One morning, when I went to see the Viceroy for my weekly interview with him, he mentioned to me, that there was this vacancy on the Court, that the Chief Justice and he had been discussing the matter but that they could not agree as the Chief Justice wanted me and the Viceroy could not spare me. I had still nearly four years left of my second term of office as member of the Viceroy's Executive Council. He said that in the end they had agreed that they would leave it to me, so that if I wanted to continue in the Council, the Chief Justice would reconcile himself to taking on one of the Muslim judges from one of the High Courts; but that if I wanted to go to the Court, the Viceroy would very reluctantly spare me. After mentioning this, the Viceroy said, "You may think over this and when you come to see me next time you may let me know your decision."

I thanked the Viceroy and said, "Sir, I can let you know now. I do not need time to consider the matter further." He smiled and said, "I am so glad you don't want to go," I said, "No, Sir, I think I would like to go to the Court." He was astonished. "At your age, considering where you are, what you have already done, having still four years more here, with all sorts of possibilities open, I am surprised you should wish to go and bury yourself in the Court where you will be out of everything."

I gave him some of my reasons why I preferred the Court, and he stood by his promise to the Chief Justice. It was agreed that the change should be made sometime towards the end of September when the Court would be about to convene after vacation. That is how I went to the Supreme Court.

**Question**: *Do you want to say a word about your reasons? I would have thought that the Viceroy's arguments would have been very powerful.*

**Khan**: They were. The reasons, those that I gave to the Viceroy, I can repeat immediately. There was something else also which I shall add and that might come as a surprise to people who think one should not be influenced by that kind of thing, but I have always been influenced by that kind of thing.

My reason was that though the greater part of my public career up to then had been what people would call political, I had never taken very kindly to politics. For one, in Government at that time, there was no question of belonging to any political party. It was a reserved government and anyone who joined it cut asunder from party affiliations. But even later, after independence when it became a matter of party and politics, I was not much of a party man. I have always carried out quite loyally my duties and obligations to the party to which I have belonged, but it has always been a somewhat restricting and irksome position. Some people take pleasure in party politics but I do not. I have been perfectly happy to work with a chief who would look after the party business, so that I could carry on my duties, departmental as well as political. On the other hand, the practice of the law and judicial work have been a much greater attraction to me since the beginning of my career. I derive more satisfaction from work on that side, and I suppose it is a good dispensation of Providence that some of us have a bent one way and others have a bent the other way.

I also mentioned one other matter to the Viceroy somewhat incidentally, "There is something else also that you might perhaps be interested in. I think I am afflicted with a weakness on the political side, which might be of some use to me on the Bench. I may be wrong, but I believe I have the capacity to see and to appreciate the other man's point of view."

When my decision came to be known, everybody was surprised. I shall, however, tell you what influenced me even more than any of the things that I told the Viceroy. In the course of the week preceding the Monday on which the Viceroy spoke to me - I think that Monday was the 16th of June - I had three dreams, one after the other, with an interval of one or two days in between. In the first dream I saw that a cousin of mine, whose name is Inayat Ullah, had arrived in Simla, in the house where I was then staying, the Retreat, which was my official residence. In the dream I saw that I was sitting in my office room in the house and the door opened and Inayat Ullah came in. He was very cheerful, almost laughing. I can still see him quite clearly, exactly as I saw him then, and the impression was so vivid that when I got up in the morning, I thought to myself, "I had better get ready quickly. Inayat Ullah is here and I must go down and join him at breakfast." Then I recalled that I had seen him only in my dream.

"Inayat Ullah" means "a favour bestowed by God." I thought to myself, this is a good dream, perhaps something good is on the way.

A day or two later I saw in my dream that a friend of mine, who had then been dead for six years, and who had been very close to me, had come and met me in the same way, very cheerfully. His name was Inamullah. "Inam" means "a bounty which signifies approval," a sort of award, and "Ullah" means "from God." then I thought, I have had these two dreams in succession, and the second is a stronger indication of good than the first one, perhaps something is in the offing.

Again a day or two later, I dreamt that I had gone to a place called Lyallpur, about 90 miles due west of Lahore to meet a friend of mine whose name was Sardar Muhammad. That would be a good indication also as Muhammad is the name of the Prophet of Islam and "Sardar" means "chief." After I had met this friend of mine, I said to myself, "Zafar Ullah is here also, I might go and meet him too. He was a namesake of mine who was also a lawyer and practised in Lyallpur. So I called on him and met him and talked with him. "Zafar Ullah" means "victory from God," or "success from God." When I woke up I was greatly struck by this sequence of dreams. A cousin of mine and another friend arrived that morning to spend a few days with me. The first thing I told them was, "I think there is going to be some change in my career." Both of them immediately said, "Have you had a dream?" I said, "Yes, I have had three," and I told them these dreams.

The next day, when I went to see the Viceroy and he mentioned the matter to me, my immediate reaction was due to these three dreams, combined with something else, which I must now tell you. Before the first of these dreams, I had gone down to Lahore to have a medical check-up carried out. There had been traces of sugar in my urine, and my doctor had warned me that I was running into diabetes, that the sugar was rising in the blood. Another friend of mine, who was also a doctor, and was at that time Director of Public Health in the Punjab, had come up for some meeting in the Punjab Government at Simla. He used always to stay with me. I told him this, and he said, "Look, do not depend only upon your regular doctor. I know he is a very able man, but this is the kind of thing that requires the attention of a specialist." He gave me the name of a diabetic specialist in Lahore, Dr. Vishwanath, a very able man, and perhaps the best in the whole of northern India, and insisted that I should go down immediately to Lahore and have a check-up by him.

I went down to Lahore. Dr. Vishwanath was extremely good to me. He devoted three whole days to a thorough check-up. On the third day, when he had completed it, we sat down and discussed everything in detail. He educated me, as it were, in what diabetes is, how it can be controlled, what I had to do and what I had to avoid. At the end of it, the following dialogue took place between us:

"Finally, I must tell you: Go slow." "What exactly do you mean by 'go slow?'" "Cut down on your work." "I cannot do that. We are in the middle of the war, and I carry very heavy responsibilities, I cannot cut down on the work. If you think this constitutes a serious menace to my expectation of life, I can resign. I can revert to my practice and then, of course, I can choose how much work I should take on.

He said, "No, no. It is not as serious as all that. But, if you cannot cut down on your hours of work, then take life philosophically." "What do mean by that?" "Well, do not worry over much." "I am doing work which needs constant attention and it carries some elements of anxiety and worry; I cannot help being anxious over things sometimes. But I am not one of those people who lose their sleep over problems which they take with them to bed." "Do you sleep well?" "Yes, I generally sleep well." "How much sleep do you have?" "I need seven hours, but if I can get a little more I feel more comfortable." "How long does it take you to get to sleep?" "Not long. Once I am in bed, and I say the last prayer, 'Lord, I commit my soul to thee...,' which takes about three minutes, I am off to sleep. Sometimes I fall asleep in the middle of the prayer." "So you never lie awake bothering over your problems?" "I cannot say I never lie awake bothering. Sometimes, but very rarely, I discover myself doing that, and then I check myself and get rid of it." "How to you manage that?" "If I discover that I am mulling over something or the other, I tell myself without actually using the words, 'You have done your day's work as well as you were able to. If you are spared tomorrow, you will take it up again. You must remember the universe belongs to God and not to you. This is the time to rest. You had better go to sleep. If you wake up tomorrow, you can take up your duties again.'" "And does it help?" "It always helps." "Well, that is what I meant by taking life philosophically."

Thus, a week later when the Viceroy asked, "Why do you want to go and bury yourself in the Court?" I thought to myself that perhaps this was my strongest reason for making the change, for that would be going slow with a vengeance. At that time, the Supreme Court had a limited jurisdiction. Only cases that involved a question of the interpretation of the Constitution could come up to the Court, and the Court was not overly-occupied. Then there was the four months' vacation in the summer. Heat is inimical to diabetes, and I felt that if I could get out of the heat during the summer, I would be doing well.

I took up my duties on the Court in early October of 1941. In February, 1942, Generalissimo Chiang Kai-Shek and Madame Chiang Kai-Shek came on an official visit to Delhi. Judges of the Supreme Court were also invited to the banquet that the Viceroy gave in their honour and thus I too had the opportunity of meeting them. Except for the fact that I was deeply impressed by his personality and was interested in what came out in the papers with reference to conversations between him and the Viceroy, I did not attach any great importance to the event, not knowing at that time that it might involve my having to go to Chungking for six months, as was proposed, but for four months, as it actually turned out.

Towards the end of April or the beginning of May, the Viceroy wrote me a letter in his own hand stating that one of the matters settled between the Viceroy and Generalissimo Chiang Kai-Shek during the February visit was that China and India should establish direct diplomatic relations with each other. The Viceroy expressed the hope that I might agree to go to Chungking for six months on deputation from the Court and open the first Indian diplomatic mission there and set things going. Later, a diplomat could take over. He explained that the assignment involved danger as the Japanese Air Force had carried out extensive bombing of Chungking, after Chungking became the capital; that there were few amenities available; that I would not be able to take my wife and daughter with me; and that on the financial side, as my salary as Judge of the Supreme Court was more than the salary and allowances of the

British Ambassador in Chungking, I would be considerably worse off by taking up the assignment. He added, "There is, however, nobody else I can think of who can carry out the assignment with as much ability and dignity as you can." He was anxious that the Chinese administration should be impressed by the fact that a man had been chosen from the top-most ranks to be India's first representative. He added some personal compliments to me.

It was not so much the contents of the letter that influenced my decision. In fact, some of the factors mentioned in the letter should have dissuaded me from accepting. Having been in the Cabinet for a number of years, and having worked with Lord Linlithgow since 1936, who had been personally very nice to me, I felt that if he had need of me, and thought that I could be useful, it would be somewhat ungracious of me to say no.

But it was a hard wrench. We had taken a house in a lovely spot in Gulmarg, in Kashmir, for our summer residence. We had furnished it exactly as our official residence in Delhi had been furnished, having gone to a lot of trouble and expense over it. We had got the same furniture-maker to make us a duplicate set of furniture and everything, so that my wife should feel it was the same home except that instead of being in Delhi it was in Gulmarg. I had been looking forward very keenly to my first vacation after a number of years, as my two war years in Government had been very strenuous. Then this came.

I mentioned the matter to my wife. She was very disappointed, but agreed that I could not help saying yes. So I wrote to the Viceroy saying yes. Luckily, the period was cut down to four months. Just when the Viceroy had asked me and I had agreed to go, the Japanese occupied upper Burma, and the Burma Road, from Burma into China was cut off, the air service that used to go from Calcutta to Chungking via Burma, was suspended. I had to wait till something else could be organized, and that gave me a few days up in Gulmarg, which instead of making my departure easier made it more difficult. The place is so lovely: my first vacation with my wife and daughter could have been so enjoyable.

Eventually I got to Chungking by what was known as the service over-the-Hump. This was a blind-flying service of DC-3s, from Calcutta to Dinjan, in Assam, and then from Dinjan over the Hump peaks, 18,000 feet high, which necessitated flying at 21,000 to 23,000 or 24,000 feet. At that time there was no question of any oxygen or any pressurization or anything of that kind, and they had to fly blind as there were no arrangements for obtaining information on weather, etc. From Dinjan the flight went to Kunming, and from Kunming it went on to Chungking, on the Yangtze where, during the months when the river was not in flood, it landed on an island in the middle of the river.

It was a weekly service that generally left Calcutta about 10 a.m. It was able to get to Chungking at about 4 in the afternoon. There were only bucket seats in the plane. It was really a freight service, but some passengers were permitted to use it. My military secretary and I, accompanied by a small staff, one superintendent and one assistant, proceeded to Chungking by that service and arrived at our destination without mishap.

The Imperial Chemical Industries had a bungalow on the south bank of the Yangtze river and it was lying vacant at that moment. The officer or officers who had been occupying it were not then in residence, and they offered to let my military secretary and me occupy it. That was indeed a great boon. Chungking is situated at the junction of the Yangtze and Kialing rivers and has hill ranges on both sides, so that it lies in a sort of trough and is very humid. Being shut in by the hill ranges, it scarcely gets any breeze at all. It is very oppressive in the summer. In the winter it is enveloped most of the time in thick mist and cloud. It was a common saying in Chungking that if there was anything worse than the Chungking summer it was the Chungking winter.

When the Japanese forces occupied Eastern China, Chungking was chosen as the capital, partly for the reason that during the winter it could not be effectively bombed: it was not visible from the air. In the summer it was vulnerable from the air and had been very badly battered during the two previous summers.

As good luck would have it - nobody knows for what reason - the Japanese did not attempt any bombing of Chungking during the summer of 1942 when I was there. I know my presence in Chungking was not the reason, but I certainly got the benefit of their restraint that year, whatever the reason. In other respects everything was almost unbearable, not only the climate, but also the filth, the isolation and the complete lack of amenities. All communication with the outside world was cut off, except the weekly air service from Calcutta. Being in China, and wartime China at that, not a drop of milk was procurable. The Chinese themselves do not use milk, so that it was not that milk was rationed: it was just not obtainable. We had taken some Lipton's tea with us from Calcutta, but we had to take it without sugar and without milk. The lack of sugar was no privation in my case as I had given up sugar because of my diabetes. Tea of any kind was scarce in China. The Third Secretary in the Australian Embassy, Keith Waller, who is now the Australian Ambassador in Moscow, used to walk a couple of miles along the ridge of the southern range of hills, where our bungalow was situated, and bring me as many books as I could read, mostly Australian fiction. His visits were a great delight and were most welcome. We insisted on keeping him with us for an hour or a couple of hours, and all we could offer him by way of hospitality was sugarless and milkless tea, and he drank quantities of it, as if it were ambrosia of the gods. When we left we still had some half a dozen tins of Lipton's tea left. We gave them to Keith and Keith felt that we had bestowed a whole fortune upon him. You can judge from that what conditions were like in Chungking.

The political and other conditions perhaps deserve an observation or two. I reported to the Viceroy from Chungking, and reaffirmed when I came back and had a long talk with him, three matters which he was rather surprised at, and I in turn was surprised that he was surprised. I told him, first: that as soon as Japan was defeated, I was quite sure that the Communists would be on top in China. He nearly jumped out of his chair and exclaimed, "Why do you say that?!" I replied, "It is perfectly obvious. They are the only organized party in China, and they are the only people who are putting up any resistance to Japan, whether it will do any good to China at the moment or not, they are getting trained and they are undergoing all the hardships. They are already very well trained.

Secondly, on the Kuomintang side, at the top, with the exception of Chiang Kai-Shek himself, and men like K.C. Wu, who had been Mayor of Shanghai but was then in Chungking and had a very high reputation, and perhaps half a dozen others, everybody else was steeped in corruption. For instance, the finance minister was Kung, brother-in-law of Chiang Kai-Shek, and he had the reputation of being the biggest crook in Asia. The man went about loaded with gold watches, chains, and knick knacks. Even his mouth was full of gold; most of his teeth, whether natural or artificial, were encased in gold. It was common knowledge that the greater part of the goods that used to be carried over the Burma Road, while it was open, were treated by Kung as his private property and were sold by him on the black market. A loan that he had negotiated with the British did not go through because he insisted that the money should be handed over to him to be employed for the purposes for which he said he wanted it, and the British insisted that they must supervise its application.

On the other hand, the upper middle class, and there were many estimable people among them, suffered great hardship because there was continuous inflation, and the value of the currency dropped everyday, and therefore prices went up every day. These people had, by that time, disposed of all that they had which could be dispensed with, and their condition was pitiable.

The result of all this corruption was that the peasant was having a very rough deal. I related all this to the Viceroy in support of my strong feeling that once Japan was out of the way, the Communists would spread all over China. He may not have considered my reasons very strong. But I was convinced that my feeling was well founded.

Number two: I told him I had heard a lot of talk about the Chinese peasant being an individualist, that he would never tolerate communism. That was all fiction. He was so much oppressed that all he bothered about was some relief from peculation and oppression and corruption. If anybody could give him some stability in conditions and some relief from oppression, he would welcome them with both arms. That the Viceroy did not like either. He found it unpleasant and disagreeable.

Thirdly, I told him that the notion that the communism of Mao Zedong and Zhou Enlai was of a pink variety of communism, that it was not deep-dyed, was all nonsense. They had all been trained in Moscow and they were 100 percent Red communists, dark red, if it was preferred, but certainly not pink.

These were the main impressions that I brought away. The impression with regard to the strong personality of Chiang Kai-Shek was greatly reinforced. He was trying to do his best. Later on he got rid of Kung, his brother-in-law. Like all Chinese he had a strong family feeling, but Madame had it in much greater strength. She was a Soong. Her brother was, for a time, Foreign Minister. You might have read in Gunther's book, the chapter on "Let Us Sing a Song of Soongs," I must say she herself had a very attractive personality. On each occasion, both in Delhi and in Chungking, when brought in contact with her, I admired her greatly. She was a gracious hostess, had a brilliant mind, and was in every way an estimable woman. I

## REMINISCENCES OF SIR MUHAMMAD ZAFRULLA KHAN 119

do not know whether she herself was concerned in any of these things that I have mentioned, but certainly, Kung, the husband of one sister was the center of corruption. Curiously enough, the third sister was the widow of Sun Yat-Sen. She is now one of the Vice Presidents of the People's Republic. At that time, she was in Chungking; she was not with the Communists. Sun Yat-Sen's son from his first wife, Sun Fo, was one of the two Deputy Foreign Ministers. It was not very easy to obtain access to Chiang Kai-Shek, who was himself Foreign Minister but Sun Fo was always available. I had a standing arrangement with the senior Deputy Foreign Minister that I would call and spend about three quarters of an hour with him every Wednesday, and he would bring me up to date on everything. As I have said the great privation there was the isolation; one did not get any news. He would also give me some sort of news with regard to the fighting, such as it was, that was going on with Japan.

I noted that although India was not yet independent and technically was not a sovereign state, I was treated both according to protocol and otherwise exactly as if I was the Ambassador of a sovereign state. So far as contact with high personalities was concerned, I found it easier than European and even American diplomatic representatives. The then American Ambassador led a very secluded life. He had weak eyes, and could not face the glare of the sun; so he had to spend most of his time in a dark room. Thus he did not go about much, but I have no doubt that his colleagues in the Embassy made up that deficiency.

The British Ambassador was Sir Horace Seymour. I recall that on one occasion he received some important message from his government which had to be communicated urgently to Chiang Kai-Shek. Now, urgency in China in those days, and particularly in Chungking, had not the same impact as it has elsewhere. He had asked for an interview but he knew from experience that it would be days before he would get the interview. In the meantime, he thought he had better have the information conveyed to him anyhow, although the discussion on it might be postponed. I had a room as my official headquarters in the British Embassy. It was very kind of the British Embassy to let us have a room because accommodations were extremely difficult in Chungking. The Ambassador said to me one day, "Sir Zafrulla, I understand you have a standing engagement with the senior Deputy Foreign Minister." I said, "Yes." "Will you be seeing him tomorrow or the day after?" I said, "Yes." He said, "Do

## 120    REMINISCENCES OF SIR MUHAMMAD ZAFRULLA KHAN

you mind doing me a favour?" and he entrusted me with that message so that I could deliver it, as he did not expect an early interview either with the senior Deputy Foreign Minister or with Chiang Kai-Shek himself.

I had a feeling not that I was taken into complete confidence - that I think with the Chinese is out of the question - but that being an Asiatic I was admitted at least to the ante-chamber of their minds, perhaps, a little more easily than a European would have been. That was about the only difference.

As I have said, I spent four months in Chungking, and in early October I returned to Delhi. Before I left Chungking, I received a communication from Sir Olaf Caroe that the Viceroy thought if I could stay a little longer in Chungking, it might be useful. I wrote back to say that I would be glad to stay on if the Chief Justice thought there was nothing which needed my attention in Delhi, but that in order to preserve my sanity I must have at least two weeks at home and could then return to Chungking.

He wrote back and said, the Viceroy thought that perhaps it was not worthwhile subjecting me to the hazards of a journey home and back. So I went back to Delhi. I sat on the Court on one case, and then I was dispatched to a conference in the Province of Quebec, in Canada. That was the Pacific Relations Conference, at Mont Tremblant.

**Question**: *Sir Zafrulla, would you like to say a few words about the meeting of the Dominion Ministers in London?*

**Khan**: Early, during the war, His Majesty's Government called what was later known as the Dominion Ministers Conference. They asked each of the dominions and also India, which was not yet technically a dominion but was in practice treated as one, to send a minister to London for a conference on such problems as the war had given rise to. This was in November, 1939, during what has been known as "the phony period of the war," that is, before Hitler started his march into Holland and Belgium and later into France.

I was asked by the Viceroy, as the senior Indian minister, to represent India at this conference; so I went along. In those days the best way to travel to the United Kingdom from Delhi was to go by train to Gwalior and catch a flying boat going to London. My young secretary and I travelled down to Gwalior and when we got to the flying boat we discovered that Dick Casey, then Finance Minister of

## REMINISCENCES OF SIR MUHAMMAD ZAFRULLA KHAN 121

Australia, was also in it and was going to London for the same purpose. I had known him during the Coronation of King George VI. He was accompanied by a General and one other delegate. We travelled together up to Marseilles. Beyond Alexandria we could only make short hops because the days were short, and under war restrictions civilian aircrafts could only fly during daylight hours below the clouds, so that they should remain visible from the ground.

We flew from Gwalior to Karachi, from Karachi to Basra, from Basra to Alexandria, taking one day for each sector. From Alexandria, we were not able to go beyond Corfu, the first day, because if we had attempted Brindisi, the sun might have set in the meantime and that would have been contrary to regulations. The next day we went on from Corfu to Marseilles. At Marseilles, we were taken to a hotel and we were at dinner - my secretary and I at one table, and Dick Casey and his people at another - when Dick came over to me and said, "Zafrulla, I have received a message here that I must not travel by the flying boat to London. So the British Consul, who brought me this message says he has sleeping berth reservations for me and my companions on the night train to Paris, and if you would wish to do the same, he says he can secure reservations for you also." I enquired, "Is the flying boat not carrying on to England tomorrow?" He said, "Yes, the flying boat is carrying on to England." I said, "Well, then, why don't we all go on by the flying boat?" He said, "It is something that I can't understand. Apparently my government wanted a guarantee of 100 percent security for me and my companions from the Admiralty, and the Admiralty said being wartime they could not guarantee even one percent security. Everybody must travel at his own risk. They would give reasonable directions and take feasible precautions, but they would not guarantee anything. The Australian government then said that in that case, we must travel overland. So we are going overland to Paris and then from Paris we shall go on to London."

I told him that as my government had sent me no such instructions and the flying boat was going on to the United Kingdom, we would carry on in the flying boat.

The next day we left by the flying boat and were flying parallel to the Franco-Spanish border towards the Bay of Biscay, when one of the engines developed trouble and we had to go back to Marseilles. The trouble was set right within an hour and we left again, and after a stop at Accachon near Bordeaux for re-fuelling, we made

Southampton before dark. We were driven to the railroad station and waited for the train. In the meantime it became dark, and there was a complete blackout. A complete blackout can be a very bewildering experience. Trains crept in like ghosts in the dark with no lights inside. To find a seat, somebody had to help you with a torch, and if no torch was available, you had to stumble over people's knees and tread over their toes and feet. As it was, my secretary had to shift for himself, perhaps he found a seat in one compartment, and I found standing room in another.

We arrived at Waterloo station and were received by Colonel Crankshaw on behalf of the Hospitality Department, and were taken in a car to Grosvenor House, where accommodations had been arranged for us. Outside, as I have said, it was absolute and complete darkness. The moment we got through the revolving doors of the Hotel, we found the inside was brilliantly lit and, of course, the contrast was very striking. We were very comfortably lodged and though we had arrived late - it was 11 o'clock - we were served a sumptuous meal. At that time there appeared to be no shortages.

The following evening I attempted to walk a very short distance in the blackout and found that I could not manage it at all; I had to beat a very hasty retreat.

Next morning, we discovered that Casey and his party had not yet arrived. They got to Paris, of course, ahead of us; before we left Marseilles, they were already in Paris. But there they had to stop for the day, for they could cross only by night, and that night nothing was available, so they had to wait for another night in Paris. They arrived in London two days after us but just in time for the Prime Minister's luncheon to the delegates. The Prime Minister at that time was Chamberlain; Churchill was First Lord of the Admiralty. Among other things, we were invited to the Admiralty one night after dinner, when Churchill briefed us, took us down to the map room and the security room, and explained all the arrangements, holding forth as eloquently as he used to.

Someone of our number asked him, "Mr. Churchill, does it not strike you that you are doing the same job today as you were doing 25 years ago? You were First Lord of the Admiralty then." He said, "Well, in a way it is striking, the same enemy, the same problems, the same preparations and arrangements." He was at his best, as I was told he always was, about midnight. When we were in the map room, he explained to us the whole organization whereby they knew the

## REMINISCENCES OF SIR MUHAMMAD ZAFRULLA KHAN 123

exact position of every vessel, Naval and mercantile, and how it was being escorted and protected. At one stage he turned to me and enquired, "What do you think of all this?" I said, "It is reassuring." "That's the word, that's the word; it's reassuring," he observed. Colonel Reitz, the South African Minister, said to Mr. Churchill towards the end, "I have been thinking how fortunate it was that our people did not shoot you when you were trying to escape from Ladysmith!" Churchill's eyes twinkled with pleasure.

We attended meetings and we met people. Then we made discreet inquiries: "Would we be able to go to the front at all?" We were told there would be no possibility of that. Colonel Reitz was very upset. I might mention that he had fought in the Boer War against the British and later he had written about his experiences in that war and called the book *Commando*. It became a best seller and subsequently wrote another book called *Out Span* as a sequel to *Commando*. He sent me copies of both later. Subsequent to our association in the Dominion Ministers' Conference, he was appointed High Commissioner of South Africa in London.

He fumed, "I dare not go back home without going to the front. My boys will say to me, 'Daddy, you funked it!' I would not be able to show my face to them." He manoeuvred, and finally it was decided that we would be taken over to the front, but that only the ministers would go; their secretaries would not accompany them. We were put in the charge of Mr. Eden, who was at that time Dominions Secretary.

We crossed over to Paris, and during our first night in the Crillon Hotel; we had our first experience of an alert. My reaction was that it was too much of a bother to go down to the cellars which were supposed to be the air raid shelter, and I just turned over in bed and fell asleep again. The next morning we were told that Mr. Eden had gone down to the cellars among the ladies in his silk pajamas suit! Obviously, the occasion left no time to bother about sartorial details.

We were bidden to lunch at Vincennes, which was the military headquarters of the French, and the lunch was presided over by a Field Marshall, their first Commander in Chief during the war. They had gone to the trouble of providing a menu card for each guest which had hand-painted on it his country's map, mine had India and Dick's had Australia. We passed our cards round, which were signed by those present. When we got to the British headquarters I got Lord Gort also to sign my card.

## 124     REMINISCENCES OF SIR MUHAMMAD ZAFRULLA KHAN

We were then taken to the Maginot Line, where we lunched with the commander of one of the forts, deep down in the bowels of the earth. The equipment of these forts was, for that time, truly wonderful. The artillery pieces were so heavy and powerful that ammunition was fed into each gun by an electric automatic arrangement. In addition to the forts there was a broad strip of other types of defences and constructions running all the way.

In the Maginot fort, at the end of the lunch, the commander decorated each of us with the Maginot badge. King George VI later went over to the front and he was also decorated with that badge. On it was inscribed the slogan "On ne passe pas," "They shall not pass," but they did pass; they passed around the Maginot Line and flew over it.

Sir Findlater Stewart, who had been for a number of years Permanent Under Secretary of State for India and who was a very good friend of mine, was at that time working in Norfolk House in St. James's Square in the war organization and war planning. He reminded me afterwards that when I came back from our visit to the front, he asked me what my impressions were. According to him, among other things, I told him that there were two factors that had struck me very forcibly in regard to the Maginot Line: One was that starting from the Swiss-French-German border, the Line came right up to the French-Belgium border, and stopped short there. It was not carried on to the Coast. What was there to prevent the Germans from coming around it, by advancing as they had done in the First World War, through Belgium? Sir Findlater said, "What is the second thing?" I told him, "What is to stop them from flying over it?"

His Royal Highness the Duke of Gloucester was at that time one of the staff officers of Lord Gort. The day that we spent looking at things at and around the British headquarters, he motored about with us, and each of us in turn was accorded the honour of sitting with him in his car for an hour or so. I am unable to recall that during the time I was with him His Royal Highness made any observation of any kind at all. It was the later part of the afternoon, it had been a long day and, no doubt, he was tired. Suddenly, he inquired of his staff officer, "What do we do next when we finish this round?" The officer said, "We go on to Lille, where the Mayor is giving a reception, and then after dinner, there is a concert. I do not know whether Your Royal Highness would like to go to the concert." His Royal Highness' reaction was sharp and conclusive, "What I say

REMINISCENCES OF SIR MUHAMMAD ZAFRULLA KHAN **125**

is 'Damn the concert!'" I had no intention of going to the concert either. I, too, was getting tired.

While I was still in England at the Dominions Ministers' Conference, a session of the Assembly of the League of Nations was called at the request of Finland, to deal with Russian aggressions against Finland. I received instructions from the Viceroy that I should represent India at this session. I took with me one of the officials in India Office, as my secretary. The secretary who had accompanied me from India became the delegation, and I became the head of the delegation to the Assembly. We went along to Geneva, where again the contrast between the brilliantly-lighted lakefront at night and the complete blackout in England was shattering.

We had to go through Paris. We flew to Paris and then took a train to Geneva. I found that in Paris they had a much more sensible system of blackout. It was complete in the sense that you could not notice anything from above, but the streets were dimly lit by heavily shaded lights, which provided just enough of a glow to enable people to find their way. I wondered why the British had not adopted that system.

During this session of the Assembly at Geneva, we solemnly expelled Russia from the League. The Assembly and the Council unanimously passed a resolution to that effect. But it was all hush-hush; nobody wished to speak out. I was the only one who did. R.A. Butler, who is now Foreign Secretary, was leading the British delegation. The Duke of Devonshire, Under Secretary of State for the Dominions, was one of the members. I had known R.A. Butler for a long time. I told him I would have to speak out. "For heaven's sake, do! We dare not, but you are free, go ahead." They did not know what Hitler was going to do next and they did not want to offend him. They were ready to expel Russia from the League on account of its aggression against Finland, but they did not wish to be too outspoken in their condemnation of aggression lest Hitler should be offended. That was something I could not understand at all. So I spoke out.

Mr. Hambro of Norway was the President of the Session, and he was intensely annoyed by my speech, so that when I finished, he leaned over and reminded the interpreter who was going to interpret my speech - it used to be consecutive interpretations in those days, not simultaneous as it is now - that the rules did not require that the whole speech should be interpreted. It would be enough to give the gist!

I reminded the assembled delegates that if they did not stand together, they would be broken one by one. Of course, it was not the kind of thing they relished hearing from somebody representing a country which was not even independent and who dared to tell them what to do. I, on the other hand, thought the occasion demanded that one should speak out one's mind boldly.

From Geneva, I took a train to Marseilles. It was a very crowded train; by that time the mobilization was in full swing and I could not get even seating accommodations. From Marseilles, I caught a flying boat back to Delhi.

**Question**: *After you came back from China as Agent General, you attended the Pacific Relations Conference at Mont Tremblant in Quebec. Would you care to say something about that?*

**Khan**: As I have said, after my return from Chungking, I sat on one case on the Court, and then there was a fairly clear run, there was not anything ready for hearing and the Chief Justice had no objection. So I agreed to lead a small delegation to the Pacific Relations Conference at Mont Tremblant.

Being the middle of the war, the journey had some interesting features. From Karachi to Cairo there was no difficulty. When we arrived in Cairo, we found that the next lap would be from Cairo via Khartoum, Juba, Stanleyville, Leopoldville, to Lagos, in Nigeria, and that was controlled by the Middle East Command. We had to wait in Cairo for two or three days and were allotted seats in the next flying boat proceeding to Lagos.

At that time, Dick Casey, whom I have already mentioned in connection with the Dominions Ministers Conference, was the British Resident Minister in the Middle East. He very kindly sent his secretary to meet the flying boat on its arrival from Karachi, with a message that he would be happy to put me up. But I preferred to stay at the hotel where accommodations had already been taken for us. I gladly agreed to go to lunch with him the next day. He was very worried over the situation in India, and we discussed whether it would be possible to do something by way of liberalizing the spirit of the then Constitution. I told him that I had already submitted a memorandum to the Viceroy, from Chungking, making certain suggestions, which I was glad to find Dick Casey thought would be

# REMINISCENCES OF SIR MUHAMMAD ZAFRULLA KHAN 127

helpful and were practicable. He said, "Why don't you, at the end of the conference at Mont Tremblant, go on to London to discuss all this there?" I told him I could not, in the middle of the war, just go where I wished and claim the time and attention of busy people, but that I would go gladly if I was asked. He said he would write to Mr. Amery who was then Secretary of State for India.

So we went along from Cairo to Lagos, making night stops at Khartoum, Stanleyville and Leopoldville. We stopped two or three days at Lagos and were put up at Government House. Sir Henry Bourdillon was at that time the Governor General of Nigeria. Then we made a short hop one afternoon by land plane from Lagos to Accra, where the Governor was Sir Allan Burns, and he very kindly put us up at his very interesting residence, Christianborg Castle, which is situated on top of a rock which rises sheer from the Atlantic for 200 feet. The same night we heard the news over the radio that all flights of aircraft, civilian as well as military were grounded, until further notice. No reason was assigned, and we did not know whether we would be able to go forward or even backward.

The next morning the mystery was resolved. It came over the radio that the American North African landings had begun. We had to wait until something could be arranged to put us across the Atlantic. The third evening, after dinner, a telephone message was received from the airport, which was under American control, that if the Governor would send his guests over within half an hour, they would be sent across the Atlantic.

At the last moment, Lady Burns very kindly pushed three sofa cushions through the window of the car saying, "Take these. The aircraft is a freighter. There may be no seats at all, and these might be of some help." We arrived at the airport and found that the aircraft was one of the freighters which carried American ferry pilots back to America. These pilots used to bring military aircraft over, to be sent across through Iran to Russia, and then went for more. There was a party of them going back to America by this freighter. We were told that there were only three chairs in the aircraft, their commander would take one and two would be left for us, which was very kind of them. The pilots themselves and the baggage would be on the floor. One of us would have to accommodate himself on the floor also.

I had in my party one lady, Begum Shah Nawaz, and our secretary Syed Bashir Ahmad. On the principle of women and

## REMINISCENCES OF SIR MUHAMMAD ZAFRULLA KHAN

children first, I allotted the two seats to Begum Shah Nawaz and Syed Bashir Ahmad and decided to lie down on the floor with my overcoat on, thinking that with the help of the cushions, so kindly provided by Lady Burns, I would be reasonably comfortable.

But that turned out to be an illusion. I lay down on the steel floor with one cushion under my head, the second under my elbow and the third under my hip, each at a strategic point, but the higher the plane got, the colder the surface of the floor became and the steel seemed to grow much harder. I could not sleep a wink through the whole night. By sunrise the next morning we made Natal in Brazil, across the South Atlantic, where we landed in an American military camp, which was in the course of being set up there. They gave us a luxurious breakfast, and we were transferred to an American military plane, with wide comfortable seats and a kitty full of sandwiches and soft drinks. There was no steward on board, and everyone was free to help himself to whatever he liked.

The ferry pilots who had been with us during the night - there were no lights and in the dark we had not been able to see each other - were now seated comfortably in the wide seats and were enjoying themselves. One of them, Murray White, who was next to us, fell into conversation with us, and after 10 or 15 minutes he said in great surprise, "Why, you are like us!" which amused me greatly. I asked him, "Did you imagine that you were locked up in that aircraft last night with three wild beasts from the jungle, and terrified lest the plane should blow up at any time?"

It might be of interest to add, by way of parenthesis, that in February last (1962), I was in Denver, Colorado, to carry out one or two speaking engagements in the University there. The very first morning I was rung up by a Colonel White. In the Air Force here, you have the same ranks as in the military; we have different ranks for the Air Force. The girl at the switchboard had said, "Are you prepared to take a call from a Colonel White? He says he knows you." I said, "I don't know any Colonel White in Denver, but anyway, put him through." So he was put through and he said, "My name is White. You may not recall me, but during the war we travelled together from Accra to Miami." I said, "Are you, by any chance, Murray White?" He answered, "It is astonishing that you should remember my first name." I countered, "Isn't it more astonishing that you should remember my name? You could only have seen it in the papers." He said, "Yes, I saw it in the papers that you were

We are grateful to Mr. Abid Mehmud, with whose efforts we were able to get these photographs from the UN.

September 30, 1947. Pakistan's membership of the UN. (LtoR) Meer Laiq Ali, Abdus Sattar Pirzada, Begum Tasadduq Hussain, M.A. Asfahani and the leader, Sir Muhammad Zafrulla Khan. (Behind). Mr. Faruqui and Mr. M. Ayub. (UN photo)

September 30, 1949. The Pakistani delegation. (LtoR) Col Abdur Rahim Khan, Sir Muhammad Zafrulla Khan ( Foreign Minister), Mian Zia ud Din, Mr. Mohammad Hasan, Mr. A.S. Bokhari, Mr. Agha Shahi and Mr. Azeezud din. (UN photo)

September 1949. (From left.) Sir Muhammad Zafrulla Khan, Col. Abdur Raheem Khan and Mr. Shahban. (UN photo)

November 14, 1952. Sir Muhammad Zafrulla Khan addressing the Seventh session of the General Assembly. (UN photo)

October 15, 1953. Sir Zafrulla with Malik Sir Khizr Hayat Khan Tiwana (Former Prime Minister of the Pre-partition Punjab province).(UN photo)

August 17, 1961. Sir Zafrulla Khan presenting his credentials as Pakistan's Permanent Representative to Dag Hjammerskold, the Secretary General of the UN. (UN photo)

November 15, 1961. Addressing the General Assembly. (UN photo)

January 29, 1962. Addressing a Press Conference. (UN photo)

January 29, 1962. Another view of the Press Conference. (UN photo)

February 1962. With French delegate, Mr. Armand Brard, after presenting the Kashmir Case at the Security Council (UN photo)

June 15, 1962. Going towards the Security Council session in his typical prayerful mood. (UN photo)

September 18, 1962. Talking with Pakistan's Foreign Minister, Mr. Mohammad Ali Bogra, just before his election as the President of the Seventeenth session of the General Assembly. (UN photo)

September 19, 1962. Presiding over the General Committee. On his right is Mr. U Thant, the Secretary General. (UN photo)

September 26, 1962. With President Ayub Khan of Pakistan just after he addressed the General Assembly. (UN photo)

September 3, 1985. The UN flag remained at half-mast at the demise of Sir Mohammad Zafrulla Khan. (UN photo).

REMINISCENCES OF SIR MUHAMMAD ZAFRULLA KHAN 129

coming to Denver." He told me he is married, and is retired from the Air Force; he had a crash, but that he is employed in the meteorological side. I had them to tea and we spent a delightful time together.

From Natal we flew on to Georgetown in British Guyana, where we spent the night in another American military camp. The next day we flew from Georgetown to Miami, where we were met by the British Vice Consul, who told us he had reservations for us the next day and the following day, both by train and by air, to New York, whichever we preferred. My inclination was to stop the next day in Miami, which none of us had visited before - I had been to America, but had not been down to Florida - and then fly the following day to New York, but my two companions thought that it would be enough to have an afternoon and evening in Miami and that they would like to go on to New York next morning by train. So I fell in with their wishes.

We stopped in New York for a few days. We were put up in the Waldorf Hotel. We went by train to Montreal and changed trains there and went on to Mont Tremblant, which I thought was an ideal place in which to hold a conference in the winter, because you could not do anything else except talk together. It was a skiing resort and the lodge and the cottages had been placed at the disposal of the Pacific Relations Institute for the conference.

Among the people I met there was Phillip Jessup, who led the U.S. Delegation. He is now on the International Court of Justice, so that our friendship has extended over 20 years.

**Question**: *What was the conference about? What was its purpose?*

**Khan**: The Conference, as its name implied, studied generally the relations between the U.S. and the countries of the Pacific region and more particularly the impact of American troops and civilians upon the countries which were represented at the conference, what problems it gave rise to, how it affected the attitude of those countries towards America, and what could be done to remedy any problems that might have arisen.

Our secretary, Syed Bashir Ahmad, was delighted with the place because he was able to take up and acquired quite a proficiency in skiing while he was there. We were altogether a very happy family. Among the people there was Lord Hailey, whom I knew from India and had known in London. Incidentally, he is still going strong; he is well over 90, and maintains a lively interest in Asian and African affairs. There were several other outstanding people whom I knew already and some whom I met for the first time.

From Mont Tremblant, I went on to Ottawa, where I stayed at Government House with the Earl and Countess of Athlone. The Earl was a brother of Queen Mary. The Countess, Princess Alice, was a very gracious hostess. The then Chief Justice of Canada, Sir Lyman Duff, very kindly invited me to sit with the Supreme Court of the Dominion, one morning, while they were in Session, a courtesy judges extend towards each other. Incidentally, I had already sat in Lagos with the Supreme Court of Nigeria and in Accra with the West African Court of Appeal. I went from Ottawa on to Toronto, and from Toronto to Washington, D.C. Lord Halifax was then Ambassador of the United Kingdom to the United States. He told me that he had received a message from the Viceroy that I was to go on to England, for consultations which I recognized must have been Dick Casey's doing through the Secretary of State. I was told arrangements would be made for my travel to London. Begum Shah Nawaz would not be able to travel with me as I would travel by the bomber flight and women were not permitted to travel this way. So arrangements would be made to send her back to India the way we had come. My secretary and I would go on to London.

So we had to go back to Montreal. We had to wait a week in Montreal for the bomber to take off. The bomber arrived the day after we arrived in Montreal, and we were taken to the airport and were briefed. We had to put on silk and leather suits, gauntlets and fur caps, etc. When we were fully accoutred for the journey, we looked like polar bears on their hind legs. The bomber, which would fly at 20,000 feet was not heated; there were no seats, mattresses were spread on the floor and plenty of pelisses and things were provided to keep us warm while we would be lying down.

After the briefing we were taken back to the hotel and were told that we would leave the next day. But next day a blizzard started which delayed our departure for a week.

We travelled from Montreal to Prestwick, making a stop at Gander in Newfoundland. As I have said, the bomber was fitted with mattresses and pelisses. The arrangement was that we would all be lying down; there were no seats, and there was no heating, and so all the mattresses and pelisses and coverings were necessary. Over our ordinary suits we had to put on a silk suit and a leather suit and

REMINISCENCES OF SIR MUHAMMAD ZAFRULLA KHAN     **131**

gauntlets and all sorts of things to protect us against the cold. There was an arrangement, we were told, for the supply of oxygen, as the bomber would be flying above 20,000 - there was no pressurization in those days - but it so happened, though we were not warned, that on that particular flight the supply of oxygen failed. Our instructions were to keep the gas masks on, so that we had the worst of both worlds - the evil smell of rubber from the gas masks and no oxygen. I noticed towards the latter part of the flight, which was also the latter part of the night, that some of the passengers were feeling rather troubled. They sat up and then leaned over and then lay back, and I could not understand why this was happening. I was not so affected myself, but some were. It was not until we had landed at Prestwick that we were told that in fact no gas had been coming through the tubes, that something had gone wrong.

We arrived in Prestwick between 9 and 10 a.m. and then were driven through the snow to Glasgow Railway Station, where we were told to take whatever we wanted for breakfast and also to provide ourselves with whatever we would need during the day, as the train that was to carry us from Glasgow to London which, of course was not very comfortable, but it was wartime and one could not expect anything better.

□ □ □ □ □

# INTERVIEW - JUNE 30, 1962

**Question**: *Last time, Sir, we were talking about your flight from the conference at Mont Tremblant to England. Would you care to say something about the journey to England in January, February, 1943?*

**Khan**: We arrived in London on 5th January, 1943, from Montreal, and I stayed on for exactly two months, until the 5th of March 1943, although it had been expected that my stay in England would not extend beyond two weeks.

In London conditions were fairly comfortable and it was remarkable that the bombing that went on created no panic or disturbance. Everything was extremely well organized.

I had been sent for, under directions from the Secretary of State through the Viceroy, to take part in consultations as to what could be done to stimulate India's war effort. I believe I have mentioned that I had, even when I was on the court, after I left the Cabinet, and

## REMINISCENCES OF SIR MUHAMMAD ZAFRULLA KHAN

also from Chungking, been sending notes and memoranda to the Viceroy urging greater association of Indians as partners in the government.

Before I left the Viceroy's Cabinet myself, in September, 1941, the Viceroy had, mainly under my advice, carried out a large measure of Indianization of his Cabinet. Now, in early 1943, we discussed in London what further steps could be taken in that direction. My discussions were carried on mainly between Sir James Grigg, who had been Finance Member of the Viceroy's Cabinet and had, therefore, been my colleague in the Cabinet and was in 1943 Secretary of State for War; Sir Findlater Stewart, who had been for several years Head of the India Office and was then on special duty in connection with the war organization and worked in Norfolk House in St. James's Square where all the war planning was done; and Sir John Anderson, later Lord Waverly, who had been Governor of Bengal and was then a member of the Cabinet and was held in very high esteem, and whose views on questions which related to India carried great weight.

We worked on a scheme, a sort of ad-hoc arrangement, under which, without any change in the constitution, the Viceroy would set up a wholly Indian Cabinet and let them work, in effect, as a responsible Cabinet, advising them and guiding them, but by common consent not overruling them, so that they could take full responsibility for their decisions and for the conduct of Government. During our discussions, Sir Findlater kept Mr. Amery informed of their trend. Sir James Grigg, who years before had worked as Mr. Churchill's Secretary when the latter had been Chancellor of the Exchequer, and who enjoyed his confidence, undertook to reassure Mr. Churchill on the feasibility of the proposal.

*[(Because of technical difficulties, the following is a summary of Sir Zafrulla's statements in this portion of the interview:*

Finally it was agreed that portfolios in this proposed Cabinet be offered to Sir Ramaswami Mudaliar (who would, without assuming the title, act as Prime Minister), Sir V.T. Krishnamachari (who would be Finance Minister, and Sir Aziz-ul-Haq (then High Commissioner in London, who would be Commerce Minister). But just at this juncture, Mr. Gandhi decided to go on a fast. Three of the then ministers in the Viceroy's Cabinet thereupon resigned. These were Mr. Sarkar from Bengal; Mr. M.S. Aney from the Central Provinces; and Sir Homi Mody from Bombay. The Viceroy held that

REMINISCENCES OF SIR MUHAMMAD ZAFRULLA KHAN    **133**

this demonstrated the impossibility of transferring any substantial power to Indians during the war. He did not criticize Gandhi for going on the fast, only the Ministers for resigning on what was not an issue that directly concerned their offices.)]

**Question**: *Would you say something now, Sir, about events in India itself, especially the attitudes towards the war by both political parties?*

**Khan**: During the first part of the war, that is to say from September, 1939 until Hitler began to move in force through Holland, Belgium and France, there was not much political activity. India, as I have already indicated, had organized a very big effort in the shape of the War Supply Organization, in which all the British countries to the east and south of Suez were represented, and that was going forward very vigorously. The political parties did not give much trouble.

On the collapse of France in June, 1940, everybody became very anxious, including the political leadership in India. It was apprehended that Germany might win the war and that would be a major disaster. All political controversies were laid aside, so much so that the Congress leadership, including Mr. Gandhi, not only expressed genuine sympathy with Britain which was now carrying on heroically in a very desperate position, but also did whatever they could through expression of their sympathy and support to create a spirit in India that we should do all we could to help in the situation.

I recall Mr. Gandhi saying that Hitler was entirely responsible for the war and that Mr. Gandhi not only wished for but prayed for the victory of Britain. That was a clear indication that they were very much afraid that if Britain collapsed all hope of independence, liberty and freedom of the triumph of humanitarian values would disappear. Everybody knew what Hitler was and what his attitude toward dependent peoples was. He had put it forth very clearly in *Mein Kampf*. But, when through the summer it began to appear that Britain would not only stand fast but that with the help that was coming from all directions, and especially from America, it might be able to prolong the struggle long enough, to emerge victorious at the end, the Congress began to develop more and more opposition, not to the war itself, but to the then constituted authority in India on the political plane, and to push forward more rapidly toward independence.

During the fall of 1940, Sir Jeremy Raisman, who was then Finance Minister, found himself under the necessity of presenting a Supplementary Budget. In the general debate on the Supplementary Budget, the Congress's attitude was one of extreme opposition, to the then form of government. To my mind - I was then in the Cabinet and was Leader of the House - that was an indication that the political leadership in India was beginning to hope that Great Britain would emerge victorious from the struggle and, in consequence, they resumed the political struggle.

But, by and large, nothing was done by any political party or group to obstruct the war effort. There was a certain amount of underground terrorism going on, and later there were disturbances in Bihar, which was very unfortunate, but looking back over the whole period of the war one would say that the attitude of the main political parties - the Congress and the Muslim League - was on the whole co-operative. At least it was at no time seriously obstructive. Such political activity as was carried on was kept within legitimate bounds.

On the other hand, there was the consideration that if all political activity was laid aside, the political objective might receive a setback. They wanted to keep the idea in the forefront, that India was doing all it could to help win the war and that India's emergence into a free independent country, in association with Britain - at that time, everybody's objective was that India should become a dominion, as it actually did become in 1947 - should not be subject to any delay once victory was won.

From then onwards, the main difficulty in the way was not the attitude of the British Government, but the deadlock between the two parties: How was the communal problem to be resolved? Everybody recognized that until there was some agreement on that it would be difficult for the British to put into effect a constitution that would set up India as a dominion.

I, myself, speaking as Leader of the House as early as the fall of 1940 in the debate on the Supplementary Budget, had announced quite clearly that we were all agreed that India should be independent as soon as possible. The only obstacle was to find a basis of settlement between the parties.

On the 15th of August, 1945, when the general election in Britain had brought the Labour Party into power, Prime Minister Attlee made an announcement in the Speech from the Throne that steps would be taken to set up India as an independent dominion as soon as possible, a promise which was fulfilled exactly two years later.

**Question**: *Sir Zafrulla, it has frequently been said, especially since independence, that from 1906 on, with the founding of the Muslim League, the British Government in India quite deliberately, as a matter of policy or at the best unconsciously, attempted to divide Hindu and Muslim interests. What is your own view on this?*

**Khan**: My view is that the deliberate policy of the British Government in England or as a major objective in the policy of any Viceroy, this is not true. The Muslim League came into being in 1906, during the viceroyalty of Lord Minto, under the guidance of such Muslim leaders as the late Aga Khan, Sir Syed Amir Ali, Nawab Salimullah of Dacca, and Mirza Abbas Ali Beg, in consequence of the growing apprehension in the minds of Muslim leadership in India that with the progress of the representative principle, which found expression in popular elections, Muslim interests would be progressively neglected, unless safeguards were devised and put into effect. Experience had already shown that the electoral system of responsibility could be manipulated to the serious prejudices of the minorities, and the Muslims, being the largest minority, had grave apprehensions on that score.

The country was still at a stage when the struggle for independence all lay ahead, but the experience already gained in the political field made the Muslims feel that some safeguards had become necessary.

Muslim public opinion later on split on whether the best way of safeguarding the Muslim position would be through co-operation with the Indian National Congress or through strengthening their own organization.

I do not think the setting-up of the Muslim League in 1906 could be interpreted as evidence of British policy to divide the Hindus and Muslims although it is true that we were still in a stage where any colonial administration would look for support wherever it could find it. It was part of colonial policy, not only in India but in other places also where similar conditions prevailed, that the administration would try to obtain support wherever it could find it, and it was imagined that as the minorities were more dependent upon the government for protection and the safeguarding of their interests than the majority was, such support may be more hopefully looked for from the minorities.

## 136 REMINISCENCES OF SIR MUHAMMAD ZAFRULLA KHAN

The allegations that have frequently been made after partition and after independence that in the later stages of the struggle it was the British Government which was putting up the Muslim League, especially after the claim for Pakistan was put forward, or that it was in any sense backing them, are utterly unfounded. The best refutation of that charge is the fact that, as I have already mentioned, from the middle of August, 1945 - during the crucial period of the last two years - the Labour Party was in power and the Labour Party had never been sympathetic towards the Muslim League, but had always been extremely sympathetic towards the Congress. Mr. Attlee did all he could and went as far as he could to preserve the unity of India and to safeguard it against being divided. It was under that desire and hope that he sent the Cabinet Mission, composed of Lord P. Lawrence, who was Secretary of State for India; Sir Stafford Cripps, who was Lord Privy Seal; and Mr. Alexander, who was First Lord of the Admiralty, to India to secure acceptance of a federal plan for an independent India.

They did a first-class job and to the gratified surprise of everybody, they did bring a settlement about between the two political parties which would have maintained the political unity of India on a federal basis, with a choice, at the end of 10 years, to be exercised only once, that the two Muslim majority zones in the federation could legislate themselves out of the federation and become independent if they were not satisfied with the manner in which the federation was working. It is much to be regretted that the plan after being accepted was sabotaged by Pandit Jawaharlal Nehru's announcement within a few weeks, putting an interpretation upon certain paragraphs of the plan, which those paragraphs were utterly incapable of bearing.

**Question**: *In February-March, 1945, you went to Great Britain to attend the Commonwealth Relations Conference. Could you tell us something about that, its particular significance at that particular time as far as India was concerned?*

**Khan**: The British Commonwealth Relations Conference of 1945 was held in London at Chatham House, the headquarters of the Royal Institute of International Affairs, 10 St. Jame's Square, during February and March, 1945. I had the honour of leading the Indian delegation to that conference. I had been the first President of the Indian Institute of International Affairs. In fact, I was the first and only President as the Institute was transferred to Pakistan on

## REMINISCENCES OF SIR MUHAMMAD ZAFRULLA KHAN 137

partition and India set up its Council on World Affairs. After its transference to Pakistan, I became President of the Pakistan Institute of International Affairs, which position I continued to occupy until 1954, when I went to the International Court of Justice. Thus, during the years that the Institute operated in India, I was its President and in that capacity I led the Indian delegation to the Commonwealth Relations Conference in London in February and March, 1945.

Except for the Secretary of the Institute, Khwaja Sarwar Hassan, who was also with us as a delegate, I believe all the other delegates were non-Muslims. We were a good delegation. One of the members was Sir Maharaj Singh, who had for a short time been Agent-General of India in South Africa. He had been in the Civil Service of the United Provinces and rose to great eminence. The other delegates also were very keen and active members of the Indian Institute.

I think we made a significant contribution to the deliberations of the conference. In the opening session, the leader of each delegation made a brief speech, reviewing the war effort of his country and making general observations on the objectives and ideals of the Commonwealth. I took advantage of the opportunity thus afforded, after summarizing India's war effort, to draw attention to the fact that while India had two and a half million people in the field in defence of the freedom of the Commonwealth, it was a great irony that India should still be a suppliant for its own freedom. I made a strong appeal to the assembled statesmen of the Empire that India should, as soon as possible, become independent.

It so happened that the juxtaposition presented by me struck the imagination of those present and also of the press. By the time we came out of Chatham House, about a couple of hours later, we found that that part of my speech had been printed verbatim in bold letters in the evening papers. That created a great stir. Finding that my plea had struck such a chord of sympathy both in the conference and outside, I then took advantage of the fact that I had been nominated as one of the two guests to respond to the toast of the guests at the banquet that was given on behalf of the Royal Institute that evening in Claridge's Hotel, in honour of the members of the Conference, to develop that theme at greater length. In that speech, I appealed to the British Government to do something positive and concrete in that behalf. I made a suggestion that even pending a settlement between the Muslim League and the Congress, as there was agreement on all sides that India should be a dominion, the same as Canada, Australia and New Zealand, the British should give effect to that aspiration by promulgating a Constitution which they deemed just and fair to all interests subject to the assurance that as soon as the two parties could arrive at a settlement between themselves, whatever they proposed would be substituted for the interim Constitution.

The entire British Cabinet, with the exception only of Mr. Churchill, was present at the banquet. Mr. Ivision Macadam, Director-General of Chatham House, had himself urged me that I should take advantage of the great impression that had been created by the few words I had said during the afternoon to push this matter further at the banquet. He had pointed out that this would be an excellent opportunity as everybody who mattered was to be present with the exception only of Mr. Churchill whose duties as Prime Minister would prevent him from attending.

Within a day or two, I was told that as the result of those two speeches Lord Wavell, who was then Viceroy of India, had been summoned for consultations to London. In this manner, apart from the contribution made by the Indian delegation through the discussions on each topic as it came up in the roundtables into which the conference was divided, we were at the very beginning able to give the principal topic on which India was interested, that is to say, to march as quickly as possible towards independence, a vigorous push forward.

Later, in India, Mr. Asaf Ali, who was one of the leading members of the Congress, told me that Pandit Jawaharlal Nehru and Mr. Asaf Ali and some of the other Congress leaders who were then in internment in the fort at Ahmadnagar in the Deccan, South India, had heard my opening speech over the radio. He described the scene to me: "We were all clustered around the receiver and we heard your speech with bated breath, especially the part beginning 'Statesman of the Empire, does it not strike you as an irony that while India maintains two-and-a-half million people in the field in defence of the liberties and freedom of the Commonwealth, it should itself be a suppliant for its own freedom.' When your speech finished, we turned off the radio and Pandit Nehru, who had been leaning forward so as not to miss a single word, sat back and he said, 'My goodness, this man says these things with even greater courage and more plainly than we do!'"

The difference between those who were fighters in the field, as it were, for independence and those like me, who were doing the same thing through co-operation with the British, was not on the objective; on that we were all agreed. The difference was one of method; and both methods were necessary; in fact they were complementary. It was not as if we thought that the co-operative method alone should have been pursued, and I doubt whether even the most extreme Congress leadership could have thought that it was not worthwhile to continue the co-operative method also. Both were necessary and were complementary to each other, though, of course, the method of fighting in the field, if I might so describe it, was much the more spectacular of the two and also involved greater sacrifices. They went to jail; they had to suffer privations, and I do not mean to imply at all that our part was in any sense as hard and as much beset with difficulties as theirs; but I do maintain that those of us who worked in co-operation, with the British, towards the same objective, did help in some ways to push the matter forward. The Commonwealth Relations Conference in February-March of 1945 was one of those occasions on which we were able to give the matter a push.

The journey to England and back on that occasion, in contrast with the journey mentioned earlier, to Mont Tremblant and then on to England and back, was a perfectly straightforward affair. By that time the Germans had been pushed back far enough to make the regular air route operable. So we went directly from Karachi, via Cairo, over the Mediterranean, on to England and back by the same route. There was no trouble at all.

**Question**: *Sir, would you tell us something about Chaudhary Rahmat Ali and his attitude towards Pakistan?*

**Khan**: I knew Chaudhary Rahmat Ali very well when he was a student in the Islamia College at Lahore, and later when he was a student in the Law College at Lahore. At that time, I was a part-time lecturer in our University Law College. Later, I knew him when he was a student in Cambridge, in the early 1930s when the Roundtable Conferences were being held in London. He used to come up to London and discuss things with some of the delegates. He had associated with him Khwaja Abdur Rahim, who was also at Cambridge at that time. The latter subsequently went into the Civil Service and rose to be Commissioner of Rawalpindi, and then resigned. He is now practising at the Bar and is also interested in industry. I might take this opportunity to mention here that when it came to partition later, I found that in the matter of preparation for putting our case before the Boundary Commission, Khwaja Abdur Rahim was the only one who had done any useful work at all by way of collecting and collaborating data on various important factors.

Chaudhary Rahmat Ali and Khwaja Abdur Rahim came to London, and we spent some time together discussing Chaudhary Rahmat Ali's then-scheme of Pakistan. Chaudhary Rahmat Ali has the credit of having invented the name "Pakistan." To my great surprise I found that, at that time he was looking only at the northwest of the subcontinent and was ignoring Bengal altogether. When I pointed out to him that in Bengal there were almost twice as many Muslims as there were in the Punjab, he was extremely surprised, and thought I was being very foolish. In a contemptuous tone he said, "Now, what is it you are saying? Punjab has 56 percent Muslims and Bengal only 54 percent Muslims."

I had to point out patiently, "That's true, Mr. Rahmat Ali, but percent means out of 100. Bengal has 54 Muslims out of each hundred of population. But how many hundreds are there in Bengal?" It took me ten minutes to explain this very elementary fact to him, that as the total population of Bengal was more than twice that of Punjab, 54 percent out of a population more than twice that of the Punjab, gave Bengal more Muslims than there were in the Punjab.

It was then that he began to think of some modification of his scheme, so as to include Bengal as part of it. He was more of a visionary than a man of affairs and was not inclined to attach much significance to the practical aspects of a problem.

His scheme involved separation and partition, but it was based on an exchange of populations, necessitating that the total Muslim population of the entire subcontinent of India should go into Pakistan.

I enquired from him who would provide the cost of the transportation of the enormous number of people affected and of their movable goods, across the subcontinent. His answer was that we would have to organize ourselves and to club together to carry out the operation. My comment was, "Mr. Rahmat Ali, if our economic position were so good as to enable us to carry out this huge operation of an exchange of populations and to pay our share of the cost of the transportation of the Muslims, we would not be doing so badly that we would insist on partition."

He was very enthusiastic and was a very devoted type of person. He was so enamoured of his idea that he could brook no criticism of or opposition to it. I did not speak in opposition to his idea, because at that time the whole thing was so academic, and we treated it as something with which these young undergraduates amused themselves during their leisure hours. None of us, at least in the Roundtable Conference, was at that time disposed to attach much importance to it or to treat it as a practical proposition. But so much was Mr. Rahmat Ali devoted to this idea of exchange of populations and that Pakistan, whether confined only to the northwest or also comprising the northeast, should accommodate within its borders the total Muslim

population of the whole of India, that when Pakistan was achieved and put into effect, he was greatly disappointed. He used to apply all sorts of opprobrious epithets to the Qaid-i-Azam lamenting that he had destroyed the whole concept with which Mr. Rahmat Ali had started.

He had settled down in Cambridge, but when he visited Pakistan he was not taken much notice of. Besides furnishing the name he did not play any active part in the promotion or the setting-up of Pakistan. He died soon after partition, a very disappointed man.

□ □ □ □ □

# INTERVIEW - JULY 7, 1962

**Question**: *Would you like to say a few words today, Sir, about your relations with Sir Khizr Hayat in the summer of 1947 and before that?*

**Khan**: I had known Sir Khizr Hayat Khan for a number of years and had admired him and his great qualities. He came into particular prominence in connection with the events we are now approaching in the spring of 1947. After the final failure of the Cabinet Mission Plan in December, 1946, the Labour Government in England, and the Prime Minister, Mr. Attlee, were faced with the problem what to do about India's progress towards independence. Mr. Attlee came to the conclusion that after the failure of this last effort, directed towards the maintenance of the political unity of the subcontinent, there was no choice left but to agree to partition and to carry it out.

So, in February, 1947, he announced his decision on partition in principle. The central point of the announcement was that His Majesty's Government would transfer power to the provincial governments that were then in power, and through them a scheme of partition would be worked out.

When I heard that announcement I felt very uncomfortable because at that time in the Punjab the administration was in the hands of the Unionist Party. Sir Khizr Hayat Khan was Prime Minister, but the majority of his followers, that is to say, members of the Unionist Party, were Hindus and Sikhs, and only a minority were Muslims. By that time, the majority of the Muslim representatives in the Punjab Legislative Assembly were members of the Muslim League, and they were in opposition. So I began to worry over what would happen under Prime Minister Attlee's scheme with regard to the Punjab, in which I was most interested both because I belonged there, and also because, as everybody knew the Punjab was the heart of the scheme of Pakistan. I knew that the Qaid-i-Azam, Mr. Jinnah, had tried to persuade Sir Khizr Hayat Khan to come to some understanding with the Muslim League, and had failed.

Sir Khizr Hayat Khan's stand had been that he supported the idea of and the demand for Pakistan, but that that related to the centre. So far as the Province was concerned, he stood by the policy and principles of the Unionist Party, as indeed Sir Sikander Hayat Khan had done before him, and he wanted to carry on the same sort of understanding which had been reached between Mr. Jinnah and Sir Sikander Hayat Khan. Now through this announcement of Prime Minister Attlee, that distinction between the provincial sphere and the centre was wiped out. The provincial governments had become, as it were, the centre of interest.

I was then in Delhi as Judge of the Federal Court of India and was not directly in politics. But I had continued to take a keen interest in the constitutional advances of India towards independence, and could not now at this last moment dissociate myself from what was going on. I certainly could not disinterest myself in the pivotal question on which the future of my people turned and in which we were all vitally concerned. So I revolved the matter in my mind through the whole night, which was most unusual with me, because when my time for sleep comes, I put aside all affairs with which I have been concerned during the day until the following morning. But that night I kept puzzling my mind over what was to be done. By the morning I came to the decision that I had better write to Sir Khizr Hayat Khan and offer him whatever advice I could in the matter. I was by no means certain in my mind that he would accept my advice, but we were good friends, and I had great confidence in his judgment and good sense and in his sense of responsibility, and I hoped that I might be able to influence him to some degree.

So I wrote a letter to him, first, putting the position before him as it emerged from the Prime Minister's announcement; secondly, his responsibility in the particular situation that had arisen; and urged very strongly upon him that the time had come, the distinction between the provincial sphere and the central sphere so far as this matter was concerned having been abolished, when he should resign and thus prepare the way for a Muslim League government to be formed in the Punjab so that they could then cooperate in this process of partition that was adumbrated in Prime Minister Attlee's speech.

As soon as he received my letter in Lahore he called me over the telephone and said he could not speak to me openly or in detail about what I had written to him because he was not quite sure that his telephone calls were not tapped, but he indicated to me that he agreed in principle with what I had written to him and wanted me to go up to Lahore immediately so that he could discuss the whole matter with me and how it was to be carried through.

So I left for Lahore that night and was with him next morning. We discussed the pros and cons of what I had written to him, not so much what needed to be done - on that he was in principle in agreement - but how it should be done. Then he brought into consultation the late Nawab Sir Allah Bakhsh Khan Tiwana, who had always been a very close friend of his and whom he often consulted over matters, and who also was a man of very strong common sense.

Nawab Allah Bakhsh Khan also agreed that on the whole he thought Khizr should resign and let the Muslim League take over. Khizr Hayat then said, "There is one other man whom I must consult or at least who ought to know what I am contemplating. He has stood by me and I just can't carry this through without his knowing what I propose to do." That was Nawab Muzaffar Ali Khan

Qizalbash, who was a colleague of his in the government. So he sent for him and when he arrived, he discussed the matter with him. All four of us were in the conversation. Muzaffar suggested that Khizr should decide to resign but should not hand in his resignation until after the budget session, which was due to start within a few days, and until after he had got the budget through. Nawab Allah Bakhsh Khan came down very strongly against that suggestion. He said to Khizr, "You either decide to resign and resign, or you decide not to resign and carry on. If after the budget session, you come to the decision that you should resign, then resign. It is no kind of decision: 'I shall resign, but I shall resign after I get the budget through.' In the first place, how do you know you'll be able to get your budget through, how the situation is going to develop after this announcement of Prime Minister Attlee? In any case you'll get your budget through with the help of your party, which is composed largely of non-Muslims, and would it not be disloyal to them to get their support for carrying your budget through and then do something which they may not approve of? You ought to make a decision one way or the other. If you decide this is not the time to resign, then do not resign and do not say anything at all about it. When the time comes in your judgment to resign, well, then look at the situation at that time and decide accordingly."

Muzaffar Ali Khan left and Khizr decided that during the course of the afternoon he must put the matter before the party. So he called a meeting of the party in his house for the afternoon. I was not present in the meeting, though I was in the house. The discussion went on for quite a long time, and I understood, after the meeting broke up, that the party very emphatically with a very large majority had advised him not to resign and to carry on. But he told them that his decision was that he was going to resign.

Before the party meeting he had gone over to see the Governor, Sir Evan Jenkins, and had warned him that he might decide to resign, in which case, he would go back to him after dinner and let him know what his decision was. The party meeting broke up just before dinner, so we dined together - the party members had left - and immediately after dinner Khizr went over to see the Governor, and told the Governor he had decided to resign and advised him to invite the Nawab of Mamdot, the leader of the Muslim League party, to form a government.

## REMINISCENCES OF SIR MUHAMMAD ZAFRULLA KHAN 145

That was how this difficulty in the Punjab was met. The Governor, I believe, was somewhat disappointed but he did not attempt to dissuade Khizr Hayat from doing what he had decided to do. He told him it was his business, and though personally he would have wished him to continue, if it was his decision to resign he must accept his decision.

I left Lahore the next day and went back to Delhi. As soon as Khizr's decision was announced, a disturbance began in the Punjab, inspired mainly by Master Tara Singh, the Sikh leader, who later on, in India, started his agitation for a separate Sikh province. He stood at the steps of the Legislative Assembly Chamber in Lahore, rattled his kirpan, that is, his dagger, and said, "This will decide." Unfortunately, that proved to be the presage to all sorts of horrible things that happened afterwards. That is a chapter that most of us do not wish to recall now, after all the horrors that happened. But that was the beginning of it, in the last week of February, 1947.

Sir Khizr Hayat Khan did a great service to the cause of Pakistan by the manner in which he acted on that occasion. It is a great pity that the part played by him at that juncture has not been properly appreciated, especially by the Muslim League.

The very first difference that arose between him and the Muslim League was that they had hoped, when he decided to resign, that he would join the Muslim League, but he would not join the League as that might be interpreted as meaning that he was still hankering after office, which he was not. He was in full sympathy with the ideal of Pakistan and he would continue to support it, but he would rather not do anything that might appear as if he was wanting to play a prominent part in whatever course affairs might take in the Province. I have always admired him for the part that he played at that time as I thought it showed great courage, situated as he was, with all the difficulties in his way. He did not consider his own position, he had no thought of any personal benefit; he did what he thought was right in all the circumstances.

The situation continued to drift through the spring and early summer. Lord Mountbatten was appointed Governor General: he came out and took stock of the situation. He went back to England and urged upon His Majesty's Government that whatever was to be done must be done quickly. The original idea had been, as indeed was announced by Prime Minister Attlee, that partition should be completed within the course of a year, and by June, 1948, the whole project should be completed. Lord Mountbatten urged that the situation was so precarious that unless something was done immediately, everything might get out of hand and nothing may be achieved.

Thus he got the date advanced to the middle of August, and the process of partition was speeded up accordingly.

The announcement of Prime Minister Attlee, of the 3rd of June, set out the final stages and the method of partition. On that I made up my mind to resign my seat on the bench and sent in my resignation to take effect on 10th of June. His late Highness the Nawab of Bhopal, who was a very good friend of mine and whom I had held in very great esteem and affection, suggested that for a year or two, depending upon how quickly matters would proceed, I should go to Bhopal and take on the duties of his Constitutional Adviser, to suggest ways and means how his interests as the ruler of Bhopal, and the interests of the Ruling Chiefs generally, might be safeguarded under the new constitution. I readily agreed, and went on to Bhopal within a few days of resigning my seat on the bench.

By that time, widespread disorders had started and the situation, even in New Delhi, which was the capital, was becoming pretty desperate for the Muslims.

I was soon sent for by Mr. Jinnah, who suggested that when the Boundary Commission was set up, to delimit the boundary between West Pakistan and India - at that time, between West Punjab and East Punjab - I should argue the Muslim League case before the Commission. Without hesitation I took on that duty upon myself.

In the meantime, His Highness the Nawab of Bhopal had suggested that I should go to England for a fortnight, while the Indian Independence Bill was in discussion before Parliament and see whether anything could be done to get a clearer assurance from His Majesty's Government with regard to the position of the Princes under the new constitution. I went over and was present in the gallery of the House of Commons when Prime Minister Attlee introduced the Bill. I was much struck by the very clear exposition that he gave of the provisions of the Bill, and complimented him later on his speech. He did not indulge in oratory, he was not much of an orator, but he explained the provisions very clearly so that everybody was able to appreciate what was meant.

One thing I was surprised by was that he made a grievance in his speech of the fact that Mr. Jinnah had not agreed that Lord Mountbatten should, under the new constitution, become the Governor General both of Pakistan and of India. I could not see how that arrangement could have worked even for a week. There were bound to be - some were already looming ahead - differences between Pakistan and India over a host of matters, and the position of the Governor General under the new constitution would be that of the constitutional Head of government. A joint Governor General would be the constitutional Head of Pakistan and constitutional Head of India, and in each capacity would be bound to act on the advice of his Cabinet. As Governor General of Pakistan he would act on the advice of his Pakistan Cabinet; as Governor General of India he would act on the advice tendered by his India Cabinet. In case of serious differences, which, as I have said, were bound to arise, what would be his position? In Karachi, he would be the spokesman of the Cabinet of Pakistan, vis-a-vis India, and would presumably address a communication to himself in Delhi, in his position of Governor General of India, urging the Pakistan point of view, and then would go back to Delhi and send a reply to Karachi from Delhi, refuting what he had written from Karachi. That is the kind of thing that was bound to happen and he would not be able to carry on in that position for more than a week or a fortnight or on the outside for a month. That so experienced a parliamentarian as Mr. Attlee should have thought that this arrangement could have worked and should have made a grievance of the fact, that it had not been accepted by Mr. Jinnah, was indeed surprising.

I was able to accomplish a little bit with regard to what His Highness the Nawab of Bhopal had in mind. The relevant clause of the Bill, which subsequently became the Indian Independence Act, relating to the Princes, provided that on the due date all treaties, engagements, etc., between His Majesty and the Indian Princes would lapse and suzerainty would disappear, which meant, in effect, that the Princes would be independent and would be free to establish such relationship as they preferred with either or both dominions. The anxiety of His Highness the Nawab of Bhopal - he was then the Chancellor of the Chamber of Princes, and in a sense acted also on behalf of the Princes - and of the Princes, was that it should be made quite clear that if they wanted to remain independent, they could remain independent, or they could accede to one dominion or the other, at their discretion.

I got in touch with several of the leading statesmen in Britain when I went over, including Lord Templewood, who, as Sir Samuel Hoare, had been the Secretary of State for India during the crucial period, and now, as Viscount Templewood, was a member of the House of Lords. We discussed this matter back and forth, and he said he would try to do what he could to get a clearer assurance from the Under Secretary of State for India, Lord Listowel, who would be in charge of the Bill in the House of Lords. So when the particular clause came under consideration in the House of Lords, Lord Templewood addressed the question to Lord Listowel whether it would be correct to assume that the meaning of the clause was that the Princes could remain independent, if they chose, or could accede to one dominion or the other at their discretion.

I imagine the Labour Government was reluctant to make this too clear, being afraid that the Congress might not like it. Be that as it may, Lord Listowel said nothing in words in reply to the question but merely nodded his head. Lord Templewood, who was an astute parliamentarian, and aware that a nod of the head could not go onto the record said, "From the nod of the noble Lord I understand that he agrees with the explanation that I have given." Thus Lord Listowel's nod was transcribed on the record.

Later events showed that whatever the letter or the spirit of the Act, the Minister for State Affairs in India, the late Mr. Vallabbhai Patel, was determined to ride roughshod over the States and the States were to be completely integrated with India.

I came back and went straight to Lahore where the Boundary Commission had in the meantime been constituted. I was in England when it was announced that Sir Cyril Radcliffe, now Lord Radcliffe, would be the umpire, both in the case of the Punjab Boundary Commission and the Bengal Boundary Commission. This meant that if the Commission made a unanimous or a majority report the boundary would be as determined by the Commission; but that in case of a tie, the umpire's decision would prevail. In each case there was bound to be a tie because each Commission was composed of two Muslim and two non-Muslim members. In the case of the Punjab Boundary Commission the two Muslim members were Mr. Justice Din Muhammad and Mr. Justice Muhammad Munir; while Mr. Justice Mahr Chand Mahajan and Mr. Justice Teja Singh were the non-Muslim members. All four were High Court judges. Later, Mr. Justice Munir became Chief Justice of the Lahore High Court

### REMINISCENCES OF SIR MUHAMMAD ZAFRULLA KHAN 149

and still later a judge of the Supreme Court of Pakistan, and then Chief Justice of Pakistan. At this date, he is Law Minister in the new Cabinet of Pakistan that has been formed this month.

A Commission composed like that was bound to be dead-locked in the sense that they would not be able to make a unanimous or a majority report. So, in effect, Sir Cyril Radcliffe would have to determine the boundary in each case.

When I arrived in Lahore - I believe it was a Monday evening - I was told that Sir Cyril Radcliffe was already in Lahore and that he had summoned the parties to meet him at 11 o'clock next morning. So we appeared before him, and he gave us directions, and set noon of the following Friday as the hour by which the parties should put in their written cases before the Commission. The following Monday arguments would start before the Commission. He himself would not sit with the Commission to hear arguments because according to him, he did not know whether his function as umpire would come into play at all or not. It was only when the Commission made a report that he would know whether he would have to function or not. But he would follow with great interest whatever was being urged before the Commission, as a transcript of the proceedings would be sent to him daily.

The following evening Mr. Justice Din Muhammad came to see me. He was very agitated and said, "Whatever you have prepared or are going to prepare, whatever arguments may be addressed to us, I have come to tell you that I have a very strong suspicion that the boundary line has already been decided upon, and that all of us will be engaged in a farce." I asked why he thought so. He said, "Yesterday, when you people left, Sir Cyril said that this morning he was going up for a flight to survey the area which might be in dispute and to see how the land lies." I asked him how would we know what he had looked at and what impressions he had formed. We would be sitting here dealing with the matter, and he would have made a survey of which we would have no knowledge. This might prove awkward later on. Sir Cyril explained that the aircraft that had been placed at his disposal was a small one, but that two of us, one from each side, could go with him. It was decided that Mr. Justice Munir and Mr. Justice Teja Singh should go up with Sir Cyril this morning.

This morning all of them assembled at an early hour at the Walton Airport from which they were to take off for the flight but there was a dust storm on and it was decided to abandon the flight.

## 150 REMINISCENCES OF SIR MUHAMMAD ZAFRULLA KHAN

Just before leaving the airfield, Mr. Justice Munir asked the pilot where they were to go. The pilot put his hand in his pocket and brought out a slip of paper which he gave to Mr. Justice Munir, saying those were his orders. Munir brought that slip away and gave it to me. This slip indicates that the directions to the pilot were to fly east to the point near Pathankot where the river Ravi emerges from the mountains and debouches into the plains of the Punjab and then to follow the course of the River Ravi up to a point in Lahore District, and then to veer left along towards Ferozpur etc. "This means that that is going to be the boundary, otherwise what was the point of going to a particular point and then following a definite course? It was not to be a flight over a certain area to survey it; this was to follow a definite line. I have, therefore, decided to go to Delhi tonight, to put the matter before Mr. Jinnah, and to suggest that Munir and I should resign from the Commission on the ground that apparently the whole thing has been determined in advance, before even the parties have put in their written cases, and that there is not much use in our going on with the Commission. Later, either a new commission can be constituted or some other method can be adopted for determining the boundary."

I said to him, "Mr. Jinnah will not be so easily persuaded by your presentation of this matter. He might pooh-pooh the whole thing. He is a lawyer, and you'd better have some legal basis for what you are going to say to him." He asked, "What do you mean by 'legal basis'?" I said, "What I suggest - I don't know whether you'll succeed with him even then - but what I suggest is that you should take up this aspect of the case with him: We have accepted Sir Cyril Radcliffe as umpire in the case, and we are bound to accept what he decides as umpire. But, as umpire, it is his duty to base his judgment on such material as is submitted to him by the Commission. As umpire, he is not entitled to receive material from other sources and to take that into consideration. What the parties place before the Commission is the material on which the decision must be made, that material, along with the views of the Commission, will be submitted to Sir Cyril Radcliffe, and on that together with the announcement, which the Prime Minister has made and which is the basis of partition he must make up his mind. Now, who suggested this trip to him? He knows nothing at all of conditions here; he doesn't even know the parties' cases. What is the meaning of this particular line that the flight was to follow? Mr. Jinnah should try to find out the meaning of this proposed trip which had to be abandoned and the significance

## REMINISCENCES OF SIR MUHAMMAD ZAFRULLA KHAN    **151**

of the line which was to be followed. If he should be satisfied that it had no particular significance at all, though it's difficult to believe that a definite line like that should have no significance, then matters may proceed. But if he is not satisfied, he should ask for an explanation: from which direction did this suggestion proceed. He can then make his point that the umpire is being influenced in a particular direction by people who are not directly concerned with this question at all and we have lost confidence in this procedure. That might perhaps go some distance with Mr. Jinnah; otherwise you have not much hope, merely because of this slip of paper."

He went to Delhi that night, was in Delhi the next day, saw Mr. Jinnah, left Delhi in the evening and arrived back in Lahore on the third morning, Friday morning, and came straight from the railway station to see me. He was very crestfallen, Mr. Jinnah had told him to go ahead and to do his best and not to worry. Sir Cyril was a responsible man and would not let his judgment be influenced by any outsider.

Curiously enough, when the award was announced, the boundary followed the line described in the 'slip of paper' except for one change, again, adverse to Pakistan, which I shall come to later.

As I have said, on Tuesday, Sir Cyril had fixed Friday noon as the deadline for filling written cases. When I had arrived at Lahore the previous evening and was received by a large number of people, including among them the Nawab of Mamdot, who was then, I believe, the Head of the Provincial Cabinet, he told me that this meeting was fixed for 11 o'clock the next morning with Sir Cyril and that there was to be a meeting with the lawyers at his house at 2:30 p.m., from which I concluded that I would then meet the lawyers who had been engaged in the preparation of the case, for I had been assured by Mr. Jinnah that by the time I arrived in Lahore I would find the whole case ready, and I would only have to take on the presentation of the case on the basis of the brief prepared by the lawyers.

So, under that impression, at 2:30 I presented myself at Mamdot Villa, the residence of the Nawab of Mamdot. I found a large number of lawyers present there, most of whom I knew very well as personal friends, some of them my seniors at the Bar with whom I had worked for a number of years. I shook hands with them all and sat down and said, "Well, now, gentlemen, which of you are working with me on this case?" Khalifa Shuja-ud-din, who was my senior at the Bar by three or four years, smiled and asked, "Which case?" "The Boundary case, of course. I was asked to meet with the lawyers working on the boundary case this afternoon, here." He said, "We know nothing at all about the boundary case! We don't know what you're talking about. We were asked to meet you here, to welcome you back to Lahore, knowing that you have come to handle this case. We know nothing at all about the case." Tableau!

To put it very mildly, I was flabbergasted, not only to learn that nobody had been paying any attention to the case, much less preparing it, but at the prospect that within less than three days - it was already the afternoon of Tuesday - I would have to present a case in writing on the partition of this part of the country. I did not know which way I could turn for any material or statistics or to ascertain the principles on which the line should be drawn, or what our case should be!

I said good-bye to the assembled lawyers within a few minutes, and then turned to the Nawab of Mamdot and asked, "Has the Muslim League Organization prepared any plan or collected any material or done anything in the matter?" He uttered a laconic "No." Everything had been left to me! And I had just come from abroad!!

Khwaja Abdur Rahim, who was then the Commissioner of Rawalpindi, was in Lahore on special duty in connection with the influx of refugees from the other side, which had already started in large volume. He had certain statistics on population prepared on his own. He came over to see me the same afternoon and handed over the material to me. This was a piece of sheer good luck for which I was most grateful. I also found that four lawyers from outside Lahore had come up to Lahore in the hope that they might be useful to me in the preparation of the case. Two of them were from Montgomery, one from Pakpattan and one from Hoshiarpur. Those from Montgomery were Mr. Nisar Ahmad and Sahibzada Nusrat Ali; the one from Pakpattan was Syed Muhammad Shah; and the one from Hoshiarpur was Chaudhari Akbar Ali Khan, who is at present Pakistan's Ambassador in Jiddah. There were also one or two junior lawyers from Lahore, who occasionally looked in and were able to assist, not so much with the preparation of the case but on any odd matter on which I needed any assistance. I am very grateful to all of them for their devoted assistance.

My anxiety now was to work day and night and get the case in readiness by Friday noon. Even now, looking back, I cannot explain how it became possible for us to produce a case, which we did by the noon of Friday.

Conditions in Lahore at that time were all topsy-turvy. The permanent pressure and anxiety was how to handle the refugee problem. Were it not that the people as a body rose to the occasion, I am sure the provincial government would have proved absolutely unequal to the task and the administration would have foundered. It was the spirit of the people that carried us through and a few devoted officers and workers, naturally, like Khwaja Abdur Rahim and his colleagues who were dealing with this influx of refugees. Trainloads came in full of dead and wounded, children with their eyes gouged out and hands cut off, women with their breasts cut off! Such savagery and inhumanity!

There was nothing to choose between the two sides. I imagine the same things occurred on the other side. That part of the country seemed to have become a howling wilderness of beasts rather than a land of human beings. All humanity had been purged out of them, all mercy and pity and human love and affection seemed to have evaporated.

Altogether a dreadful business. I hate to recall it. One had to work under those conditions, so it was not very surprising that everybody was at sixes and sevens and nothing could be arranged for certain. Before leaving Mamdot Villa I had requested the Nawab of Mamdot to arrange that by 8 o'clock the next morning I should have two stenographers at my disposal, at my residence which was almost opposite to the Villa, who would work in relays, and I should have the usual office equipment, pencils, papers, typewriters. He had assured me that everything would be in readiness by 7:30.

So I went back and started working on whatever material was available, and worked late into the night. I started again early in the morning, and after breakfast I was ready at about 7:30 and inquired whether the stenographers had arrived. There was nobody. At a quarter to eight there was nobody. Eight o'clock, nobody, not a pencil, not a sheet of paper, not a typewriter, not a stenographer. Again, I had recourse to Khwaja Abdur Rahim, whose tent-office was fortunately right opposite to me on the same road where I was staying, and he very kindly offered to send over his two stenographers, who came over, and I started dictating.

I do not know how I got through that delicate and complicated task within the space of two days, and got the draft ready by

## REMINISCENCES OF SIR MUHAMMAD ZAFRULLA KHAN

Thursday night. On Thursday night I insisted that at least two of the Punjab ministers, Mian Mumtaz Daultana and Sirdar Shaukat Hayat Khan, should come over and read through the draft. I was submitting a case on behalf of the Muslim League and somebody on behalf of the League had to give me instructions! I dared not submit a case which might afterwards be repudiated. Sirdar Shaukat Hayat Khan could not come; he had high fever. But Mr. Mian Mumtaz Daultana very kindly came along. He said it was not necessary for him to read the draft that had been prepared as they had all full confidence in me, but I told him that this was not a matter of confidence but a matter of instructions and that I must have somebody's instructions. I insisted that he should read right through the draft and put his imprimatur on it.

So, he very kindly read through the draft, praised it very highly and said he agreed entirely with it. The next morning I put the final touches on it, and by noon we were able to deliver the document to the Commission.

Immediately thereafter I went on to the Friday service at the mosque, where I was asked to take the service, and I earnestly urged the congregation that they should be very diligent in prayers that all should go right, as I was much afraid that over portions of the Punjab the Muslims would have to face the days the Muslims in Spain had to face under Isabella and Ferdinand. Unfortunately, that apprehension proved to be only too well-founded.

The following Monday arguments started before the Commission. The case was argued very well on all sides. The Hindu case was put by Mr. M.C. Setalvad, who is now the Attorney-General of India. He had been asked to come up from Bombay to do so. He was assisted by very able lawyers, among them Bakhshi Tek Chand, who was a retired judge of the Lahore High Court, and had been for many years the ablest lawyer at the Lahore bar. The Sikh case was put by a gentleman who later became the Advocate General in East Punjab. It is not necessary to go into detail about what was said, but the main contest centred around the Gurdaspur District, Ferozpur District and parts of the Jullundur District. The crux of the matter was how to interpret and apply the expression "contiguous Muslim majority areas and contiguous non-Muslim majority areas."

We rested our case on the tehsil, or sub-district being adopted as the unit for the purpose of determining contiguous majority areas. One could take the village as a unit, but that would mean the boundary line would be a completely crazy one. It would not be possible to determine by villages, where the majority on one side ended and on the other side began. Or one could take a police station as a unit, but even that would be too small and the boundary line based on that unit would not be a practical one at all. One could take a subdistrict, as we did, or one could take a district as a unit. The choice was a difficult one. If a district were taken as a unit, then the notional partition which had already been put into effect for purposes of administration ad interim, would have to be confirmed, and that would give the whole of the Gurdaspur District to Pakistan. But the risk was that if we confined our case to districts, it might be assumed that we were happy with the notional partition and our claim might be whittled down further to our serious prejudice. Adopting the tehsil as a unit whould give us the Frozepur and Zira tehsils of the Ferozpur District, the Jullundur and Rahon tehsils of Jullundur district and the Dasuya tehsil of the Hoshiarpur district. The line so drawn would also give us the State of Kapurthala (which had a Muslim majority) and would enclose within Pakistan the whole of the Amritsar district of which only one tehsil, Ajnala, had a Muslim majority. It would also give us the Shakargarh, Batala and Gurdaspur tehsils of the Gurdaspur district. Or we could take what in the Punjab are known as Doabs, that is to say, the areas between two rivers as the units. If the boundary went by Doabs, we could get not only the 16 districts which had already under the notional partition been put into West Punjab, including the Gurdaspur District, but we would also get the Kangra District in the mountains, to the north and east of Gurdaspur. Or one could go by Commissioners' divisions.

Any of these units being adopted would have been more favourable to Pakistan than the present boundary line. The tehsil was the most favourable unit. In actual fact the boundary line was drawn much to the prejudice of Pakistan.

It was known in advance that there would be no unanimous or majority report. The non-Muslim commissioners took one view; the two Muslim commissioners took another view; and consequently the umpire had to make his award. After the umpire had studied the records he had discussions with the members of the Boundary Commission in Simla. We were told by the Muslim commissioners that while Sir Cyril was not quite definite and clear with regard to the Gurdaspur District, he was quite clear that two subdistricts of the Ferozpur District - the subdistrict of Ferozpur itself and the subdistrict of Zira - being Muslim majority areas and contiguous to the rest of the Muslim bloc would form part of Pakistan.

About the time when it was expected that the award would be announced, a communication was received by the then Governor of West Punjab, Sir Evans Jenkins, from Mr. Abel, subsequently Sir George Abel, the Private Secretary of the Viceroy, Lord Mountbatten, over the telephone, on the basis of two documents drawn up by Mr. Beaumont, Private Secretary to Sir Cyril Radcliffe, describing the boundary between West Punjab and East Punjab, one tracing it out on a map; the other describing it from village to village. The Governor was told that this was the award, and that it would be announced within 48 hours. The Governor was asked to take, in consultation with his Chief of Police, such measures as may be necessary to give effect to the award when it was announced. One has no doubt that a similar communication must have been made to Mr. Trivedi, who was Governor of East Punjab.

No award was announced within 48 hours. As a matter of fact, the award was not announced till eight or ten days later. By that time Sir Cyril Radcliffe had left the subcontinent.

The notes taken by Sir Evans Jenkins of the Communication made to him by Mr. Abel showed the two subdistricts of Ferozpur and Zira, as we had expected, part of West Punjab, and consequently of Pakistan. But when the award came out, eight or ten days later, these two subdistricts were put in India. No explanation has hitherto been furnished why this modification took place. I have before hazarded an explanation; I hazard it again for the purpose of this record. It seems to me that unless a clear and convincing explanation is forthcoming to displace this hypothesis, this is almost the only thing that could have happened. We must remember that at that date there was as yet no Pakistan and consequently no Pakistan government. There was only the Provisional Government of India of which Pandit Jawaharlal Nehru was the Prime Minister and head of government.

Mr. Trivedi, the Governor of East Punjab, an ICS officer, was under the authority of the Provisional Government; so was Sir Evans Jenkins, the Governor of West Punjab. It stands to reason that when Mr. Trivedi received this Communication from Mr. Abel, the Viceroy's private secretary, he communicated its gist, probably through a personal visit, to the Prime Minister. The significance of the Ferozpur subdistrict going to Pakistan, was that it would include the headworks of the Satlej Valley canals system that are situated just outside the Town of Ferozpur, which, under that arrangement, would be included in Pakistan. The whole of the water of that canal system flowing through those headworks went to Pakistan and Bikaner, one of the Indian states - 83 percent to Pakistan and 17 percent to Bikaner.

The Bikaner State and the Jaisalmer State both in Rajputana would be contiguous both to Pakistan and to India; therefore, they could accede either to Pakistan or to India. It was well known that the rulers of both these States were not at all anxious to accede to India. They thought they would get a better deal by acceding to Pakistan.

This canal, which took off from the Ferozpur headworks and which went to Bikaner was in a sense Bikaner's lifeline, the only irrigation system that state had. If in addition to the desire of these two rulers to accede to Pakistan, not because they had more love for Pakistan than for India, but mainly because they thought that India's policy towards Indian states would be one of rapid integration and Pakistan might not proceed so rapidly or to such an extreme length and they might be able to make better terms with Pakistan, the Maharaja of Bikaner found that the control of the waters that came into his state, upon which the prosperity of the state depended, was in Pakistan's hand, that might prove a decisive factor in impelling him to accede to Pakistan.

In view of that contingency the inference is almost irresistible that Mr. Nehru must have approached Lord Mountbatten to procure a modification of the award in that respect. There is no other explanation, why, after the award had been communicated to Mr. Abel, Sir Evans Jenkins and Mr. Trivedi (and almost certainly to the Viceroy) and had no longer any authority to modify the award, the award was modified. This aspect did not come to the knowledge of the Pakistan authorities until months later, whereas it was presumably within Mr. Nehru's knowledge through Mr. Trivedi from the outset. The Governor of West Pakistan owed no duty to anybody, except the Central Government of India, of which the head was Prime Minister Nehru. Mr. Trivedi also, also owed no duty to anybody except to Mr. Nehru. So it was quite right of Mr. Trivedi to let Mr. Nehru know what the proposed award was, and the Governor of West Pakistan was under no duty to let anybody on the Pakistan side know, since Pakistan had not yet come into existence and nobody on that side had any right to know what the decision was.

The greater part of the Gurdaspur district being included in East Punjab, and therefore in India, was a great blow to us, and that was something that made the intervention of India in Kashmir possible. That was the only part in the plains through which India had access to Kashmir; otherwise, though India's boundary still would have run along the boundary of Kashmir for some distance, it would be over and across high mountains with no road running through. The only road that could go from India to Kashmir, and even that had to be built over a great part of its length and had to be through the Gurdaspur district.

Gurdaspur district had four subdistricts: One, Shakargarh, to the west of the Ravi River; that was included in Pakistan, because at that place the Ravi River became the boundary; and three to the east of the Ravi River, that is to say, Gurdaspur subdistrict itself, Pathankot and Batala. All these three were included in India and gave India access to Kashmir through the plains.

Incidentally, my own house was 11 miles from Batala in the subdistrict of Batala and that also fell within India.

The modification of the award in respect of the Ferozpur and Zira tehsils, led directly to the Indus waters dispute. India having obtained control of the headworks at Ferozpur could easily turn off the water, as it did later, and that brought on that dispute. Thus the two big disputes between India and Pakistan resulted from these two portions of the award, which could not be justified on any basis whatsoever. In the Gurdaspur district the Muslims had a majority. In the subdistricts taken separately, they had a majority in the Shakargarh tehsil, west of the Ravi, and they also had a majority in the Batala tehsil and a majority in the Gurdaspur tehsil, but not a majority in the Pathankot tehsil. If Batala and Gurdaspur had gone to Pakistan, Pathankot tehsil would have been isolated and blocked. Even if it had been allotted to India it would have been possible for India to get access to Pathankot through the Hoshiarpur district, but it would have taken quite long to construct the roads, bridges and communications that would have been necessary for military movements.

As part of the machinery for sorting out things in connection with the partition, a tribunal had been set up for the distribution of assets under the chairmanship of the ex-Chief Justice of India, Sir

Patrick Spens, now Lord Spens. This tribunal heard the parties, sorted out the assets, assessed what was due from one side to the other, and gave its award. In making its assessment, it took into account the Indian claim that the irrigation system in what was the old undivided province of the Punjab had been much better developed in the portions which had gone to Pakistan than in the portions which had gone to India. The claim was put forward that all this development had taken place at the joint expense of the province, but that the benefit of the major portion of it was now enjoyed by Pakistan, and that Pakistan must pay compensation for the excess share of this development that it enjoyed. The tribunal took that into account in making its award and compensated India for having obtained a smaller share of this joint development that had been made at joint expense. The day after the tribunal made its award India diverted the waters at the Ferozpur headworks asserting that Pakistan was no longer entitled to these waters of the Beas and Sutly Rivers through these headworks. Pakistan was, almost at its birth, threatened with extinction, for without these waters the greater part of West Pakistan would be turned back into a desert waste.

On the 4th of May, 1948, a provisional agreement was arrived at between the Government of India and the Government of Pakistan, which provided that, leaving the legal position aside, India would let this flow of waters into Pakistan to continue for a period but that it would have to be progressively reduced and Pakistan in the meantime should investigate alternative sources of substitution for these waters. This agreement was subject to the condition that Pakistan should pay into the State Bank of India, or whichever bank may be specified, a certain assessed amount in escrow to be taken by India as compensation for the use of these waters by Pakistan, if the final decision should be in favour of India. This amount was not to be handed over to the Government of India, but was to remain in the Bank as a guarantee that in case it was found that Pakistan was not entitled to these waters, the amount would be available to India as compensation.

Later on India took up the position that Pakistan was not entitled to any part of these waters and that India, as the upper riparian owner was entitled to divert the whole of this water for its own benefit without any regard to the historical uses which had already been established.

## REMINISCENCES OF SIR MUHAMMAD ZAFRULLA KHAN

Mr. David Lilienthal, who had been Chairman of the Tennessee Valley Authority was on a visit to the subcontinent and happened to fly over the Indus Valley. He wrote an article for the *Saturday Evening Post* setting out what the consequences of this dispute over the waters were likely to be, to both sides, and drew particular attention to its impact on the economy of West Pakistan. He suggested that the World Bank should offer its good offices to the parties for the purpose of resolving this dispute on the basis of certain principles which should be accepted by both sides, namely that established uses should be respected, that if extra water was available from all these rivers, there should be agreement as to how that should be shared for the purpose of the development of the whole of the Indus Basin, the part that was in Pakistan as well as the part that was in India, and how the costs of such development should be apportioned.

The World Bank's good offices were accepted by both sides and a prolonged series of investigations and discussions took place under the auspices of the Bank. At long last agreement was reached which was incorporated into a treaty and is now being worked out on the spot. One part of the agreement was that India should enjoy the waters of the eastern rivers and Pakistan should replace that water by means of replacement works and channels from the western rivers, India paying the cost of the replacement. But when the costs of replacement were assessed, India said the amount was beyond its capacity to pay. Through the good offices of the bank it was arranged that it should pay as much as it was able to, and that the rest would be made up by friendly powers, like the United Kingdom, the United States, Australia, and some of the Colombo power. In respect of the works for future uses, as distinguished from established uses, Pakistan was to bear the cost of its own works and India was to bear the cost of the works on its own side.

I understand that some difficulty has since arisen. The basis on which the costs of replacement were calculated has already ceased to operate, because the costs of these works have gone up so much that the amounts then assessed are no longer sufficient to cover them. How that is to be worked out I do not know but I believe some sort of negotiations are going on with the Bank on that aspect.

□ □ □ □ □

# INTERVIEW - JULY 28, 1962

**Question**: *Sir Zafrulla, one thing that interests me and interests many people is the reasons why someone like yourself, who has served united India for so many years, finally took the decision to support Pakistan. Would you care to say a word on that?*

**Khan**: I was not directly in politics between 1941, when I took my seat on the bench of the Federal Court of Delhi, and the 10th of June, 1947, when I resigned from the Court. But, of course, my interest in all these matters was still very keen, and in my early years on the Court, as this record will show, I went on urging upon the Viceroy indianization of the Cabinet and practical progress towards independence. I was not only sympathetic towards what the Muslim leaders wanted to safeguard, but was most keen that we should fully safeguard our future position. Till the summer of 1946, however, I had not made up my mind finally that Pakistan was the only or the most feasible solution of that problem. In the summer of 1946, when the Cabinet Mission succeeded in obtaining the agreement of the Muslim League and the India National Congress on their plan, I breathed a sigh of relief. I was conscious of the undoubted advantages which would accrue to the whole country and, of course, also to the Muslims as a section of the population, from the political and economic unity of India. Now that a plan had been accepted which Muslim leaders thought would give them a fair chance of cooperating in building up the country and would safeguard their faith, culture and special interests and which they were willing to try for ten years and then make their final decision, I thought this was a good way out of the difficulty. As a matter of fact, I greatly admired Mr. Jinnah's strategy that having pushed the matter as far as it was possible for it to go, he was willing to try an alternative which seemed to him feasible and practicable.

Then that plan was wrecked - I am afraid quite deliberately - by Mr. Nehru, who had, shortly after the plan was accepted by both sides, become President of the Congress, and as President made authoritative statements which were utterly inconsistent with the clear wording of the Cabinet Mission's Plan. Thereupon, I became convinced that no kind of agreement which might be entered into would be faithfully kept by the Congress or the leaders of the majority community and that, it was too great a risk to accept anything which could not be enforced if they were not willing to carry it through.

Finally, when in the December of that year even Mr. Attlee's attempts to put the pieces of the Cabinet Mission's Plan together failed - he had sent for Mr. Jinnah and Mr. Nehru, to London, and he tried his best but did not succeed - then no doubt was left in my mind that the only way out was partition.

So you may take it that the final change in my mind and attitude started with the Cabinet Mission's Plan. At first I thought we had a fair enough substitute, at least for trial for ten years, and then when that was torn up, the rebound was that nothing else was now feasible.

In fact, though that does not strengthen the argument, even a person like Mr. Attlee, who was dead-opposed to partition, was finally convinced that the only solution was partition. All my subsequent experience has confirmed that nothing else could have worked.

**Question**: *In the summer of 1947, wasn't it, you became Adviser for a number of the Princes. Would you care to say something about that?*

**Khan**: I have already touched upon that. I had known His Highness the Nawab of Bhopal for some years. Perhaps I had known him more intimately than I knew any of their other Highnesses. I was never very intimate with them as a group; but with some of them I had good personal relations, including the Maharajah, whose hospitality I had often enjoyed in Srinagar whenever I had been on a visit there, whether as a Minister in the Viceroy's Cabinet, or later as a judge of the Court.

As soon as the announcement of Prime Minister Attlee was made on the 3rd of June, I made up my mind to resign from the Court and to revert to practice at the Bar. This resolve was strengthened when His Highness of Bhopal inquired whether I would be willing to act as his Constitutional Adviser for a few months, or longer, in case of need.

The Maharajah of Indore was also associated with him in making this suggestion. On one or two occasions, the Chief Minister of Bahawalpur, Mr. Gurmani, who was a friend of long standing, approached me for advice. As soon as I resigned from the Court I moved down from Delhi to Bhopal, which I made my headquarters, but I was not allowed to remain there long at one stretch. I was first asked by Mr. Jinnah, as I have already related, to take on the Muslim

League's case and to present it before the Punjab Boundary Commission, and later he asked me to lead the first delegation of Pakistan to the United Nations.

It was not until I returned from the Assembly's session in New York in December, 1947, that Mr. Jinnah asked me to join the Pakistan Cabinet. Thus, though for over six months I acted as Constitutional Adviser to His Highness of Bhopal, except during the first two months or so, I was not able to spend much of my time in Bhopal. Towards the end of the year, when I was asked by Mr. Jinnah to join his Cabinet as Foreign Minister, I put the matter to His Highness and he very graciously agreed to let me go. He realized that for the Princes it was no longer a question of constitutional advice or the drawing up of treaties and agreements embodying safeguards. It was a direct conflict with Mr. Patel, who was determined to get rid of what he and his colleagues in the Government of India thought was an anachronistic system and to absorb the Princely states into India. So, when I put the matter to His Highness, he said, "Sir Zafrulla, we know the fate that is awaiting us. We shall try to make the best terms we can with the government of India, and I should not deprive Pakistan of your services if they are needed." He not only very kindly let me go, he enquired how I proposed to travel to Pakistan from Bhopal.

I told him I proposed to go down to Bombay by train, because it would be unsafe to travel through the troubled areas of East and West Punjab, and from Bombay I would either travel by sea or perhaps fly to Karachi. His Highness said he would not let me expose myself to any risk whatever. Even getting down to Bombay by train was not altogether safe. So he put his larger aircraft at my disposal. He asked me to take my wife and child and a couple of my servants with me, and as much of my personal effects and belongings as could be conveniently carried by air. He very kindly obtained a through-clearance from the Government of India so that the plane would not have to land at the border for clearance and could fly straight to Karachi. He kindly gave directions that the rest of my effects should be sent to Karachi via Bombay by sea. He was very helpful indeed in every way.

I took over as Foreign Minister of Pakistan on the 26th of December, 1947. I had not been much in touch with His Highness on Indore. I visited him once or twice at Indore, but Mr. Patel and Lord Mountbatten proved too much for His Highness and he crumpled up at the very start and accepted without demur whatever they proposed. His Highness of Bhopal had also in the end to accept the arrangements they proposed, but perhaps he was able to make a better bargain. He was then the Chancellor of the Chamber of Princes, but I was not advising him in his capacity as Chancellor, but only in his capacity as Ruler of Bhopal.

**Question**: *Would you care to say something, Sir Zafrulla, about your views of Mr. Jinnah and Mr. Liaqat Ali Khan?*

**Khan**: I had many opportunities of working with Mr. Jinnah, even when I was in government, though people did not know it. Behind the scenes there was a good deal of intimacy between us two. There was at one time an impression that perhaps we did not see eye-to-eye with each other. That was entirely wrong. I was willing to help as much as I could from my side, and he occasionally gave me advice and often asked for my views. Except perhaps for Liaqat Ali Khan later, who became his first lieutenant in the political field and possessed more of his confidence than any of his other colleagues, I was closer to Mr. Jinnah than other people who worked with him.

But when that is said it does not mean being very close and intimate. Mr. Jinnah's personality did not encourage intimacy. Whatever Pakistan owed to human agency for coming into being, it owed 99 percent of it to Mr. Jinnah. But Mr. Jinnah's was a personality which had more of the head than of the heart. I do not mean to say his heart was not in what he was doing, he was completely devoted to the ideal of Pakistan, but he did not encourage affectionate intimacy. He appreciated loyalty and devotion; in fact, he appreciated them so much that where he suspected any lack of them he was unforgiving. On the other hand, if he was assured of a person's loyalty to himself and to the principles for which he stood, he could forgive him a good deal.

He had all the devotion that he asked for. He never asked for any affection, and even those who were not only willing but yearning to yield him affection, found no opportunity of making that offer nor were they encouraged to do so. Liaqat Ali Khan, at least in some respects, supplied the deficiencies from which Mr. Jinnah suffered.

There was complete accord between Jinnah and Liaqat Ali Khan. They understood each other and appreciated each other even when they were not in complete accord with each other. I know of occasions when Liaqat Ali Khan loyally gave effect to Mr. Jinnah's views, though he could have wished them different. On his side Mr.

Jinnah accepted from Liaqat Ali Khan what perhaps he would not have accepted from any body else.

Liaqat Ali Khan did not have such a cold, sharp incisive intellect as Jinnah had. He was slow and deliberate. He was prepared to ask for and accept advice. He could modify his own view if he felt somebody else's would achieve the objective better. He was much more human than Mr. Jinnah. Later on, when Pakistan was set up, and he became Prime Minister, people had more to do with him than they had to do with Mr. Jinnah during his brief term as Governor General. He did not treat himself as a purely constitutional head of government but even then Liaqat Ali Khan was Prime Minister and as he was more approachable and necessarily had to be much more in contact with people, Mr. Jinnah's coldness affected the situation much less than it would otherwise have done.

There were occasions when differences arose between the two, but they never came visibly to the surface. They managed to adjust themselves to each other quickly.

Mr. Jinnah's health began to deteriorate visibly after Pakistan had been set up, and he had a very difficult time, though he made a valiant struggle. It was only just over a year that he was at the head of the government.

With me his relations, as between Governor General and Foreign Minister, were extremely good. Political or constitutional theories regarding the Constitutional Head of government and the effective head of government had not much interest for me and I was able to report to him almost as freely and in as much detail as I did to Liaqat Ali Khan. Occasionally, when Mr. Jinnah took particular interest in a matter, I could report to him perhaps even ahead of discussing the matter with Liaqat Ali Khan. There was no question of short-circuiting either. Mr. Jinnah was quite certain, so far as I was concerned, that I was not keeping in mind any distinction as to the form of government under the parliamentary system and the constitutional head of government, and he was quite happy. I got a great deal more help in that way from him, because he was interested in questions of foreign policy, and discussed them freely with me.

On one occasion, he raised the question of responsibility in the Cabinet. He said, "We must come to some clear understanding. If you want me to be a purely constitutional head of government, I am quite willing to carry on on that basis. But then the people must know where the responsibility for decision rests. It must be made quite clear publicly. On the other hand, if you are willing to accommodate yourselves to the position that on matters of outstanding importance, we put our heads together and in case differences arise and cannot be resolved, you would be prepared to accept my point of view, then equally we can carry on on that basis, and then also the people should know how we are carrying on. I do not attach too much importance to constitutional theories and I am willing to fall in with whichever way of conducting business should appeal to you."

There was this sort of steel inside the velvet: I am prepared to fall in with your views, but the people must know. The people must know meant that the people would not tolerate that situation; they would insist that he should have the last word.

Then he asked for our views. Liaqat Ali Khan tried to play safe; he would not go as far as Jinnah perhaps had wished him to go. I suppose he was conscious that he, as Prime Minister, carried the responsibility for decisions, though he was quite willing, both in the way of reporting to Jinnah and asking for his advice to work in accord with him. But he was somewhat reluctant to yield the whole position, and, of course, he spoke on behalf of the Cabinet, he was the head of the government. Mr. Jinnah was anxious to know the views of each minister, and as I was next in order of seniority, he asked me for mine. I said, "The Prime Minister has spoken for the Cabinet. All I wish to add is that so far as my portfolio is concerned, my fear is not that you might interfere too much with my conduct of foreign affairs; it is that you may not be able to afford enough time to give me the guidance that I may need from you." I confess that was a somewhat diplomatic kind of reply, but it seemed to please him.

Fate intervened in a way, and matters did not come to a head. After this Cabinet meeting, in which the position which he wished to occupy was more or less accepted by the Cabinet, his health began to deteriorate faster than it had done during the previous months. He experienced a sort of cycle: he would improve a bit but not as much as he had done before, and then he would go down again, and then next time he would not be able to win back to the same degree of strength. He went to Quetta to recuperate, and returned to Karachi a few hours before the end.

Liaqat Ali Khan was a good chief to work with. He was pro-nothing, and he was con-nothing. He looked at everything from the point of view of Pakistan. I never detected any kind of bias in his temperament, either for or against persons or causes or anything; he was devoted in every way. During the four years that we worked together, I never had any suspicion that there was any member of the Cabinet who was not completely loyal to him. Subsequently, during my years at The Hague (1954-61), his widow, the Begum Ra'ana Liaqat Ali Khan, who was our Ambassador at The Hague throughout that period, repeated to me several times that her late husband had often said to her that I was the only member of his Cabinet on whom he could rely completely. This came to me as a surprise, and I said so to her, "It was very kind of him, Ra'ana, but I do not take that as a special compliment. After all, one has got to be loyal to one's chief. What merit is there in it?" She said, "Well, he thought there was particular merit in your case, not that he had any reason to suspect that you would not be loyal to him, but because he suspected, he may have had cause to, that some of the others were not quite so loyal."

I said, "I can tell you quite honestly that I never felt that any of my colleagues was not completely loyal to the Prime Minister." She said, "Well, that is proof of your own complete loyalty, because anyone else who was not quite loyal would not mention anything to you which may have sort of smacked of his loyalty."

We got along extremely well and I particularly appreciated sometimes in his public speeches, sometimes in conversations with others, when I was present, instead of saying "Zafrulla did this, or the Foreign Minister did that," he would refer to me as "My Foreign Minister." I was always deeply touched by the pronoun, "my Foreign Minister," and now, thinking back, after his tragic end, I feel he identified himself more completely with himself than perhaps I was conscious of.

Our relationship was not only intimate; it was affectionate on his part, and he rose steadily in my estimation, so that the news of his assassination, which reached me in New York - it was given to me over the telephone by a press correspondent - came as a very great personal shock. I recall the observation I made immediately to the correspondent: "The hand that released that bullet has released a whole collection of misfortunes. You cannot assess at the moment what this tragedy might mean to us." That was the beginning of the deterioration in the political field which continued till the take over by the present President in October, 1958.

**Question**: *Would you care to say something, Sir, about your activities as Foreign Minister in these first four years of Pakistan?*

**Khan**: It was actually the first seven years of Pakistan because I remained Foreign Minister of Pakistan from the 26th of December, 1947 until 7th of October, 1954.

There were the administrative problems which all the ministers were facing in setting up their ministries in working order, because we had all to start from scratch. I had the additional problem of setting up a foreign service, because under the British, though some of us had received training in almost everything else - I myself had been a Cabinet Minister holding various portfolios from 1932 to 1941 - the foreign and political portfolios were the Viceroy's own reserve. There was very little material available from which we could put together a foreign service. We had to search for suitable personnel far and wide.

That was, however, not so difficult as some of the external problems that overtook us immediately. I had already been to the United Nations, leading the first delegation of Pakistan when we were admitted to membership of the Organization in late September or early October, 1947. But even before I took over as Foreign Minister, we were overtaken by the Kashmir problem, which had been in ferment since August, 1947.

On the first of January, 1948, the matter was taken by India to the Security Council. I was conscious that this was likely to happen the moment I took charge of my portfolio, but in the very first meeting of the Cabinet, on the 26th of December, in which I was sworn in, Mr. Jinnah directed that I should go to Rangoon to represent Pakistan in the Burmese independence celebrations. These were scheduled for the 4th and 5th of January. I suggested that if he should agree to sending Sardar Abdur Rab Nishtar, who was in the Cabinet and had a much more presentable personality than I had and much more photogenic - a very handsome, strapping man - that would leave me time to get to learn something about the Kashmir problem, which if it was taken to the Security Council at an early date, would find me utterly unprepared.

But Mr. Jinnah in his usual forthright manner laid down the law and said, "You are Foreign Minister; it is your business to represent the country in the independence celebrations of a neighbouring country, and you've got to go. You'll have plenty of time for the

REMINISCENCES OF SIR MUHAMMAD ZAFRULLA KHAN    **169**

Kashmir question." There was nothing more to be said about it. Off I went to Rangoon two or three days later.

Conditions in Karachi at that time were very difficult. I had taken my wife and daughter with me from Bhopal to Karachi, but there were no accommodations for us at Karachi. I was staying as a guest with my friend, Syed Amjad Ali, and my wife and daughter were staying as guests with my wife's younger sister, whose husband had already been posted at Karachi and they had an apartment allotted to them. Our things were lying scattered about anyhow. In the middle of all this I had to go to Rangoon, whence I returned on the 7th of January. The flying boat by which I was travelling was met at Kurangi Creek by Mr. Hilali, one of our officers in the Foreign Service, now our High Commissioner in New Delhi and lately our Ambassador in Moscow, who told me that India had taken the Kashmir case to the Security Council and that the Security Council was meeting on the 12th of January to hear the case. My passage had been booked for the following afternoon from Karachi to New York, and I had to get ready to leave as quickly as I could.

It was very difficult to get ready in such a short time, with my personal belongings scattered about and not knowing where anything was, not knowing where the relevant documents could be got hold of. Chaudhri Muhammad Ali, who later became Finance Minister and was for some time Prime Minister, was then Secretary General to the Cabinet and was to accompany me, also Mr. Ayub, who is at present our Ambassador at Bonn.

I left it to them to collect whatever relevant material was available. There was no time to read anything. We literally stuffed all the documents etc. into a gunny-bag, for we had no other receptacle available, and we started on our journey to New York. We took a Pan-American plane but, as it turned out, fortunately, by the time we arrived in London, they discovered there was some mechanical defect that had to be attended to, and we were detained in London for a day. This gave me an opportunity of studying some of the documentation and to start preparing our reply to the case that India had presented to the Security Council. I was able to work one whole day in London and to dictate the first draft of our reply.

Then we started from London and carried on after a stop in Shannon, as far as Gander, Newfoundland. In Gander, we were detained by bad weather. There were several feet of snow, and we were accommodated in wooden cabins at the airport - they were

## 170          REMINISCENCES OF SIR MUHAMMAD ZAFRULLA KHAN

heated - and the stenographer who accompanied us started typing out what I had dictated in London. Unfortunately, he was in the next cabin to mine and the partition was very thin so that I could not get any rest. His constant pounding of the keys forced me to keep awake also.

When we arrived in New York, we were met at the airport by our then Ambassador in Washington, Mr. Hasan Ispahani, and our Consul General in New York, Mr. Shaffi. They told us that not knowing where or when we might be able to arrive, the Ambassador had made a request to the Security Council that the hearing of the case be postponed by a couple of days, and the Security Council had fixed the 15th of January for opening the hearings on the Kashmir case.

During the time thus gained we were able to get our documents together, and make some study of the case; and then the hearings started. I mention these details to give an idea of the background against which one had to work, apart from the nature of the problems themselves which were complicated and confusing enough.

It is not necessary to go into the details of the Kashmir case here. Everybody knows that the Security Council started very well. The members were very keenly interested and were anxious that a speedy solution to the dispute should be found along lines upon which both Pakistan and India, appeared to be agreed; that is to say, that the question of the accession of the state of Jammu and Kashmir to Pakistan or India be settled through the freely-expressed wishes of the people of Kashmir, to be ascertained by means of a free and impartial plebiscite to be held under the auspices of the United Nations. As a matter of fact, at the stage members around the table were rather surprised at how much agreement there was between the two governments, despite the differences that had arisen, and they thought it would be easy to prescribe what was needed in order to insure a fair and impartial plebiscite.

The Right Honourable Philip Noel Baker, who was then Secretary of State for Commonwealth Relations and had come over himself to represent the United Kingdom in the Security Council discussions on Kashmir, worked extremely hard to build an agreement in the Security Council itself on what needed to be done before we should separate. He has on several occasions since told me quite plainly how distressed he was that right in the middle of his efforts, when he had, every hope that at his instance Sir

## REMINISCENCES OF SIR MUHAMMAD ZAFRULLA KHAN 171

Gopalaswami Ayyangar and Sir Girja Shankar Bajpai would succeed in persuading Prime Minister Nehru to go along with the proposals laid before the Security Council, Mr. Attlee intervened and upset the whole business. On two occasions, separated from each other by an interval of years, he used the same expression, "And then the disastrous telegram arrived from the Prime Minister." He himself did not tell me, but at the time when this happened, Ayub, the Secretary I have already mentioned, was able to report to me on very good authority that for a day or two Noel Baker had contemplated resigning rather than readjust himself to the new directions from London.

Thus, the failure of the Security Council to secure an early settlement of the Kashmir dispute is attributed largely to the unfortunate intervention of Mr. Attlee from London. That took place probably at the instance of Lord Mountbatten, who must have been moved by Mr. Nehru to intercede with the Prime Minister. The argument used may have been that if the Security Council persisted in laying down the conditions they had set out in the draft resolution for securing a fair and impartial plebiscite in Kashmir that might push India into the arms of the USSR; the kind of argument that had been repeatedly used not only over this problem but over others also, and not only by India.

India's attitude had been that whereas they made repeated professions, "we shall withdraw our armies as soon as law and order is restored and the raiders have gone out of Kashmir, and the decision must be made by the people of Kashmir, freely, without any interference." There was an undercurrent of persistence that the Security Council should not go beyond ordering Pakistan to do whatever it could to get the raiders of the tribal areas out of Kashmir and it should be left to India to ascertain the wishes of the people on the question of accession. The Security Council repeatedly rejected this idea. What the Security Council desired was not only a cessation of fighting and restoration of law and order but also that the plebiscite should take place under conditions which would ensure beyond doubt that it was fair and impartial. That was the crux of the matter.

The intervention of Prime Minister Attlee, resulted in the abandonment by the Security Council of its resolution of February 6, 1948, which six of the members had sponsored and which was about to be voted upon when the Indian delegation withdrew from the Security Council to go back to New Delhi for consultations. By the time they came back, all the strings had been pulled and a very much watered-down resolution was proposed and finally adopted on the 21st of April.

The later stages are details of the Kashmir dispute. That is the one big issue which has all through the years, right up till now, divided these two neighbouring countries who otherwise have many fields in which they can usefully and fruitfully co-operate, not only in the general international interest but also in their own interests.

**Question**: *Is this what Krishna Menon is referring to when he says now that India never agreed to a plebiscite? Is he referring back to this particular discussion?*

**Khan**: No, as a matter of fact when he says that India never agreed to a plebiscite, he knows that he's not telling the truth. Later, under this resolution, which I said was greatly watered-down, a commission was set up and they went over to the subcontinent and travelled backwards and forwards between Karachi and New Delhi and finally they obtained the agreement of both governments to two resolutions which they had proposed, one dated the 13th of August, 1948, and the other, the 5th of January, 1949. Those resolutions fairly and squarely proposed a plebiscite for the purpose of ascertaining the wishes of the people of the State and laid down the conditions under which its fairness and impartiality could be insured. Mr. Krishna Menon knows he is not speaking the truth in saying that the Indian Government had never agreed to a plebiscite. As a matter of fact, during the last debates here, he went so far as to say, "My Prime Minister has never used the expression plebiscite in connection with Kashmir." In reply to him I was able to cite a dozen public announcements by his Prime Minister where he had used the expression plebiscite in connection with Kashmir. Mr. Krishna Menon just goes on saying whatever he feels would suit his case.

Then, soon thereafter, in addition to Kashmir, we had another major dispute with India which arose out of the diversion by India of the waters of three Punjab rivers, which denied Pakistan its existing uses. That created a major problem. This question has fortunately now been tied up in a treaty through the good offices of the World Bank, who worked very hard over it. I had to take part in the discussions on that question also. My first visit to New Delhi after partition was in connection with that dispute.

These were two major questions that I had to deal with, though the waters question was not strictly within my portfolio, but it did affect our foreign relations. Then we had to establish our relations with other states, to settle our orientation towards international problems and our policies in the United Nations.

In the United Nations, we were at the very beginning of our membership confronted with the problem of Palestine. Pakistan took up with great vigour the advocacy of the Arab cause. Later on, all questions of self-determination and independence, the question of Tunisia, the question of Morocco, the question of the ex-Italian colonies which resulted in the independence of Libya and trusteeship for Somalia, Pakistan took a leading part. So that though we were later-comers in the United Nations - we were admitted only in 1947 - Pakistan pulled more than its weight in the early years of its membership in the United nations over all these matters.

□ □ □ □ □

# INTERVIEW - SEPTEMBER 15, 1962

**Question**: *The last time, Sir, we had been talking about the United Nations and the Kashmir issue, and I wonder if today you would want to go on from there, after the passing of the resolution, to the working of the UN Commission.*

**Khan**: One development that took place after the passing of the resolution and before the Commission came over to the subcontinent, was that about the middle of the last week of April our then Commander-in-Chief, General Gracey made a report to the Prime Minister, who was also Defence Minister, that India was preparing to mount a military offensive in Kashmir, and what its consequences would be, in case India proceeded with what appeared to be obvious was its design, both for Kashmir territory and for Pakistan.

When that appreciation was considered by the Prime Minister and the Cabinet, they decided that if India mounted a military offensive that would be against the spirit of the Security Council Resolution of the 17th of January, 1948, which both sides had accepted and in which both sides had been told not to do anything which might further exacerbate the situation and that it would be necessary to put in regular Pakistani forces to hold the line.

That is what in fact happened; India started the offensive and Pakistani troops were engaged. Prime Minister Nehru protested, but we were awaiting the advent of the Commission on the subcontinent. The Commission gathered together at Geneva sometime during June and arrived in Karachi on the 7th of July, 1948. They came to make a formal call on me. I entertained them at tea and also had the relevant maps suspended on the wall of my sitting room, to explain to them what had happened between the passing of the resolution of the 21st of April and the time that the Commission came to the subcontinent. They were now confronted with a development which they had not contemplated while they were studying the case in Geneva, and this they regarded as a new element in the situation, which, indeed, it was.

Pandit Jawaharlal Nehru, Prime Minister of India, has gone on asserting that Pakistan put in its regular forces and tried to conceal this fact from the Commission but could not succeed in doing so and had later to admit that this had been done. That is not correct. The Commission was told by me at the earliest what the situation was.

India also raised certain objections on this later in the Security Council meetings. One was that we did not inform India in advance of what we proposed to do. This obviously was absurd. India did not inform us of what they had proposed to do. The situation being as it was, we had to take appropriate measures on our side.

Secondly, that we did not inform the Security Council, but nor had India informed the Security Council that they intended to mount a military offensive. As to the Commission, I have explained that we informed the Commission as soon as it arrived in Karachi. There was no question of our having concealed the fact from the Commission till we could no longer deny it. We had never concealed the fact that from the first week of May of 1948 our regular forces were engaged in Kashmir.

Pandit Jawaharlal Nehru himself has gone on saying that from the beginning of May they had proof that our regular forces were engaged in the fighting in Kashmir. We had never denied that from the beginning of May they were so engaged. Yet, he has sometimes made the assertion: "The Foreign Minister of Pakistan stated before the Security Council repeatedly that the regular Pakistani troops were not engaged on that front, and then, of course, it was discovered that they were." I made that statement before the Security Council in the months of February and March. Our regular forces were not engaged till early May. There was no contradiction.

Whether the Prime Minister of India made these assertions and charges because he was confused over the dates, or because knowing the dates, he thought it would create some feeling against Pakistan, I do not know. I have stated the facts to clear up the situation as far as the dates were concerned.

The Commission found themselves confronted with this new element in a problem that was already complicated. They discussed matters with us in Karachi, and then they went to Delhi, and they did that several times. In the end they produced what is known as "The Commission's Resolution of the 13th of August, 1948," which the Government of India accepted. The Government of Pakistan did not reject it, but intimated to the Commission that the resolution stopped halfway. It sought to stop the fighting that was going on but it did not spell out the obligations of the parties with regard to the plebiscite.

That consideration must have appealed to the Commission, for it began to work on the second part and eventually towards the end of December they presented their second resolution which is known as the "Resolution of the 5th of January, 1949." It was presented to the representatives of both sides in Paris because the Assembly session was taking place in Paris, and the Commission was also working in Paris. Both governments accepted it within two or three days of each other during the last days of December, 1948.

The Resolution is dated the 5th of January, 1949, but in pursuance of that resolution, the ceasefire was agreed upon on the 31st of December and was put into effect on the 1st of January, 1949. Then the Commission gathered together again in the early part of the year in Delhi and asked both sides to send their representatives to meet it in Delhi so that the Truce Agreement could be settled.

At the meeting in Delhi the Commission asked our representatives whether they had a plan for implementation of the first part of the resolution with regard to the withdrawal of Pakistani Armed Forces from the Azad Kashmir side and the withdrawal of the bulk of the Indian forces from the Indian-occupied side of the ceasefire line. They had their plan ready and they submitted it to the Commission. They asked the Indian side whether they had a plan ready, and they said they had but it had not yet been submitted to the Commander-in-Chief who was out of Delhi and there would be a delay of a day or two.

When the Commander-in-Chief came back to Delhi, the Prime Minister was not there, and there was a little further delay. When they submitted their plan to the Commission, they stipulated that the Commission was not to disclose it to the representatives of Pakistan, and not even to transmit it to the Security Council, till an agreement was reached, when the agreement could be published.

The Commission found itself in a difficult position. I imagine a certain amount of discussion went on between the Commission and the representatives of India. Eventually the Commission in its report to the Security Council recorded its views that neither qualitatively nor quantitatively did the plan constitute compliance with the Resolutions. The two resolutions of the Commission had provided that the tribesmen and other elements who had entered Azad Kashmir for the purpose of fighting should go out. This had been achieved shortly after the ceasefire and the Commission had so certified. Then a Truce Agreement was to be reached between the two governments providing for the complete withdrawal of the Pakistani forces and the withdrawal of the bulk of the Indian forces. The Pakistani forces were to begin the withdrawal and thereupon the withdrawal of Indian forces was to begin. The two withdrawals were to proceed simultaneously until the whole of the Pakistani forces and the bulk of the Indian forces had been withdrawn. At that stage, the Plebiscite Administrator would take over and he would then carry out the final disposal of the forces on both sides in order to ensure the freedom of the plebiscite, the security of the state, the maintenance of law and order. That is where the thing got stuck. No Truce Agreement was reached and the Commission reported that they could not usefully carry on. The Commission was dissolved and a U.N. representative was appointed with all the powers of the Commission to try to get a Truce Agreement and to carry on with what began to be known as demilitarization and then to arrange for the organization of the plebiscite.

Sir Owen Dixon, who was a Judge of the High Court of Australia and subsequently became Chief Justice of Australia, was appointed U.N. representative. He went over to the subcontinent and carried on discussions with both sides. He recorded his conclusion that he was convinced that he could not get any plan accepted by Pandit

# REMINISCENCES OF SIR MUHAMMAD ZAFRULLA KHAN

Jawaharlal Nehru which would ensure the freedom and impartiality of the plebiscite.

But he could not just stop there. His directive from the Security Council was that if he could not obtain implementation of the Resolution of the Security Council, of the 21st of April, 1948, and the Resolutions of the Commission, he should try some other method of bringing about a settlement of the dispute.

He proposed that the two Prime Ministers should agree to go into conference with him on a plan which he would develop in detail but the central feature of which would be that it would provide for certain areas of the State contiguous to India which had a clear non-Muslim majority acceding to India and the Azad Kashmir territory with its solid Muslim population acceding to Pakistan, leaving the future of the rest of the State, including the Valley, to be determined by a Plebiscite.

He came to Karachi with that suggestion from Delhi and assured us that he had been told by the Prime Minister of India that he was willing to go into the proposed conference to discuss such a plan, and asked whether our Prime Minister would be willing to do the same.

Our Prime Minister was very doubtful whether anything would result from such an effort, but in the end he agreed and Chaudhri Muhammad Ali, who was then Secretary General of the Cabinet, and I communicated to Sir Owen Dixon the Prime Minister's acceptance of his proposal. Sir Owen Dixon thought he could now go ahead and elaborated his plan. He said it would take him five days or perhaps a week to complete it and he would then fix the time and place of the meeting with the two Prime Ministers.

He sent a telegram to Pandit Jawaharlal Nehru that he had obtained Liaqat Ali Khan's assent to such a meeting and now proposed to proceed with the elaboration of his plan. Promptly came a reply from Pandit Jawaharlal Nehru that this was the first that he had heard of this plan and would Sir Owen Dixon go to Delhi and discuss it with him.

Sir Owen Dixon told me he was surprised at this message but that as the Prime Minister had asked him to go to Delhi it would be discourteous to refuse. He went to Delhi, and when he came back he told me that he had been met at the airport by Sir Girja Shankar Bajpai, who was then Secretary General of the India Foreign Ministry and he said to him, "Sir Girja, it was, of course, perfectly opened to the Prime Minister to say that he had considered the matter further and he had come to the conclusion that he was not prepared to take part in the proposed conference, but how is it that he says this is the first he has heard of it? You were present when I discussed this matter with him. He urged me to go to Karachi on the assumption that he was prepared to come into conference on a plan like that."

Sir Girja Shankar's comment was, "Sir Owen, I imagine the Prime Minister must have been overcome by temporary amnesia."

His effort having thus come to an end he submitted his report to the Security Council. He said at one place in his report - and India tried to make much of it later - that when he found that he could not make any headway with Prime Minister Nehru who insisted on having it declared that Pakistan was an aggressor, he told Prime Minister Nehru that he could not decide this question, nor had the Security Council authorized him to do it, but that he was prepared to assume for the purpose of carrying the matter forward that Pakistan's action was not in conformity with its obligations under international law. But even that did not help him to make any progress, and his attempt to formulate an alternative plan also fell through.

Thereafter, Dr. Graham was appointed U.N. Representative and he made several efforts to persuade the two governments to agree to a scheme of demilitarization. Sometimes India urged that demilitarization should be completed in one process and that nothing should be left to the Plebiscite Administrator in that context, and sometimes they said they did not like it done in one process; sometimes their objection was to numbers, sometimes to Azad Kashmir forces. To each proposal of Dr. Graham they had some objection.

We met in Karachi with Dr. Graham. He went to Delhi. We were asked to meet him in Geneva. Several meetings took place; he made several proposals, but either both sides were dissatisfied with his proposals, or India rejected them and Pakistan was willing to accept them, but nothing came of them.

The matter was repeatedly taken to the Security Council. The Security Council went on affirming its previous resolutions. In the meantime, India went forward with setting up a Constituent Assembly in Kashmir, which was to frame a constitution for Kashmir, and to settle its future affiliation. We brought this to the notice of the Security Council. India, through Sir B.N. Rau, its then

Permanent Representative at the United Nations, gave solemn assurance that though they could not stop the Constituent Assembly when it should be convened from passing any resolution which they might choose to pass, even on the subject of the accession of the state, anything they did in that respect would not affect the Security Council or the obligations that India had undertaken.

We had expressed an apprehension, which, unfortunately, has subsequently been proved only too well founded, that once the Constituent Assembly was set up, it would be invited to pass a resolution affirming the accession which the Maharaja had purported to carry through. It would then be claimed that that amounted to a plebiscite. India said no, that wasn't their intention at all. The Prime Minister of India went on saying publicly, in Parliament and outside, that this was an international dispute and that it could not be settled unilaterally by one party, and that in any case, it could not be settled by the Constituent Assembly that might be set up in Kashmir.

During the last discussion of the question in the Security Council during the spring and early summer of this year, that position was quite clearly taken up by India, namely that the matter has been settled, there is no longer any dispute, the people of Kashmir have decided, the accession is confirmed, and that the whole business is at an end. If that is not a unilateral decision of an international dispute, I do not know what is.

The last draft resolution before the Security Council, dated the 22nd of June, which was vetoed by the U.S.S.R., and, therefore, was not formally adopted but had obtained seven votes in support of it, proposed that the two parties should get together and try to work out a settlement. The whole matter is in that very unsatisfactory position. The dispute exists. It is keeping the two countries apart and prevents cooperation between them on matters and in spheres in which obviously they ought to cooperate together for their mutual benefit. On both sides feelings flare up. The situation becomes acute. An atmosphere of tension and distrust is maintained. In no sense, can the matter be treated as having been settled. As I stated before the Security Council in the debates that took place earlier this year, "Fifteen years have passed, but even if fifty years were to pass, the people of Kashmir will never reconcile themselves to the present situation. The matter will be settled only when those people can freely decide what they wish to do; accede to India, accede to Pakistan, or whatever else might appeal to them."

**Question**: *What was the role of Sheikh Abdullah during these years? Have you any views on that?*

**Khan**: Sheikh Abdullah was undoubtedly the most popular leader in Kashmir when this trouble started. Before Independence, he had started a movement in Kashmir called the "Quit Kashmir Movement," that is to say, that the Maharajah should quit Kashmir and the people should be at liberty to set up whatever form of government they desired.

Then Partition came and Sheikh Abdullah, obviously distressed by the turn things had taken, and anxious to do whatever he could to speed matters toward getting law and order restored and getting the tribesmen out of Kashmir, reconciled himself to the situation that the Maharaja had offered accession to India. In fact, the Maharaja's letter of accession, no doubt under the suggestion of Mr. Menon, who was then advising him - not the present Defense Minister of India but the then Political Secretary of India - stated that he intended to associate Sheikh Abdullah with his Prime Minister in the administration of the state. In his reply to the letter, Lord Mountbatten expressed the satisfaction of his government over this. Thus India claimed that the undoubted representative of the people of Kashmir was in support of the accession and was associated with the administration. Shortly after Sheikh Abdullah became the Prime Minister of Kashmir.

His effort was that the special position of Kashmir vis-a-vis India should be recognized and Kashmir should be completely autonomous and should later settle for itself what it wanted to do. Whether he intended later just to affirm the accession or to let the people decide whatever they wanted to do, is not quite clear. But as time passed and he found that India was steadily working towards greater and greater integration of the state with India, and towards its eventual absorption by India, differences began to arise between him and the Government of India. In the end he was set aside and Bakhshi Ghulam Muhammad took over the administration of the occupied part of Kashmir.

Sheikh Abdullah was taken into custody under the preventive provisions of the law applicable, and was kept in custody for quite a long period. He was released about four years ago, and after a few

REMINISCENCES OF SIR MUHAMMAD ZAFRULLA KHAN **181**

weeks was taken into custody again. He was then charged with various offences against the government.

For three years and a half preliminary proceedings went on against him in the magistrate's court, and finally a whole list of charges was framed against him by the magistrate and against those who were being tried along with him, I believe in last January. It appears that the trial is now about to start. A trial that has taken four years in starting, how long it will take in concluding, we do not know.

Quite recently, Sheikh Abdullah has made a statement that approaches have been made to him that he could be restored to the position of Prime Minister, if he will agree to the complete integration of Kashmir to India. He has reiterated that the people of Kashmir must be left free to decide what they wish to do. That has been his position for some time, and that is his principal offence; it does not matter whether it amounts to a criminal offence or not, but that is what the Government of India will not tolerate.

**Question**: *In these years, from 1948 to 1954, when you were in the U. N., Sir, what other issues do you feel, were important and that Pakistan played a part in?*

**Khan**: Almost the moment Pakistan became a member of the United Nations in 1947, the most important issue then under discussion was the question of Palestine. Pakistan took it upon itself to become the principal non-Arab advocate of the Arab cause in the United Nations and it fought strongly the proposal with regard to the Partition of Palestine and the setting up of the State of Israel. The resolution was adopted towards the end of November, a great tragedy which has had many dire consequences.

For one thing, it has driven a wedge between the United States and the West generally and the Arabs. The United States' vehement advocacy of the cause of Israel and the manner in which the resolution on Partition was finally pushed through, perhaps deserve a little explanation.

On the Wednesday before Thanksgiving, the debate was to be concluded in the General Assembly and the vote was to be taken late that afternoon or that evening. On the counting of heads, after members had declared their support of the scheme of Partition or their opposition to it, it was quite clear that the resolution did not have a two-thirds majority. Among others, General Romulo, the Permanent Representative and Ambassador of the Philippines, had gone to the rostrum and in a passionate speech declared that his country was opposed to partition and that his instructions were to vote against it.

The delegate of Haiti had gone to the rostrum and declared himself in the same vein. Liberia had not gone to the rostrum but Mr. Dennis, the leader of the Liberian delegation, had given me his assurance that his instructions were to oppose Partition. But he had added that they were likely to be under great pressure from the United States and that he was not sure that his instructions may not be changed.

About lunch time it began to be rumoured that the President, Mr. Aranha of Brazil, intended to adjourn the meeting that afternoon until Friday morning without taking a vote. Foreign Minister Fadhil Jamali of Iraq and I went to see him in his room in the Assembly immediately after lunch and asked him whether this was his intention. He told us that he intended to adjourn the session because he had been told by Trygve Lie, the Secretary General, that the staff would not be willing to work late, this being Thanksgiving Eve.

We suggested it would not be necessary to sit very late. He said he had still five speakers on his list that would take the whole of the afternoon, possibly a part of the evening also, and if the voting started then, what with explanation of votes and points of order it would take us quite far into the evening. Fadhil Jamali and I were two of the five speakers whose names he had on his list and we told him we were prepared to withdraw our names to make it easier for him to dispose of the item by dinner time, but we could not move him.

The curious thing is that ever since then, not only the staff has worked late on Thanksgiving Eve but the Assembly has sat regularly on Thanksgiving Day till 2 P.M. This was only an excuse to get an adjournment so that those who were in support of the resolution could make their last-minute efforts to wean away some of those who were opposing the setting up of the State of Israel. But even if the President had not been so willing to fall in with the wishes of those who were supporting Partition, the adjournment could have been carried by a simple majority, and we could not have blocked it.

The session was resumed on Friday morning, and in the meantime, strings had been pulled. The representative of Haiti met me in the lounge and, with tears literally coursing down his cheeks,

REMINISCENCES OF SIR MUHAMMAD ZAFRULLA KHAN    **183**

said, "Mr. Minister, what can I do? I have now received instructions that in spite of my speech, in accordance with the instructions of my government, and my declaring that we were opposed to Partition, I have now to vote for it."

General Romulo had in the meantime left for the Philippines, but the Philippines voted for the resolution. Mr. Dennis was still there, but as he had apprehended, his instructions were changed and he voted for Partition.

So, through these manoeuvres, enough votes were shifted to push the resolution through.

I have stated the exact facts and to our minds it has been absolutely clear, and, nothing has so far happened to shake us from that belief, that it was the personal intervention of President Truman that brought about these changes. It is obvious that these three votes, Haiti, Liberia and the Philippines, could only have yielded to pressure from Washington.

Partition was carried through, and one significant aspect was that that has been the only major question since the United Nations was set up on which the USSR and the USA voted on the same side.

Why was the USSR anxious to carry through the Partition? Subsequent events have shown that the USSR has not been too fond of the Zionists or of the State of Israel. What they wanted was to drive a wedge between the United States and the Arab states. That has been one major consequence, so far as the West is concerned, of the manoeuvring that then took place.

It might be asked what was President Truman's interest? President Truman's interest was perfectly obvious. He was a candidate for the presidency the following year and his position was none too strong. There was a rift in his own party. The Jewish vote was a very strong factor in the situation. Eventually, he won the election and won it easily, but in the fall of 1947 Jewish support must have appeared vital to him.

It is only fair to add, however, that President Truman had been consistent in his support of the Zionists. Mr. Ernest Bevin, the Foreign Minister of the United Kingdom, is on record as having stated in the Assembly that in 1946 he had almost succeeded in bringing about an agreement between the representatives of the Jewish Agency and the Arabs, in London, on the basis of restricted immigration into Palestine, when President Truman's open

## 184 REMINISCENCES OF SIR MUHAMMAD ZAFRULLA KHAN

telegram, urging the British to permit immediate admission of 100,000 Jewish immigrants into Palestine, forced his hand and destroyed the last chance of a settlement.

The setting up of the State of Israel has created a problem in the Middle East which there appears to be no means of resolving. It is all very well to urge that the State of Israel is an established fact; but that does not resolve the problem. It is one of those problems that has its roots in history and it is very difficult to see how peace can be brought to that region with the intrusion of an incongruous, hostile and extremely dynamic element in the heart of the Arab world.

It is no use going on saying that the Arabs are being unreasonable. This is a matter in which history, emotions, fears are all inextricably mixed together. That the Arabs are not united and constitute a congress of comparatively weak states does not help the matter; it only makes it worse.

**Question**: *How close was the vote at the time?*

**Khan**: I think they carried it by four or five votes. They got some of the Latin Americans also.

**Question**: *So, the fact that these three states voting for it, changing their position, made a very considerable difference.*

**Khan**: It made a crucial difference; as a two-thirds majority was required, two affirmative votes were needed to balance one negative vote. If those states who had declared from the rostrum that they would vote against the resolution had voted against it, the resolution could not have been carried. All this was done over the Thanksgiving adjournment.

Well, that's a pity.

Some people might say, "If the resolution had been defeated, what could have been done?" If that resolution had not gone through - it was towards the end of the session - the matter would have remained unsettled, but we had urged that a special session be called in the following spring, and that would have been some weeks before the Mandate would have expired. An effort could then be made along the lines that a group of Zionists themselves, a small group but an important one, had urged. That group was led by Dr. Judah Magnus, who was President of the Hebrew University of Jerusalem. I had met him in Jerusalem in 1945 and we had discussed this problem. He had said in very clear terms, "Nothing will work which has not the support, or at least the acquiescence, both of the Arabs and of the Israelis, and I am working for that." His idea was a bi-national state on the basis of 50:50, irrespective of what changes might take place in population. He realized that for a long time, the Israelis would probably be in a minority but if representation in the legislature, services, allocation of grants etc. were on the basis of 50-50 so that neither side would dominate, he thought the plan could work.

I do not know whether it could have worked, but it appealed to me. I tried for it during the United Nations debates but I could not get enough support for it. Dr. Judah Magnus was so keen on it that while the debate was going on he telegraphed a whole-page letter to the *New York Times*, which was published, making a very strong appeal to the Assembly not to force Partition through but to work for something on which the agreement of the Jewish Agency or of the Zionist leaders and the Arabs could be procured.

By this time the situation has completed a full circle. I cannot speak on such a delicate and important matter on behalf of the Arab states, or indeed, on behalf of anybody. But my own conviction is that today a settlement can be reached between the Arabs and the State of Israel on the basis of all the resolutions of the United Nations on Palestine, provided the State of Israel would be prepared to settle on that basis, but it is not. They have repeatedly declared that the extra territory that they have incorporated in the State of Israel is theirs in full sovereignty: "The Arabs fought us; they lost. We have gained this territory as the fruit of victory. We will not settle on any other basis."

Yet they go on complaining: "The Arabs will not make peace." You cannot have peace on the basis of fruits of victory. The moment you talk of the fruits of victory, you are talking war and not peace.

The Arabs themselves will never propose a settlement on the basis of all the U.N. Resolutions. But I feel if the State of Israel were prepared to agree to something on that basis and someone else, in the exercise of good offices or of mediation, tried to bring about a settlement on that basis, a live and let live kind of situation could be reached, which, in course of time, could develop into closer relations.

Short of that, I doubt if anything would work.

A slight variation of approach could be if the State of Israel could accept in principle that those of the Arab refugees who decide to come back and would be prepared, let us say, to take the oath of allegiance to the State of Israel and to settle down as peaceful citizens would have their properties restored to them and those who do not wish to come back would be paid full compensation for their properties and the State would assume ownership of their properties. The problem of the refugees could be put out of the way in that manner and the way would be opened for a settlement on the status of the City of Jerusalem and the frontiers.

But, again, the attitude of the State of Israel is: "What we have got we shall keep, and the Arabs must just accept the situation." It is not easy to work out a settlement on that basis.

It is one of those very unfortunate situations which I am afraid, is going to plague us for a long time to come.

Another group of questions in which Pakistan has been very keenly interested is decolonisation. It played a very prominent role in the disposal of the ex-Italian colonies, and took a leading part in the discussion of the problem of Tunisia and Morocco, and later of Algeria. It has naturally been very keenly interested, being itself an undeveloped country, in all efforts in the economic field for the raising of the standard of living in the under-developed countries, and towards economic development. Pakistan has been a member of the Economic and Social Council. Our representative on the Council, Syed Amjad Ali, who subsequently became our Ambassador in Washington, was also during one session, President of the Economic and Social Council.

On the whole, even before we became parties to treaties with some of the Western powers, our policy was one of support of freedom and liberal doctrines and attitudes. Our relationship with the Western powers has always been friendly. Then came our treaty relationship with some of them, as evidenced by SEATO and CENTO.

It has sometimes been said that under those treaties we have not only undertaken certain specific obligations, on a mutual basis, but that we have let the Western powers establish bases in Pakistan. There are no bases of any power, Western or Eastern, in Pakistan. We have only treaty relationships within the framework of the United Nations with some of the Western powers.

In that context, perhaps I might make this one comment: Pakistan is somewhat puzzled with regard to the attitude of the

United States towards that kind of relationship. The tendency, which has been freely expressed since the death of Secretary of State, John Foster Dulles, by President Eisenhower and even more clearly by President Kennedy, has been to regard Non-alignment as the more acceptable position, and consequently not only to welcome Non-alignment but to encourage it. One has the feeling that the United States is not happy in the juxtaposition of this kind of treaty relationship. That has made the authorities in Pakistan think a little more realistically over this matter and to see whether any adjustment has become necessary. I do not think Pakistan has, so far, shifted its position, but it has been studying the situation and considering whether a continuation of these treaty relationships is serving any very useful purpose.

**Question**: *After these years in the United Nations, you went to the World Court. Would you care to say something about those years at the World Court?*

**Khan**: I was elected to the Court on 7th October, 1954, in a pending vacancy occasioned by the unfortunate death of Sir B.N. Rau after he had served less than two years on the Court. I became a member of the Court on that date and completed the remaining portion of Sir B.N. Rau's term on the Court, which ended on the 5th of February, 1961.

I can, without hesitation, characterize that period as the happiest part of my public career. I must say, however, that I have always liked my work throughout my law practice when I was at the Bar, and later as Cabinet Minister in the Government of India, and then as Judge of the Supreme Court of India, and then as Foreign Minister of Pakistan. Being on the Court, which I then treated as retirement from political life, I was in a milieu that I liked best.

Then, we were on the whole, a very happy company in the Court. My relations with all my colleagues were extremely friendly. I was rendered very happy by the fact that after I had been only three years on the Court, my colleagues elected me Vice President. It was a mark of their confidence in me, and also, I think, of their affection for me. The feeling that one stands in that relationship towards one's colleagues, is perhaps the most satisfactory part of any career.

I found the work very agreeably and extremely interesting. One felt that, however slowly, one was building up the foundations of the structure of international law which is so essential in this age if the rule of law is to prevail in the world.

Each individual case that came before the Court had several features of interest. I was always very deeply interested, both in the purely legal and juristical aspects of the questions involved, and also in the human aspects.

My relations with the staff of the Court were extremely friendly - I think more intimate perhaps than those of the other judges; but the judges and the staff of the Court worked together very harmoniously.

The seat of the Court is at The Hague, in the Netherlands. My residence at The Hague enabled me to appreciate the many good qualities of the people of the Netherlands. They have carried out an extensive program of reconstruction after the very heavy losses they suffered during the War, first at the hands of the invading German forces - Rotterdam was almost reduced to rubble - then at the hands of the Allies who were coming in and the retreating Germans who opened some of the dikes causing heavy damage and ruining their very valuable orchard lands and crop areas. Not only did the Dutch accomplish all that reconstruction and rehabilitation but then they had to readjust their economy as a result of the independence of Indonesia. Now, for some years, they have been helping other countries to develop their economies.

I found life in The Hague agreeable in every way. The Hague has now grown into a large town. At one time it was known as the biggest village in Europe and it has retained many of the characteristics of a village. There are no skyscrapers at all; in fact, not very many high buildings, and that is due to the fact that the soil is not firm enough for very high buildings to be erected; the subsoil water is so near the surface. The Hague and surrounding areas are in fact below sea level. But it is a very pretty place in its own way, with its canals, its parks and all the greenery about. The climate during the greater part of the year is not very agreeable; there is a strong wind most of the time, but it is healthy. The health statistics of the Netherlands are the best in Europe.

The atmosphere is very intimate and friendly; practically every educated Dutchman and woman speaks English, so that one did not feel excluded.

**Question**: *What were some of the cases that you were involved in that interested you most during those years, Sir?*

**Khan**: The very first case I participated in was the Nottebahm Case. It raised an important point of International Law. Mr. Nottebahm,

REMINISCENCES OF SIR MUHAMMAD ZAFRULLA KHAN **189**

who had German nationality had been established in Guatemala for a number of years. He had carried on a very successful business there and had acquired a lot of property.

After the war had broken out in Europe, but before America had entered the war, he had gone to Germany, and during the return journey had stopped in the Principality of Liechtenstein and had there complied with the various requirements laid down for obtaining Liechtenstein nationality, and had then returned to Guatemala. Then the United States and some of the Latin American states, including Guatemala, entered the war, and the Government of Guatemala took action against him and his property as an enemy alien, treating him as a German subject, disregarding his change of nationality.

He was interned and his property was sequestered. After the war, when he regained his freedom, he represented to Liechtenstein that not only had he suffered loss and inconvenience but that the international rights of the Principality of Liechtenstein had been denied when his nationality was not recognized. Thus, the Principality instituted the case against Guatemala to have it declared that Mr. Nottebahm was a Liechtenstein national and should have been so recognized by Guatemala and that the latter should not have proceeded against him and that it should now restore his property to him, and should pay him compensation for the inconvenience he had suffered.

That raised a very interesting question: When is a state under obligation to recognize the nationality conferred by another state upon a non-national? The Court declined to pronounce upon the question whether as between Liechtenstein and Mr. Nottebahm a bond of nationality and allegiance had or had not been established in consequence of the naturalization proceedings which Mr. Nottebahm had gone through. That was a matter wholly within the domestic jurisdiction of Liechtenstein. The Court found that though Mr. Nottebahm had visited the Principality of Liechtenstein and had stayed there for a period, while these proceedings were carried through, and had obtained a certificate of nationality, no bond or connection had been established between Nottebahm and the Principality of Liechtenstein. He did not take up residence there; he was not employed in any connection with any of the affairs of Liechtenstein; and after having gone through this procedure, he went back to Guatemala and never returned to Liechtenstein.

Neither at the time of his visit nor later did he establish any bond or any liaison with the Principality. The Court held, therefore, that Guatemala was under no obligation to recognize his Liechtenstein nationality and was within its rights to treat him as a German national and consequently, as an enemy alien when war broke out between Guatemala and Germany.

It has become almost a rule that when a case is brought to the Court, the respondent state raises preliminary objections to the jurisdiction of the Court. When that happens, the Court must first take up that question and decide whether it has jurisdiction in the matter and only if it holds that it has, it goes on to have the pleadings completed and to hear arguments on the merits and to give judgement.

The Portugal-India case went through both these phases. Portugal claimed a right of passage between coastal Daman and two small enclaves inside, which right of passage, it alleged, India had obstructed and had thereby been guilty of a breach of international obligation. India raised six preliminary objections to the jurisdiction of the Court. Four of these the Court overruled; two were joined to the merits. After hearing arguments on the merits, the Court overruled these two objections also, and held that Portugal had succeeded in establishing a right of passage for its nationals, for civilian officials and for goods and merchandise, but had not succeeded in establishing a right of passage with respect to armed forces or armed police or arms and ammunition. On the question whether India had or had not been guilty of breach of international obligation by refusing all passage, the Court held that in view of the exercise of the right of passage, in the circumstances then prevailing, the apprehended effect upon its own internal law and order situation, India had not been guilty of any breach of obligation in denying all passage. Portugal had conceded that the exercise of the right of passage was subject to the control of the territorial sovereign and that apprehension of adverse effect upon its own law and order position by the grant of right of passage was a sufficient justification for a suspension of the right of passage.

Another case that established an important principle of international law, was the boundary case between Honduras and Nicaragua. In 1904, Honduras and Nicaragua had agreed to appoint His late Majesty, King Alfonso XIII of Spain as arbitrator in connection with their attempt to settle the boundary between them.

A commission which both sides had appointed for that purpose had demarcated the boundary, beginning from the Pacific to within a few hundred kilometres of the Atlantic; but then differences arose and the commission could not carry on. These differences were referred to the arbitration of King Alfonso XIII, who gave an award in 1906, which was by and large in favour of Honduras.

Nicaragua expressed its gratitude to the King for having graciously taken the trouble to settle a dispute between two neighbouring friendly states. The President of Nicaragua sent a telegram to the President of Honduras congratulating him on his victory and added, "What is a tract of land as compared with the maintenance of friendly relations between two neighbouring states." The Nicaraguan Parliament also approved of the award, so that the matter appeared to have been settled.

But later, Nicaragua began to have second thoughts, and in 1912 it repudiated the award and had raised questions with regard to the validity of the appointment of the King as arbitrator and the validity of the award. The United States tried to intervene in the dispute but it did not succeed in bringing about a settlement. Finally, the Organization of the American States persuaded the two parties to submit the dispute to the International Court of Justice.

As the matter was taken to the Court by agreement of the two States, no question as to the jurisdiction of the Court arose. The Court went through the usual procedure of receiving detailed written pleadings and hearing oral arguments, and finally handed down its judgment. It held that the appointment of the King as arbitrator was validly made in accordance with the terms of the relevant treaty; and, having been accepted by both parties, who had submitted their cases in detail to the King, was no longer open to question on the ground of alleged failure to comply with the terms of the treaty. Had there been any such failure it would have been cured by the subsequent presentation of the case before the King and by the acceptance of the King's award.

On the second question, it held that the award was valid, that none of the objections taken to the award had been established; that the award was not, as Nicaragua had contended, incapable of being put into effect on the spot and that, in any case, having accepted the award, it was not now open to Nicaragua to question its validity.

That judgment again cleared up two important points with regard to international arbitration. First, when a state becomes a

192          REMINISCENCES OF SIR MUHAMMAD ZAFRULLA KHAN

party to arbitration and submits its case and pleads before the arbitrator, it cannot subsequently take advantage of any irregularity in the appointment of the arbitrator and question the validity of the appointment of the arbitrator.

Secondly, once an award is handed down, a party that signifies its acceptance of the award or acquiesces in the award, cannot afterwards turn round and question the validity of the award.

**Question**: *In a case like this, when, as you say, the two sides present their briefs, does the Court, in addition, investigate the situation?*

**Khan**: If the written pleadings show that the parties are agreed on the facts, no further investigation is necessary and the Court proceeds on the basis of the written pleadings. If the relevant facts should be in dispute, the Court has power to issue a commission to investigate and report on the facts.  Both parties would be represented before the Commission. The Court can hear witnesses itself, as it did in the Temple Case, between Cambodia and Thailand. It has all the powers which any other Court has for the purpose of ascertaining the facts.

In what is known as the Corfu Channel Case, between the United Kingdom and Albania - this case was heard and decided before I joined the Court - all these procedures were gone through. The case was brought to the Court on the recommendation of the Security Council.  The facts were that a squadron of the United Kingdom Navy was steaming up the Corfu Channel, which is an international channel and is also territorial waters of Albania, and it encountered mines in the channel. Two destroyers suffered damage and some of the personnel were killed and or injured.

The United Kingdom took the matter to the Security Council. The Security Council recommended that the two parties take certain questions, which the Security Council formulated, to the Court, and they were taken to the Court. Later, Albania denied the jurisdiction of the Court. The Court held that Albania having once submitted to the jurisdiction of the Court, its subsequent repudiation of jurisdiction did not operate to deprive the Court of jurisdiction.

The case involved several technical questions and the Court appointed a commission of experts to investigate and report on them. Finally the Court decided that the mines had not been laid by Albania, but that Albania was aware of the existence of the mines and, was thus under international obligation to give warning of the

REMINISCENCES OF SIR MUHAMMAD ZAFRULLA KHAN    **193**

mines to the British squadron as soon as it learned that the squadron was to pass through the Channel.  Having failed to give that warning, it had been guilty of a breach of international obligation and was therefore liable in damages to the United Kingdom.

For the assessment of damages, the Court again appointed a commission and on the basis of the report of the commission assessed damages in an amount a little in excess of that claimed by the United Kingdom.

There was a counter-claim by Albania.  Sometime after the incident in which the British destroyers had been damaged, the British Navy had carried out mine-sweeping operations in the Corfu Channel.  Albania complained that in doing that, they had contravened Albanian sovereignty.  The Channel was part of Albanian territorial waters and the mine-sweeping operations had been carried out without Albania's permission or consent. Albania had not asked for any damages but had stated that it would be content with a declaration.  The Court did declare that the mine-sweeping operations had contravened Albanian sovereignty.

Incidentally, so far as I am aware, that is the only judgment of the Court which has remained unsatisfied.  Albania has not carried out the judgment.  The Court is only a judicial organ; the executive organ of the United Nations is the Security Council.  The Charter lays down in Article 94, that if a judgment of the Court is not carried into effect, the state in whose favour the judgment has been given may move the Security Council and the Security Council may, after hearing the parties, take such action or make such recommendations as it may deem necessary to give effect to the judgment.

**Question**: *Were there any other issues in the Court that you found particularly interesting?*

**Khan**: The jurisdiction of the Court in contentious cases can be availed of only by sovereign states.  Individuals cannot be parties to a case before the Court.  But as the Nottebahm case illustrates, a state may take up the case of a national, where it finds that the respondent state or any of its organs have denied relief to the national or subjected him to treatment which involves a denial of the international rights of the state itself.

The Norwegian Loans Case is an illustration.  The Government of Norway and some co-operative societies in Norway had, during the last years of the last century and the early years of this century, raised loans in the international market. It was alleged on behalf of the French bond-holders, at whose instance France instituted the case before the Court, that the bonds contained "the gold clause," that is to say a stipulation that repayment of the loan and payment of interest would be made in terms of the gold franc.

In the wake of the First World War, almost every country, at one time or the other, went off the gold standard and passed legislation that all obligations which had been expressed to be fulfilled in terms of gold would now be fulfilled in terms of the currency of the country. Norway had done the same, and thus a dispute arose between the bond-holders and the borrowers, who claimed that they were entitled to be paid in terms of the gold value of the franc, which, incidentally, was sixty four times the value of the franc. The French Government took up the case of its bond-holders and asked the Court for a declaration in terms of the claim of the bond-holders.

Norway filed preliminary objections to the jurisdiction of the Court, one of them being that the Court had no jurisdiction, inasmuch as the French declaration accepting jurisdiction of the Court contained an exception to the effect that the Court would not have jurisdiction in a case which the French Government had determined was a matter falling wholly within its domestic jurisdiction.

Norway contended that by virtue of the doctrine of reciprocity it was entitled to take advantage of the exception contained in the French declaration, and that the Norwegian government having determined that this was a matter falling wholly within its domestic jurisdiction the Court had no jurisdiction.

The Court accepted the plea and the French application was rejected.

Another case in which the case of an individual was the Guardianship Case. It related to the custody of a minor girl whose father was a national of the Netherlands and whose mother had been a Swede. The father, a shipowner, had married a Swedish national and they had lived the greater part of their married life in Sweden. The only child was a daughter. The mother died, and the child's custody was handed over by the Swedish courts to her maternal grandparents in Sweden. The child had lived all her life in Sweden, had never been in Holland, and did not know the Dutch language. There was no dispute with regard to the guardianship of the child's property, which she had inherited from her mother, for it was

## REMINISCENCES OF SIR MUHAMMAD ZAFRULLA KHAN 195

recognized that the father was the guardian of the child and of her property.

The father had taken proceedings in the Netherlands Courts with regard to the guardianship of the child and had been duly appointed the guardian. But when he claimed the custody of the child, the Swedish courts held that the custody of the child had been entrusted to the child's maternal grandparents not under the law of guardianship but under a special Swedish law regulating the welfare of minors. In this case, it had been found that the minor suffered from nervous depression, and it was necessary that she should be taken special care of. It was claimed that this took the case out of the purview of the Law of guardianship.

The Government of the Netherlands took up the case of its national, the father of the minor, and filed an application against Sweden, asking the Court to declare that under a Private International Law Convention relating to Guardianship, to which both States were parties, and which provided that in case of a dispute arising under the Convention, the Court would have jurisdiction, the father was entitled to the custody of the minor. The Court held that the Swedish law did not fall within the purview of the law of guardianship but related to all minors, whether their parents were alive or not and whether a question of guardianship was involved or not, who needed special care. The case was, therefore, not governed by the Convention.

My own approach to the case was based on the relevant material and the provisions of the international Convention. But to me this distinction between guardianship and custody did not come as a surprise, inasmuch as Muslim law makes a clear distinction between guardianship, which it calls *Wilaya*, and custody, which it calls *Hazana*. Under Muslim law, guardianship of minors belongs to the father, and in default of the father, to the paternal grandfather, and in default of the paternal grandfather, to the male paternal relations in order of propinquity.

On the other hand, the custody of a male child up to seven years of age and the custody of a female child throughout minority, belongs to the mother and in default of the mother, to the maternal grandmother and thereafter to female relatives on the mother's side in order of propinquity. All of them would have to be exhausted before custody would go to the female relations on the father's side.

196    REMINISCENCES OF SIR MUHAMMAD ZAFRULLA KHAN

The distinction between guardianship and custody is based on the claims of natural affection and the practical considerations affecting the welfare of minors. Thus, the administration of the property of the minor and making arrangements for its upbringing and education and making provision for the costs, and also guardianship for marriage, all belong to the father, and male relations on the father's side.

But, the actual care and upbringing, and the custody of the minor, belong to the mother and the female relations on the maternal side.

**Question**: *How much of this has been written into the Pakistan law, by the way, or how much is just accepted in interpreting it?*

**Khan**: So far as Pakistan is concerned, in all matters of personal relationships, such as, marriage, divorce, guardianship, custody, inheritance, succession, gifts, wills, legitimacy, etc., it is statutorily provided that Muslim Law shall apply to Muslims. We do not write the Muslim Law itself into our statute books except when some doubt is cast on what the law is on a particular point. Then we pass a declaratory law, saying this is the law. The Muslim law is based on the Qur'an and the Sayings of the Prophet and the writings of the jurists. When a question of Muslim law arises, it is enough to show from the writings of the jurists that the preponderance of opinion is in support of one position or the other, and the court decides on that basis.

**Question**: *In a case like this, this kind of question with regard to guardianship and custody, this would be assumed, it would be clear enough in customary law ...?*

**Khan**: Not customary law, because that is quite a distinct concept; but under Muslim Law, yes, it is quite clear; there is no doubt about it.

**Question**: *And this would be within a Pakistan court?*

**Khan**: Yes. As a matter of fact, even non-lawyers, know that guardianship of a minor under Muslim Law belongs to the father and custody belongs to the mother, in the case of a male child up to seven and in the case of a female child throughout minority. We think that this is in perfect accord with the claims of nature, as well as with the proper upbringing of the minor. A minor needs affection and a type of personal care which only a mother or a women in *loco maternis* can supply.

# INTERVIEW - SEPTEMBER 22, 1962

**Question**: *When you returned to the United Nations, Sir, in the summer of 1961, what were the problems then that you were concerned with? Perhaps if you can categorize them to some extent, colonial issues for example. Would you say that this is one of the leading issues in the United Nations at the present time, the problem of bringing former colonial powers into the United Nations?*

**Khan**: My term on the International Court of Justice finished on the 5th of February, 1961. I had been on the Court six years and four months, which was the unexpired term of Sir B.N. Rau, whose place I had taken on the Court.

My name was up for re-election before the United Nations during the 1960 session of the Assembly, along with those of my four colleagues whose term was also due to expire in 1961, but none of us was re-elected. So I had thought to myself that now, at long last, I could retire. I had taken up my residence temporarily at Cambridge, England.

I was fairly content with my life there as it was beginning to develop, and I might perhaps have chosen Cambridge to settle down in for the greater part of the year for it was difficult for me to face the summer back home in Pakistan. I had suffered from diabetes for more than twenty years. Of course, I would have gone home for the winter every year.

In the beginning of July, our President, when he was on his way to the United States on his State visit, suggested to me in London that I should come to the United Nations as Permanent Representative of Pakistan. I have been keenly interested in the United Nations - all through 1947 to 1954, I had led the Pakistan delegation to the General Assembly as Foreign Minister. I agreed and took up my duties at the United Nations on the 12th of August, 1961.

The first thing that struck me immediately was the tremendous increase in the membership of the United Nations that had taken place during the period that I had been away. I had left the United Nations in the fall of 1954 and in December, 1955, "the package deal" had gone through and was followed by a large accession of membership in the United Nations, mainly from Asia and Africa and later progressively from Africa. It took me a little time to get to know even the leading personalities representing the new members;

but I was fascinated by the new character the United Nations had assumed. For the first time, it appeared to me that the membership was balanced. In the years prior to 1955, the United Nations had worn a Western aspect. For us, despite the ideological conflict, the Eastern states of Europe and the USSR, are also Western countries. So also are the Latins. There were very few of us from Asia and Africa. Now Afro-Asian membership was rapidly approaching 50 percent of the total membership.

That made a lot of difference to the emphasis that was brought to bear upon different categories of questions. The increase in the membership from those areas did not start new questions and new problems. They were already there. The process of decolonization, for instance, was already in progress and that is what brought these newly independent nations in.

With their coming in, the pace of decolonization began to be stimulated and more and more emphasis was laid upon it; that was quite natural. For instance, so many African countries were already free but so many were not yet free, and those who were free naturally could not feel happy - they could not even feel completely free themselves, as we in Asia too had been feeling: we did not feel completely free until our brethren in Africa and Asia who were not yet free also attained their freedom. This is one aspect which the Western powers, especially the colonial powers, had the unity of outlook of the African and of the Asian peoples.

I recall, in that connection, the conference on Indonesia that was called by Prime Minister Jawaharlal Nehru in Delhi in January of 1949, which I also attended. I fell into conversation, the first afternoon, at a garden party which Prime Minister Nehru had given for the delegates to the conference, with the Ambassador of the Netherlands in New Delhi. When I told him my reactions to the last "police action," so-called, that had been carried out by the Dutch in Indonesia on the 15th of December, he said to me, "We can understand a certain amount of reaction in Asian countries over this, but we cannot understand the sharpness of the reaction, for instance, in Pakistan." I had been told the same thing by Jonkheer Von Karnebeck, the Dutch Minister in Karachi. He said, "After all, even if we have done wrong, it is the people of Indonesia who are affected by it, not the people of Pakistan."

My reply had been, "Jonkheer, that is the mistake you people go on making all the time. You do not seem to realize that if any of you

## REMINISCENCES OF SIR MUHAMMAD ZAFRULLA KHAN 199

do that kind of thing to any of us, our reactions are exactly the same as if you had done it to us. Once you realize that, it may be easier to work out solutions." There is nothing artificial about that; it is our blood. We are all one, and we are all race-blind and colour-blind. It does not make any difference what a person's colour is or what his race is. Blood is not the line which divides humanity; indeed there are no lines. We are all human beings, and we cannot see why one section should continue to dominate over another section. Why the West cannot understand this is very surprising to us.

As I have said, these problems were already there. But when more and more of the lately dominated peoples came in and they became conscious that while they were free, their brethren were not, naturally more and more emphasis was laid upon that aspect. During the 15th and 16th Sessions, certain resolutions were adopted to step up the pace of decolonization still more.

That question is not merely one of the problems before the United Nations, but holds the forefront of the stage at the United Nations. The next in order, and of almost equal importance, is the question of economic development of the underdeveloped countries. Political freedom is a very desirable objective in itself: it is not merely a means to an end, it is one of the ends. But it is only one of the ends. In its turn, it becomes a means towards the attainment of greater welfare, higher prosperity of the people concerned so that human life should become more worthwhile for them. The maintenance of international peace and security also is a means to the same end. It is now being more and more sharply recognized that the common man should now enter upon his inheritance of a fuller, richer and happier life. The emphasis has been mounting in that direction.

We are all very keenly interested in the maintenance of international peace, because if peace is not maintained, none of these ideals can be progressed towards; everything would go by the board. But we want it recognized more and more, that even the maintenance of international peace is not the ultimate end; it is a very necessary, very essential condition for the achievement of the common good of all of us, and that is that human life everywhere should become fuller, richer and happier.

Another thing I noticed to my joyful surprise was that the representatives of these new members exhibited a high sense of responsibility. This did not apply to all individuals; as a matter of

## REMINISCENCES OF SIR MUHAMMAD ZAFRULLA KHAN

fact, it was not true of all individuals even among the representatives of the older members that have been independent and sovereign for centuries. But it was true of enough individuals among the representatives of the new members, to give me a feeling of reassurance. I did not experience a single moment of disappointment over the quality of their representation. On the other hand, I am surprised why this is not more fully recognized. One often hears, "Now that the majority is going to be Afro-Asian, what will happen?" They do not look at what has failed to happen so far: at no time have the Afro-Asians shown any tendency to take the bit between their teeth and to run away with the whole contraption.

Look at the major decisions that have been taken. They are still, more or less, along the old pattern. Only the emphasis, as I have said, on certain questions, has shifted. Once the speechifying is done, and the process of give and take, behind the scenes, has run its course, the resolutions that are carried have the concurrence of the major groups in the United Nations. To the extent that that represents a change, it is a healthy change. It means that the older members are beginning to appreciate the point of view of the newer members and thus there is greater understanding and a more eager disposition to co-operate in the pursuit of the objectives and purposes of the United Nations set out in the Charter. Some of us, naturally, have a keener interest in and work harder for certain things; others work harder for other things. It is a sort of division of interests on a basis of understanding, appreciation and co-operation that is beginning to develop.

One aspect of the increasing membership is that the younger members of the missions of new members, at the level of counsellor, first secretaries, second secretaries, etc. are the people who will in the next decade be the policy-makers of their own countries. It is a very good and healthy development that they are being trained for those responsibilities in this atmosphere of co-operation and give and take. All this will be reflected through them in the policies of their countries.

The United Nations is indirectly helpful in another direction. Not all new states - and, indeed, not all the older states - can afford to maintain diplomatic missions in the capitals of all other states. Part of that lack of diplomatic representation is got over through bilateral and multilateral conversations, negotiations, settlement of formal matters - sometimes even of important matters - that are

### REMINISCENCES OF SIR MUHAMMAD ZAFRULLA KHAN 201

carried on behind the scenes. So that, in a sense, each mission at the United Nations carries on a double function: One, its accreditation to the United Nations, where we all work together for common purposes; secondly, it fills in the gaps in its country's diplomatic representation abroad.

For instance, Pakistan is not directly represented in several of the newly-independent states, and, indeed, not even in all the older states. My mission here, under the directions of my government, often takes up questions with the representatives of different countries and we get them settled here or get them moving. It is true, they do not involve issues of crucial importance, but they take the place of the daily routine of diplomatic exchanges. The United Nations is becoming a centre for that kind of activity also.

**Question**: *Would you say that the United Nations is more homogeneous, more of a genuine organization now than it was when you first came to it?*

**Khan**: In the sense that it is not now so one-sided, yes. Up until 1955, it was an organization representing mainly Europe and the Americas. There were only a few Asiatic members and two or three Africans. It is better balanced now.

**Question**: *Has it developed an esprit de corps, a feeling that the United Nations has a kind of life in itself?*

**Khan**: I believe so.

**Question**: *The same sort of thing that you mentioned about the World Court, for example. Would you find that?*

**Khan**: Not to the same degree. The Court is a much smaller body and all of us concentrated all the time on the same problem with the same objective and when we had finished with one, we took up the next one. Here, the problems are varied, numerous and conflicting, and not only does the emphasis vary, interests also clash. But here also we are engaged in similar activities in pursuit of common overall objectives and are oriented, more or less, in the same direction. That helps to generate a spirit of co-operation.

**Question**: *What about the Cold War issue, in this last year particularly, in the United Nations? Is this an issue that is always in the forefront of your work?*

**Khan**: It affects us all the time; but some members are rather cold towards the Cold War issue. They certainly consider it is a problem;

## 202    REMINISCENCES OF SIR MUHAMMAD ZAFRULLA KHAN

but, some of them, while they are ready to assist both sides to be reasonable, are not overly preoccupied with it.

On the other hand, there are certain powers that are directly involved in the Cold War issues and we cannot help being drawn into them from time to time. The United Nations is now approaching universality, and the different shades that pervade the relationships between the states outside are reflected inside the United Nations also.

**Question:** *What about Disarmament? Is this a genuine concern of a large portion of the membership?*

**Khan**: It is becoming more and more so, because it is felt that both security and prosperity are tied up with it. You cannot feel wholly secure under the uneasy equilibrium brought about by the atomic or nuclear deterrent. At any time, the wrong lever may be pulled or the wrong button pressed and the world might blow up enveloping everything in ruin.

Again, rapid progress towards the prosperity of the human race as a whole cannot be made when such a large proportion of the resources available - and more especially of the new sources of power that science has placed at the disposal of man - is directed towards the manufacture of armaments, rather than towards the beneficent service of humanity.

Mankind today as a whole is much more interested in this problem than it was at any time before. That interest has become so much keener because there is a feeling that, given a certain degree of confidence, Disarmament is practicable. Up to a certain time, with conventional weapons it was felt it was difficult because nobody would be willing to give up his advantage and most of the time the powers were engaged in manoeuvring for position. A certain amount of that still continues, but the great powers also seem to be genuinely anxious for Disarmament, for the choice has been narrowed to destruction or bankruptcy. So there is some hope.

The emphasis in the current Session of the Assembly is on making a beginning with something or the other, the banning of nuclear tests, stopping the spread or the manufacture of nuclear weapons, safeguards against sudden attack etc. Progress in the scientific field might show the way towards a treaty banning nuclear tests permanently. It seems now to be established that nuclear tests can be detected without inspection. Scientific means have now become available by which it can be determined beyond doubt whether a test has taken place. May be science might show the way, first, towards the banning of tests and restraining them, and next, towards Disarmament.

At the bottom of the whole problem is a lack of the minimum degree of confidence in the motives, intentions, and the determination to carry out obligations, of each side.

**Question**: *Would you care to say something, Sir, about your election to the office of President of the General Assembly?*

**Khan**: Well, yes, but it will take a little explanation. When I arrived in New York last year, Ambassador Shahi, who was my number two here, while we were still at Idlewild, in his briefing of me on what the situation was, told me what was likely in respect of the Presidency of the Sixteenth Session. He said there were two candidates: Ambassador Mongi Slim of Tunisia and Ambassador Ali Sastroamidjojo of Indonesia; and it was expected that Ambassador Ali would withdraw, provided the Afro-Asian group would pledge their support of his candidacy the following year, that is, for the current session which is now in progress.

I told Ambassador Shahi that would be all right with us. We would be quite happy, but that my personal reaction was that an Asian should not follow immediately upon an African in the Presidency. I had ever before arrival here, from Cambridge and London, sensed the feeling which already existed and which has become sharper and sharper, that now that the Afro-Asians had increased their voting strength, they were likely to steamroller things in the United Nations. I felt we should not do anything to strengthen that impression. I thought we could reasonably claim the Presidency in alternate years. That would be a satisfactory arrangement, as we now had almost 50 percent of the voting strength, and it was likely to go beyond 50 percent in a year or two. But I was strongly of the view that we should not hold the Presidency two years running.

In February or March of this year, it became clear that Ambassador Ali Sastroamidjojo would not be available. I started a suggestion in certain sections of the group that if Ambassador Amadeo of Argentina could be available, we should let the Latins have the Presidency. Ambassador Amadeo had proved so efficient a chairman of the First Committee, which has very often been regarded as the first step towards the Presidency, that I thought he would make an excellent President.

I consulted certain delegations, and they all said, that if the Latins agreed with us that they would help us to secure the Presidency each alternate year, we would be quite willing to support Ambassador Amadeo. Right in the middle of all this, there was a political upset in Argentina, and Ambassador Amadeo resigned. Thus he was no longer available.

At that stage, certain Asian candidates let their names be circulated for the Presidency. I was not thinking of myself in that connection, but an approach was made to me by the Chairman of the Afro-Asian group, Ambassador Rifai of Jordan as to whether I could be available. I told him what I had been thinking and said that though Ambassador Amadeo was not available, we might still consider some suitable Latin American candidate. He was, however, very insistent, and two or three names were already being mentioned from among the Asians and he and some of his colleagues thought that I would be the most suitable and would I let my name be mentioned. I put him off.

He came a second time, and a third time, and finally I agreed to put it to my government. I gave them the background and asked them how they felt. They thought I should put forth my candidacy, and I did.

It was clear from the outset that none of the other three candidates whose names were mentioned at that time could be said to be sure of being elected. Within a week, or two weeks, it became clear that I stood a good chance of being elected.

The Japanese intimated to our government that they had been quite serious in their candidacy but since I was now a candidate, they had no desire to contest the Presidency with me. That was very good of them. The third candidate also fell out fairly early - he had not yet formally put forward his candidacy. Ambassador Malalasekra of Ceylon, who had formally put forward his candidacy, remained in the field.

He was supported by the Eastern European states, which was a factor that was likely to stand in the way of the Western states giving him their support as a group. Out of the Afro-Asian group, he got the support of a few Asian countries - India was his principal supporter and canvasser - and, of course, Ceylon, Burma, Cambodia and Laos, and there may have been one or two more, but we doubt it. Outer Mongolia went with the Communist group. He may also have got the votes of two or possibly three of the African states. He

## REMINISCENCES OF SIR MUHAMMAD ZAFRULLA KHAN    **205**

had Cuba's support, but I doubt whether he got any other Latin Americans. From the beginning, it had been said that Ambassador Malalasekra would get between 25 and 30 votes, and that estimate proved to be correct.

On the ballot, he obtained 27 and I obtained 72 votes; four ballots were declared invalid. I was told later that they were declared invalid because they were marked "Pakistan," and did not have my name.

The system of voting is somewhat confusing. For the Presidency, the name of the candidate should be inscribed on the ballot. For the Vice Presidencies, the names of the countries should be inscribed, and for the Chairman of committees, the names of individuals. Some of the newer countries were, perhaps, not familiar with that distinction, and put down the name of the country and not of the candidate. One ballot contained the name of Ambassador Mongi Slim, who was the outgoing President.

I am glad to say that my personal relations with Ambassador Malalesekara continued friendly throughout. I took very little part in canvassing for the Presidency. Of course, my colleagues in the mission here did what they thought was necessary, and quite a large number of friends in other delegations also helped. I have no doubt the Ministry in Karachi instructed our Representatives abroad to do the necessary canvassing.

I have always been shy and somewhat inhibited in canvassing for myself. I can be a good canvasser for someone else, whether a state or an individual, but it is very difficult for me to make the request, "Will you kindly vote for me?"

**Question**: *There was considerable publicity, especially in some of the papers, about the letter Ambassador Malalesekara wrote that got published wrongly in the Canadian papers. Did that have any effect on his candidacy?*

**Khan**: I do not think so. I do not think it affected a single vote. People were surprised and some were amused over what had happened. Some felt sympathy towards Ambassador Malaesekra that he was put in a position of embarrassment. But I do not believe the incident affected a single vote. The situation before that letter became public was almost exactly what the actual voting disclosed. It is now obvious that it could not affect adversely those who were supporting him because the main group of his supporters was the

Eastern European group, plus Cuba, and they were opposed to the West anyhow. As this letter contained several reflections adverse to the West, they rather rejoiced in it. The Western group, as a whole, were not very favourable to Ambassador Malalesekara's candidacy anyhow.

**Question:** *You mentioned Cambodia and Laos and some of the other countries as supporting him. Was this on religious grounds, or ...?*

**Khan**: Ceylon's relationship with those countries was, on account of their religious and cultural ties, closer than Pakistan's. So in a way they would feel they were closer to Ambassador Malalesekara.

**Question**: *What about the problems facing the current Session of the United Nations and the general atmosphere within the Assembly?*

**Khan**: The problems are well known. There is, of course, the cluster of problems connected with the Cold War, some of which are on the agenda and possibly some others may be added. Some that are not on the agenda continue to cast their shadow on the work of the Assembly and its approach towards the questions on the agenda. For instance, the Berlin question is not before the United Nations, but everybody is conscious of it; and though it is in the background, it affects the attitude of at least some members towards some items on the agenda.

Then, there is the question of Disarmament, which is pressing more and more upon the consciousness of the delegates. Then there is the financial provision for peace-keeping operations, in which context the advisory opinion of the International Court of Justice will come under consideration and let us hope will be accepted and endorsed by the Assembly. The colonial question, and the question of the quicker development of the resources of the developing countries are two of the major questions: some of the other items are offshoots from these.

On the maintenance of international peace and Cold-war problems, the speech of Foreign Minister Gromyko yesterday left many of us more apprehensive than we were before he spoke. He was not only very rigid on the questions of Berlin, Disarmament, nuclear tests and Cuba, but on Berlin and Cuba he seemed to utter veiled threats. I did not feel, when I was listening to him, that this was just propaganda. I have an apprehension, certainly with reference to Berlin, that the Soviets have come to some decision with

## REMINISCENCES OF SIR MUHAMMAD ZAFRULLA KHAN  **207**

regard to the timetable of what they intend to do: for instance, a separate treaty with East Germany, and leaving West Berlin to settle questions of access, etc. with the East German Government. Should that happen, it would give rise to major problems affecting the maintenance of international peace.

Also, with regard to Cuba, the words and tone were menacing. One realizes, on the other hand, the situation with regard to Cuba vis-a-vis the United States of America and the South American states, especially those that are around the Caribbean. It is too early to make an assessment, but I had a sense of uneasiness at the end of that speech.

On decolonization, we shall probably not be able to go very much further than we did last year. Portugal seems determined to hold the line, as it were, with regard to Angola and Mozambique. The outcome is still in the dark. On the other hand, the Afro-Asians are determined to press the matter forward. A resolution of the type that was carried last year will be carried again this year, but it will be wise of Portugal to take note of the mounting indignation among the Afro-Asian countries over its attitude.

Nobody is likely to be deceived by the fiction that Angola and Mozambique are a part of metropolitan Portugal. This kind of theory was advanced by France with regard to Algeria, and it did not help towards a solution of the situation at all. It is open to everybody to go and see for themselves. If territories were part of metropolitan Portugal, the people would be treated like any other section of the Portuguese people. They are not so treated. A little is perhaps being attempted by way of providing educational facilities and roads etc., and possibly a handful of Angolese are being trained for better positions in the administration, but that's not the end of the matter by any means. It is not even the beginning of a solution.

Of all colonial problems, probably that is likely to raise more heat and dust than any other. Southern Rhodesia is another very difficult problem, and the difficulty is enhanced by the constitutional position. Southern Rhodesia, though not independent and sovereign, is, under the constitutional arrangements already in force, mistress of its own internal affairs. Britain has little authority and less power to attempt a solution. No decision can be made in the United Nations without the participation of Rhodesia, and Rhodesia cannot participate directly because it is not independent. So, it is, in a

**208** REMINISCENCES OF SIR MUHAMMAD ZAFRULLA KHAN

sense, a case of long-distance shooting, those directly concerned cannot be brought to face the situation here.

An attempt was made to leave the question out of the agenda of this session, because it had been dealt with very recently in the adjourned session in June. It was not to be expected that much progress could be made between June and, say, the end of this year. But the Afro-Asian states were insistent that the matter must be brought up for discussion again in this session. Last year's resolution directed that the committee should report to the 17th Session. The committee prepared its report and submitted it, but the 16th Session was under adjournment and had not been concluded, though the adjournment had been for the sole purpose of dealing with Rwanda and Burundi. When the Session was resumed for the purpose of dealing with Rwanda and Burundi, a motion was adopted that it should also consider the report of the committee in regard to Southern Rhodesia. Thus the report was dealt with in the resumed session, and now it has come up in the 17th Session.

**Question**: *What about South Africa?*

**Khan**: South Africa again will raise a good deal of controversy. This fall South Africa will be discussed in another forum. The International Court of Justice will deal with the problem of South West Africa on the application of Ethiopia and Liberia, representing the remaining African states. On the 2nd of October, the Court will take up the hearing of the preliminary objections of the Government of South Africa to the jurisdiction of the Court and it is expected to hand down its judgment by the middle of December, possibly earlier. If the Court holds that it has jurisdiction, then in 1964-1965, it will be ready to deal with the merits of the question. The pendency of the matter before the International Court of Justice will not affect the overall question being discussed in this Session. There will be a great deal of pressure and possibly an attempt to get a resolution through asking for sanctions against South Africa.

Last year, our delegate on the Special Political Committee presented a resolution proposing oil sanctions against South Africa. We were of the view that a resolution proposing general sanctions, even if it was carried, would be difficult to enforce. Sanctions limited to oil are more easily enforceable and could be very effective. The economy of a country, industrialized to the degree to which South Africa is, could be brought to a standstill by the denial of petrol.

## REMINISCENCES OF SIR MUHAMMAD ZAFRULLA KHAN    209

On the other hand, the oil-producing interests would not be very adversely affected, because the total consumption of petrol in South Africa is not so high that the loss of that market would affect materially either the price or the disposal of the petrol produced. That proposal did not get the wholehearted support of even the entire Afro-Asian group, because some of the oil-producing countries were apprehensive of its effect on them.

This year, I believe, another effort will be made to get through a resolution recommending general sanctions. I am very doubtful whether it would obtain a two-thirds majority, and even if it does, I doubt whether any concrete measure will be put into effect, beyond its serving as notice to South Africa that things are getting more and more difficult for them and that they had better pay attention to world opinion on this problem. From that point of view, it might perhaps do some good.

But I have little hope that the present administration of South Africa will be moved by anything of this kind. In fact, it is becoming more and more intransigent. Its latest law, known generally as the "Law of Sabotage," is a very savage measure. Indeed, it can scarcely be called a law. It is more or less an executive measure. Under it, almost any action may be taken against anybody on the ground that what he has said or done constitutes a menace or an injury to the state. The "state," of course, means the white population, or even only the Boer population.

The situation is getting more and more difficult. They seem deliberately to have taken a stand which means all or nothing. In the conditions of today, no state can get away with that. If the issue is deliberately cast in the form of all or nothing, it is more likely to result in nothing rather than in all. The policies of the present administration, if persisted in, will only lead to ruin. I believe I have a fairly sympathetic understanding of their difficulties - it is no use pretending that they are just acting out of malice; they are faced with real difficulties. But I am convinced that their own interest demands that some other solution must be sought whereunder something may be yielded in order to save the rest.

For instance, they could easily safeguard their economic interests if they were prepared to give up, gradually, their position of political dominance. But they seem to feel that once they give way on that, everything would be lost. I do not agree. Everything may be lost, say, in half a century, in the sense that white dominance may disappear. But in half a century the world will have a different complexion from what it has today. People go on thinking of half a century hence or a century hence as if conditions will continue as they are today. The world will not continue in anything as it is today; mankind is on the march and it is the era of change.

On the other hand, if the present situation is sought to be frozen, it is bound to blow up. You cannot maintain a situation like the present one in a country like South Africa. When it blows up, nothing will survive, I mean, from the point of view of the whites, and that would be a great disaster. It will not be a victory for either side; it will be a disaster for South Africa.

I hope they may begin to appreciate where their long-term interests lie.

I can appreciate that it is very difficult for them to face a radical change in the present situation. They have all been brought up in it, and are oriented in it. It is taboo for them to think of the indigenous population or the Cape Malays or the brown or the Chinese people as human beings possessing equal rights with them. The Boer is very rigid. On the other hand, he is, as the world goes today, on the whole religious. He is a reader of the Bible; he is anxious to uphold the standards and values laid down in the Bible. He believes in the fatherhood of God and the brotherhood of man. But his definition of man is confined to the white man. That is not only utterly wrong, it is also utterly unrealistic in today's conditions, from the point of view of their own interests. But they will not see it.

**Question**: *In reading over the transcripts of what you have said so far, one thing that struck me is that, I think it is true that you are the only figure who was prominent in public life, that is, in actual participation in the government, in India in the 1930s and 1940s, who is still playing a public role. One question that interests me is what differences do you see now, in looking back, between your years as minister in Delhi, of the Government of India, and your functioning as minister in an independent Pakistan? Any striking differences?*

**Khan**: It was a completely different world, a different atmosphere altogether. A minister in the Government of India before independence was in a sheltered position and was not in public life in the sense in which a minister is in a government which is responsible to the legislature and is responsive to democratic processes.

The fundamental difference between the then constitution of India and the constitution of any independent sovereign state was that the responsibility of the Cabinet was through the Viceroy, to the Secretary of State for India in England and through him to the British Parliament. Ministers were appointed for a period of five years. Occasionally, the incumbent was given an extension of six months or a year at the end of his term. The appointment was regarded as the culmination of a man's public career. The Indian members of the Council - the first one was appointed in 1909 and from 1921 onwards three were appointed - well, were generally taken from public life but sometimes a senior Civil servant was also appointed. They were not called ministers but Members, meaning Members of the Executive Council of the Governor General. The institution had been set up in the time of Warren Hastings in 1772, and had continued, with certain modifications, up to 1941, when the enlargement of the Council took place. Up to 1941, the Council had consisted of six Members, the Commander-in-Chief and the Viceroy. From 1921 to 1941, the composition of the Council had been three Indians, of whom one was Muslim, and three British, the Commander-in-Chief who was always a British military officer, and the Viceroy, who was, of course, British. So that there were three Indians to five Britishers.

To be a Member of the Council was to be at the top of public office in India. The position had great prestige, and in some respects a Member had more authority than a minister. There was no question of joint responsibility as in the case of a responsible Cabinet, though the name "Cabinet" was used for the Council. Each member was responsible for his own department to the Viceroy and through the Viceroy to the Secretary of State. Subject to that, he could do almost anything on matters which under the Rules of Business did not require the Viceroy's approval or reference to the Council. In Council, decisions were taken by majority, and in case of a tie the Viceroy had a casting vote. But the spirit in which business and administration were carried on and policies were determined varied from Viceroy to Viceroy. For instance, Lord Willingdon brought a liberal outlook and a strong common sense to bear on his exalted task and proved a more successful Viceroy than Lord Linlithgow, who succeeded him, was undoubtedly abler, but was handicapped by rigidity of temperament and a narrow outlook.

Lord Willingdon followed a working rule, from which I never saw him swerve, that if his three colleagues were agreed on a matter he always supported them. Then if the British Members did not agree and even the Commander-in-Chief was opposed, making it a case of four against four, Lord Willingdon would use his casting vote and thus the Indian view prevailed. But he did not stop there. He urged the Secretary of State to accept the decision. The Secretary of State had the ultimate authority and could overrule the Viceroy and the Council combined, even in cases where the Council was unanimous. The attitude of Lord Willingdon helped greatly towards the smooth working of the Council.

With Lord Linlithgow everything changed. The more he sought support for a particular view, the more dissent was registered and the more manoeuvring took place.

In February 1940, when my first term of five years was about to expire, I was asked whether I would be prepared to carry on for another full term. On my intimating that I would be prepared to do so, the King reappointed me for another full five years. That had never happened before. But it was then recognized, that the whole system would soon come to an end and the Secretary of State may have thought the second five-year term may not be completed. What in fact happened, as already stated, was that in 1941 I accepted a vacancy on the Supreme Court of India and went to the Court. But before I went to the Court, I prevailed upon the Viceroy, and he was good enough to support my suggestion and to put it to the Secretary of State, that the Council should be both enlarged and Indianized. That measure was taken simultaneously with my moving from the executive side to the judicial side.

On the other hand, my tour of duty as Foreign Minister of Pakistan was under a completely different system, under which the Ministry was responsible to the Legislature and the Head of state, was a Constitutional Head of Government, not having much direct power, though he had more than a limited monarch has. The Constitution was a written one, with a certain number of safeguards embedded in it. Responsibility was through the Prime Minister to the Legislature, and the Prime Minister could get rid of a colleague so long as he possessed the confidence of the Legislature. It was an entirely different system altogether.

I called for certain adjustments: working in a greater team spirit with one's colleagues, I had tried to do that already when I was in the Government of India, taking due note of the views of the legislature, how much value they attached to a particular point, and the criticism

## REMINISCENCES OF SIR MUHAMMAD ZAFRULLA KHAN    213

that was expressed there. In my case, it proved to have been a period of training for the new system of responsibility to which I was able to adjust myself quite easily. In fact, those of us who had some experience of the old system were able to adjust ourselves more easily to the new system than those who came newly to it and had not been tarnished with the old brush as it were. I think experience of cognate matters - it does not matter in what capacity - always helps one to make an adjustment more easily than coming new to a subject altogether.

**Question**: *In looking back over these years, Sir, your public life almost began with the First World War, didn't it?*

**Khan**: No, no. With the First World War, I had just started my law career. I got into the provincial Legislature for the first time in 1926.

**Question**: *Do you have any general comments, as you look back over those years, any unifying threads of your whole life that you see?*

**Khan**: A sense of responsibility and of devotion to duty must always be the main factors in a public man's life. With those, shortcomings or deficiencies may be bridged over; without those, no type of merit, brilliance, or intellectual capacity is of much avail.

□ □ □ □ □

# INTERVIEW - OCTOBER 26, 1963

**Zafrulla Khan**: Talking informally was much easier; it was just natural. I am terrified of these machines.

**Question**: *Well, we just won't look at it at all.*

**Zafrulla**: That makes no difference.

**Question**: *Well, probably the first thing we should go into is your actual election as President of the General Assembly. So perhaps you'd like to talk about the three phases of that: first, your experience in the United Nations, and consequently, your availability as a well-known member of the international community. And then, you might want speak to the point of previous experiences as an officer or as a sub-officer in international organization. And then we can go off into the nomination and the electoral process.*

**Zafrulla**: When I came back to the United Nations in August, 1961 as Pakistan's Permanent Representative, I had already been quite familiar with the United Nations as, from 1947 through 1954, I had led the Pakistan delegation to the United Nations General Assembly. In 1947, when I led the delegation, I was not yet Foreign Minister, but I was called upon to take up the portfolio as soon as I returned from the Session. Through the later years of that period, I led the delegation as Foreign Minister, and I used to stay on during the whole of the Session.

So, to the then-membership, at least, I was well known. But the membership of the United Nations increased very rapidly after 1954, so that when I came back in 1961 I had to establish contacts with the new members. It was not difficult or time-consuming. What helped was that, somewhere deep in my nature, there must be a fund of affection just for people as people. Meeting people from any part of the world is not difficult for me, and I found it easy with the African members, who are very responsive to anybody who takes an interest in and has some affection for them. I now feel that I am much more intimate with some of them than I am with some of the others.

So, within a few weeks, I began to feel at home in the United Nations once more. In the beginning, I had felt somewhat at sea. When I came back, the scene appeared somewhat unfamiliar, or perhaps both familiar and unfamiliar. By February or March of 1962, people were beginning to talk of the Presidency.

When I was asked what my views were, I expressed myself very strongly in favour of the rotation of the Presidency among various groups, and from that point of view I did not think that it was desirable that a President from Africa, as Mr. Mongi Slim, the President of the 16th Session was, should be followed immediately by one from Asia.

When I gave expression to this view, I found it met with a certain amount of approval among the Arab and some of the African delegations. The idea was acceptable to them, provided the Afro-Asians could have the Presidency each alternate year as they were even then approaching fifty percent of the membership.

We checked up with the Latins, who were quite willing to accept this idea, and they were also quite willing to furnish a candidate for the Presidency of the 17th Session. Finally, we agreed that if Ambassador Amadeo - who was the Permanent Representative of Argentina and who had been Chairman of the First Committee in the 16th Session and had done the job extremely well - was willing to be a candidate, we should go ahead with that idea. He signified his

REMINISCENCES OF SIR MUHAMMAD ZAFRULLA KHAN    **215**

willingness; but almost as soon as this was agreed upon, the government in Argentina was upset and Ambassador Amadeo resigned. I understood that his government had asked him to carry on, but he said that in principle he could not, and so he was out of the picture. While those of us who had thought along these lines were still looking for some Latin who would be willing himself and would be acceptable to the others, an Asian colleague circulated his candidature for the Presidency, so that my original idea could not be carried through.

Two other colleagues, representing Asian states, who did not formally circulate their candidacy, had expressed a wish to run for the Presidency. At that stage, the Chairman for that month of the Afro-Asian group, Ambassador Abdul Monem Rifa'i of Jordan, asked to come and see me in my office.

He came and asked me to let my name go forward for the Presidency. I told him I still thought it was not proper that an Asian should follow immediately upon an African. One or two other matters also stood in the way, and I told him I was not available.

For about six weeks I held back but, finally, on the insistence of Ambassador Rifa'i and some other friends in the Group, I put the matter to my government and they at once cabled back: "Certainly, if you feel there is a fair chance." It was under those circumstances that my candidacy was circulated.

I had not had any experience in that kind of work because I had not done even a chairmanship of committee, which is really the training ground for the Presidency. My own feeling still is, after having been President, that the chairmanship of a committee is a more difficult job than the Presidency of the Assembly. There is more rough and tumble and thrust and parry, and manoeuvring for position in committee than there is in the Plenary. The Plenary goes forward not so much at a leisurely pace - but with more dignity, and time is available to the President for consideration of this and that. But in committee the chairman has often to make decisions on the spot. In any case, it is a good training group for the Presidency and several Presidents in the past had been chairmen of committees. I had not that experience.

From the beginning, it looked as though the contest would be confined to Ambassador Malalesekara of Ceylon and myself - and there was little doubt that I would keep ahead of him and be elected.

## 216 REMINISCENCES OF SIR MUHAMMAD ZAFRULLA KHAN

In fact, his support never went beyond his initial estimate at the time when he circulated his candidacy.

I felt that, on the interpretation of rules and on determining points of order and points of procedure, I might perhaps not be found adequate; at least, standing by myself. Previous Presidents always had had the great advantage of having Andrew Cordier sitting in their left. He was a man of great experience and of very sound judgment. One could always be sure that he would feel it in his bones if a problem was boiling up and was likely to come to the surface so that he could warn the President. But he was no longer with the United Nations and that was a lack which made me a little anxious.

The election took place and I had 72 votes as against Ambassador Malalesekara's 27. Four ballot papers intended for me were invalidated because they bore the name of my country and not my name. One matter that the President always has to make very clear is that in these elections, certain ballots are cast for countries and certain ballots are cast for individuals. For the Presidency, you must vote by name for the person, not for his country. For the vice-presidencies, you vote for the country, not for the individual. When a country is elected to a vice-presidency, anybody representing that country can discharge any functions pertaining to the vice-Presidency. For instance, when the President is not available and he asks one of the Vice-Presidents to preside, anybody from the delegation can carry out that function; and the same is the case with attendance in the General Committee. The General Committee is composed of the President, the Vice-Presidents and the Chairmen of Committees. So far as the Vice-Presidents are concerned, any member of their delegations can sit. The Chairmen of Committees, again, are balloted for as individuals, not as countries. Thus new members, if the matter is not clearly explained, may fall into some confusion.

There is another factor which operates: those who can understand the language in which the President is conducting the business of the Assembly, can make these distinctions more easily than those who have to listen to him through interpretation. If the President conducts the business in French, for instance, then for those delegates who do not know French the matter has to be explained a little more clearly and in simple language and with emphasis on the points which have to be taken care of.

Having had that experience of losing four votes in the election, although it made no difference in the result, I took very great care myself that when I announced the elections I should make the points which were likely to cause confusion in anybody's mind very clear. Sometimes it is very necessary to know how many names might be put down, whether of countries or of individuals, on a ballot paper; if more are put down the ballot paper is invalidated.

The election went through, and perhaps at the outset I might say that throughout the 17th Session not a single point of order was raised on which I was called upon to make a ruling. So that even I could not test myself whether I would have proved adequate.

**Question**: *Upon being elected, what were your feelings towards the goals and objects of the President of the General Assembly? Did you think you were going to play a particular role in a particular direction?*

**Zafrulla**: I had not thought of cataloguing them in any way, but I knew in the first place that my first duty was that the business of the Assembly should be conducted in an orderly manner and with dispatch, but dispatch should not mean hurrying through the items; it should merely mean that one should keep in mind the time factor and that the best use should be made of the time available. That is about the only matter on which I expressed an opinion ahead of my being elected. Somebody asked me in the Delegates' Lounge, "What is it that you intend to do when you become President?" I said, "For one thing, I intend to follow the British system of punctuality with regard to meetings rather than what has become normal in the United Nations." I was asked what I meant and I said, "What I mean is that the second stroke of Big Ben when striking the hour of two in the afternoon, has scarcely stopped its reverberations by the time the Speaker has called the House of Commons to order, and I intend to carry on in that way." To my surprise that worked. I had some doubt whether the Assembly would wish to adopt that practice, and I had no means of enforcing it, but I suggested it and they went along with it, and we found that that was of great benefit. For one thing it saved time. During the three or four preceding sessions the waiting period, after the time fixed for the opening of the meetings, had extended to as much as 40 minutes, sometimes three-quarters of an hour, and that was a great waste of time each day, in the morning and in the afternoon, both in the plenary and in the committees. Before the opening of the meetings, the delegates arrived in fairly

**218** REMINISCENCES OF SIR MUHAMMAD ZAFRULLA KHAN

good time, but they would go into the Delegates' Lounge and cluster around the bar or sit in the Lounge smoking their cigars or cigarettes and discussing this and that. That kind of thing has its uses but there are times for it. My feeling was that we should begin the day with full attention to the work at hand and that the time for other things could be found later. That's what happened. The meetings started punctually at 10:30 in the morning; almost everybody came directly to the meeting, and came alert to the business, in the mood to take up the day's work and get along with it. So that, in the time that was available, by starting punctually, we did a great deal more than we used to do previously.

**Question**: *Had any governments tried to feel you out as to what course you might take as the President of the General assembly as part of the electoral manoeuvring which goes on to be President?*

**Zafrulla**: There were, of course, when it became quite clear that I would be the choice of the Assembly, attempts to find out which way my mind was leaning or which view I was likely to take upon certain questions; but that I considered perfectly legitimate. I think that not only is there nothing wrong with it, but that it is quite right that delegations should try to find out. Even during the Assembly, I was occasionally asked, "Were you under pressure on this question," and I replied, "No, I was never under any pressure." My colleagues sometimes came and discussed these questions, having known that they were to be taken up in the Assembly, and they were perfectly right in doing so. It was a compliment to me also; they knew that whatever view I would take as President would be effective, and it was helpful to me to know the views that were held by different sections over certain questions, because occasionally I would have to choose between them and it gave me a sort of advance notice of their attitudes.

Another matter that I had in mind was that if possible one should promote cooperation in the chamber by working behind the scenes to some degree, although the President, of course, must not be a partisan of any section. He is the servant of the Assembly, and whatever his own personal views or the views of his government over any particular question that might come before the Assembly, those should become irrelevant. He should concentrate on promoting cooperation, helpful-ness, dispatch and wherever possible give and take so that things should not drag out too long. People should get to some kind of a decision or something which would prevent a resolution being adopted by 51 to 49, where a simple majority would do, or by just two-thirds, where two-thirds was needed; that did not carry much weight. That meant that some major group or some combination of groups was either opposed or had abstained, and that took away a great deal from the moral force of the recommendation. After all, the Assembly only recommends. Under the Charter, the Assembly cannot, itself take or authorize executive action; that is the business of the Security Council. The Assembly can only make recommendations and a recommendation has value only as the moral judgment of the Assembly. If it was made unanimously or with near-unanimity, under today's conditions of membership, it would be the moral judgment of the world, as it were, and that is its real value. I think the President can contribute a great deal towards bringing that about.

**Question**: *I think that gives us a very good idea of the preceding events before your election, and perhaps now we ought to turn to the experiences which you had as the President, and the obligations of the presidency, what had to be done on the floor everyday, what had to be done with the agenda, and so on.*

**Zafrulla**: The obligations are nowhere laid down; if they were, they would be both helpful and also obstructive. It was perhaps part of wisdom that nobody had attempted to lay anything of that kind down and that applies to everything in the United Nations. Things are expressed in general terms and that leaves room for a good deal of leeway and adjustment to each situation as it might arise.

The element of dispatch had become rather important, for the previous session, the 16th, had extended over five and a half months. The President of that Session, feeling that the session had taken too long, had left a memorandum of his views on the steps that should be taken to pull up the procedure so that the work could be carried on with dispatch. Dispatch in itself is desirable but also the representation of member states could not be kept up at the desirable level if the session were to extend over a long period. The principal delegates have other duties also, they would go away, and leave the work in the hands of the members of the Permanent Mission. That is not a very effective way of attending to the business of the Assembly. But there were other things apart from punctuality which were needed to save time and to help concentrate on the business.

Two things that I had in mind were: one) I took a little more interest in the framing of the agenda for each day's business than my predecessors might have done. I have no means of judging - perhaps they did it, too. But I began to feel from the way in which the Secretariat expected the thing to run, that perhaps not as much attention was being paid to that aspect as it deserved. I took care that once the General Debate was over, whenever a meeting of the Plenary was scheduled, and it had to be scheduled more often than not, there should be enough work to keep it occupied for the whole period of the sitting, that there should be no wasted loose ends. That also saved a lot of time. During previous Sessions, towards the end of the Session, evening sittings had become the normal course, which put a very heavy strain on delegates: to have a morning sitting from 10:30 to 1:00; then the afternoon sitting from 3:00 to 6:00 and then start the evening sitting at 8:30 and carry on until perhaps midnight. When could they have any rest or respite? When could they sit back and consider the questions that had come up or put their heads together along with their colleagues and other delegations?

Having secured the fullest cooperation of the Assembly on whatever I had proposed, I thought it was due to them that I should not unduly lengthen their hours of work. Thus, I believe during the 17th Session we had the fewest evening sittings of any Session, and also not a single Saturday-morning sitting. There used to be several in previous Sessions. That gave everybody time to sit back, to study and to prepare for the next sitting.

In this business, and in every other business indeed that related to the conduct of the business of the Assembly, my Chairmen of Committees also were very helpful. I suggested to them fairly early that they should have a timetable for each item which their committee had to deal with, and as soon as they found that their committee was falling behind the provisional timetable that they had made, they should start having evening sittings rather than wait until more than half the Session was over and everybody started saying, "We are falling behind. We must have evening sittings and catch up." I felt this would also have a psychological effect: If the delegates felt that if they fell behind, they would have to sit in the evening, they would probably work a little more diligently and make the evening sitting unnecessary. That proved to be the experience of the Chairmen of Committees.

Another thing that helped was that I gave as much advance notice to the Assembly of the proposed timetable as was possible in the circumstances of each week's work. As soon as I was able to have some idea myself of what the Assembly should be doing the following week, I told the Assembly what I had in mind, and that helped in two ways: one was that if anybody had any objection to it or found it inconvenient, they could always come round and tell me, and I went as far as I could to suit everybody's convenience. Secondly, they had time to prepare for items. If they knew a certain item was coming up the following week, they had time for preparation and were ready for it when it came up. On very few occasions did one have to postpone something because the Assembly was not yet ready to deal with it, and when one had to do that it was not the result of any lack of information which they could have had from the President; it was due to some element inherent to the subject itself, perhaps some attempt at a compromise was being made, or some other factor made it convenient or helpful to deal with it a little later. Even that saved time.

I believe during the 17th Session the Assembly began to feel that the Presidency was being run in partnership. The President was keen and anxious to know their views and kept in touch with delegations. For the purpose of maintaining continuous contact with my colleagues, I declined to make use of the beautiful suite provided for the President, at the top of the Secretariat building on the 38th floor, at the other end of the corridor from the Secretary-General's suite. They showed it to me the day I was elected. I had never been there before. I asked, "Well, when do I have to use it?" They said, "You come in here in the morning, and then you come in in-between, whenever you like, and again after the meeting in the evening." I said, "No, I will not do that. There is a small room behind the podium on the same level as the Assembly floor which the President normally uses, and I shall always use that room. Any of my colleagues, who want to see me at anytime, can just get up from their seats and come around to that room." I adopted a regular routine: in the middle of each sitting when the business was running smoothly, I would hand over the Presidency to one of the vice presidents and I would withdraw to this room, and that was the signal to any of my colleagues who wanted to come around to discuss anything that they were free to do so. I always left my door open. Nobody had to announce himself. They, of course, saw if somebody was talking to me already and would not come in, but the door was always open and everybody was welcome. I think this, too, helped a lot. As soon as the afternoon meeting was finished, I made a bee-line for the Delegates' Lounge; not so much out of a desire to get to know what

## 222    REMINISCENCES OF SIR MUHAMMAD ZAFRULLA KHAN

they were thinking but to be in contact, because the podium, though it is right in the middle of the Assembly chamber, is a very lonely place. The very first day after the first sitting, I felt very cold - not physically but just as if I had been left out in the cold - and not in touch with my colleagues, and I took that as a great privation. Thereafter, I kept in constant touch with them, which helped a lot because the observations which my colleagues made without reference to any particular item but just generally concerning their views of things conveyed a good deal to me, which I could take care of, so that in a sense they were guiding me and I could give effect to what they wished done. In the end, I think the partnership proved, if I might venture to say so, a complete success.

**Question**: *Were there any other innovations of techniques, such as your use of the room behind the podium or your more careful planning of the agenda which you implemented?*

**Zafrulla**: On two or three problems I announced in the Session that the parties concerned should get together and come to some agreement, which obviously meant that if they wished me to assist, I was ready to do so. That's what happened, and we discussed things behind the scenes, and we untangled the situation and then the matter went through the Assembly very smoothly.

For instance, the question of the timing of the elections of the Security Council, the Economic and Social Council and the Trusteeship Council raised some difficulty. There were conflicting views: some delegates thought the elections should take place late in the session and some thought we should get them out of the way fairly early in the session. I had already announced a provisional date. All the candidates, naturally, were anxious to have them out of the way. Some, who were potential candidates, thought that with more time they might perhaps be able to put their candidacies in better shape. Whatever the motives, there was this serious difference, and it took me the better part of two days to smooth it out; but it was smoothed out and the actual elections to all these three bodies went through in the space of 55 minutes which was a record. No seat in the Security Council was split; the three candidate countries were elected for a full term, and also the previous year's split seat was filled. For the Economic and Social Council and for the Trusteeship Council not even a second ballot was necessary. For the Security Council only one second ballot became necessary.

One can have a good deal of difficulty with regard to elections; it is no reflection on the present President, who is indeed doing extremely well in every respect, that this year's Security Council elections have already occupied two full sittings of the Assembly and the third seat has not yet been filled. Two seats were filled fairly quickly, and the contest over the third seat got into a tangle and there is likely to be a split seat again.

**Question**: *One of the very interesting experiences which you must have had concerned your relations with the professional staff of the United Nations. Andrew Cordier, who had been there previously to help advise the Presidents, filled an important place. Being on the podium, as you say, was an isolated position; one had to have all sorts of sources of information. So what was your relationship with the Secretary-General and his professional staff and with the other delegations in getting the business done?*

**Zafrulla**: First, let me say a word with regard to Andrew, who has been through many years a very good friend and whom I admire greatly; a man who has made a contribution to the work of the United Nations which perhaps it is too early to assess at its true value. He had been a tower of strength for each succeeding President, and I was the first President to be deprived of his very valuable assistance and cooperation. That was one cause of my being a bit anxious. C.V. Narasimhao, who took his place, is a very able officer, but it was his first year also. Where only ability and intelligence were concerned, of course, there was no lack; but where the kind of experience that Andrew had was needed, having an instinctive feeling of what was going to happen, how things might pan out, what might boil up, that naturally C.V. Narasimhao could not claim, and I too had not any means of knowing. That was something that nothing could be done about and I was very sorry that Andrew was not there to help.

Barring that, the whole staff of the Secretariat, everybody, from the top to the lowest level, has had throughout my complete admiration and my gratitude for the way they worked. I believe they work like that with every President. In that way every facility is provided for the President of the Assembly, every assistance is given, everything is done to make his work as easy as possible and to make things run smoothly. In this connection, I must mention the very valuable help that Mr. Malania gave me - he is the principal assistant to the President in Assembly affairs, and he has to keep in touch

**224** REMINISCENCES OF SIR MUHAMMAD ZAFRULLA KHAN

with delegations continuously - and I knew that his work hours extended from before 9 O'clock in the morning till after midnight. If he did get any rest he must have got it on Sundays but whether he got it on Sundays, I don't know. He was absolutely indispensable! His temperament was so calm; he never got into any flurry, was never excited, and was a tower of strength.

The Secretary-General himself does not participate in any way in the proceedings of the Assembly, though he considers it his duty to be present as much as he can. Thant and I were very good friends even before he was elected Secretary-General - first temporarily and then for a full term - and there has been complete understanding between us throughout. Thant knew I was being very sincere when I told him fairly early in the Session that I knew how much he had to get through in a day and that I on my side would have no feeling that he was deserting me if he could not be by my side all through the proceedings; that whenever he felt he should withdraw and carry on his own work, he was welcome to do so. I think, in that way at least; I was being of some help to him, which he appreciated.

**Question**: *Relationships with the professional staff of the United Nations must be quite different from those with either national figures or large blocs within the General Assembly on particular issues. And another interesting part of this relationship is your relationship as the Permanent Representative of Pakistan toward the Pakistani delegation. Can you describe the kind of feelings which you had there?*

**Zafrulla**: My delegation were occasionally unhappy, not acutely I hope, that though I had not laid down any barriers between them and myself - as a matter of fact, I always attended my office here in Pakistan House in the morning for two or two and a half hours before I went down to the Assembly - yet they had a natural feeling of restraint in discussing with me matters that fell within the purview of the Presidency. The nomination of members to certain committees was left to me and I knew the desire of my delegation that Pakistan should be nominated to this or that committee; but I made it absolutely clear that my being President in a way disqualified Pakistan for anything to which I had the nomination. So, they could not get onto either of the two committees which they regarded as very important, to which the nomination was to be solely mine; but they did slip through onto what was known as the Working Group on the financial questions, for though the nomination was by

REMINISCENCES OF SIR MUHAMMAD ZAFRULLA KHAN    **225**

me the Chairman of the Fifth Committee, to whom this group pertained, while sending me the resolution for the expansion of that group by the addition of six more members, also sent me the names of the six countries which the committee desired should be nominated. So I was left with no choice, and as Pakistan's name was included in that list, that is how it got in. I found nomination to the other committees a much more difficult business than any other thing I had to do as President. Everybody wanted to get onto the Committee of Seventeen, which was to be expanded to a Committee of Twenty-four, and almost nobody wanted to get on to any other committee, because whenever I made an approach I was told, "Well, this, we are not interested in," or something to that effect. In the end I was able somehow to set up the committee and I believe they have done very well. But this is part of the day's work; you have to take on responsibility and you have got to make decisions.

On one or two occasions, individual members of my delegation came and told me something that they had learned that might arise in the Assembly, but that was quite fair. But my delegation did not try to influence me on anything one way or the other. Some others did, and as I have said that is quite legitimate; that is, if they feel the President has a view with which they differ and that it would be of some advantage to them that he should know their view, and if possible should accept it, well, they try. But the President comes to his own decision after he has heard everybody.

**Question**: *With a large Afro-Asian bloc being half of the United Nations and with a Western bloc and a Socialist bloc facing each other antagonistically on Cold-war questions, did this present a problem when you did assign committee posts and when you tried to develop this broad consensus so that the UN could move ahead?*

**Zafrulla**: No, that did not present any problem because there are traditions in respect of apportionment of these things, though one took some soundings with regard to individual countries. Now, supposing I knew that the East Europeans were entitled to one or two nominations to a committee, I tried to ascertain which of their members would they wish to be nominated, and that happened with regard to every group: one tried to find out and then one tried to do one's best. It always happened that the East Europeans were quite clear and precise: if they had only one nomination, they gave me only one name. But sometimes I had more names than there were nominations for a group: then I had to make my choice.

**226** REMINISCENCES OF SIR MUHAMMAD ZAFRULLA KHAN

**Question**: *Were there any particular issues during the 17th Session of the General Assembly which gave you bad moments: the question of credentials, the People's Republic of China or Nationalist China, or any other recurrent sort of crisis topics which come up on the agenda annually?*

**Zafrulla**: No. Looking back immediately when the matter was fresh in my mind, in the last Session, I had no feelings at all that anything had given me a bad moment. Occasionally, I found that somebody, some delegation or a certain number of delegations, desired something conducted in a different way from the way I would have preferred. But then I always knew that I was the servant of the Assembly, and when a desire became clear to me and if the rules gave me discretion, I tried to exercise the discretion not as I would have wished but as they wished, because what I would have wished had nothing to do with the matter. Sometimes I gave it expression; that is, that I wished it one way, but that I was equally happy to do it another way.

**Question**: *One of the obvious aspects of your job was one of representation. You were the embodiment of the General Assembly and as such was no doubt called upon to be at every social gathering and at every meeting in which the UN General Assembly needed a symbolic representative. Would you like to comment on the social obligations of that high post?*

**Zafrulla**: The social obligations are very heavy, extremely heavy, during the Session. I have known evenings and one was a very wet evening, what any Westerner would have described - I do not describe the weather in those terms myself - as miserable. There were four receptions to go to and not only in the United Nations - in the United Nations only one, and at the most two, can be held at a time, but not two major ones - and they were strung out throughout the Island of Manhattan, the last one being at the top story of the newly built, very beautiful home of the Chase Manhattan Bank. I had to start uptown - you have to form some sort of a plan - and I went to all of them and most evenings there was a black-tie dinner. I started my work very early, I generally left my apartment at 7 O'clock, after breakfast, and half an hour of brisk walking, the greater part of it through Central Park, and arrived in my office at about 7:30, and then carried on until late.

I had to do something about it because after a fortnight I began to feel the strain. I had to get the minimum modicum of sleep that

I needed. I must say that hostesses were very indulgent and they understood that I would have to retire earlier than other guests and they always let me go at 10 O'clock. They not only let me go but they did it very graciously. That helps me even now; some of them who get to know my habit of keeping early hours, even suggest, "Well, Zafrulla, perhaps it is getting late for you. If you wish to leave, it would be all right."

But I do feel that that side is getting very burdensome, not merely for the President - the President considers it a moral obligation to go to every one of these functions and I think it is right that he should - but it is getting very heavy for the principal delegates also. Sometimes it becomes almost ridiculous: we chase each other in our motor cars, all up and down the city; we spend more time in the streets than at the receptions. It is time that the delegations put their heads together to see how this burden can be reduced.

The other day, Ambassador Binze, who is a good friend of mine, suggested that the African states should content themselves with, say, four receptions during the session: one in September, one in October, one in November and one in December, and perhaps the Asians could do the same. If something of that kind could be agreed to, there would be more time for work, for necessary rest, for reflection, etc. It is true that sometimes you can transact a little business also during these receptions and dinners, but the time consumed is out of proportion to any business that one transacts.

There is another matter on which I felt very strongly. I think the time has come when the various groups in the Assembly should agree upon a pattern for the rotation of the Presidency among groups. For instance, the Afro-Asians - they have the voting power to bring this about anyhow and could claim the Presidency every alternate year. Smaller groups could have it every third year or once in four years. I think if some pattern were set, say a cycle of ten years or twelve years, and then each sizable group would know they would have it once or more during those years, they could produce a candidate that would be acceptable to all.

In that connection, I do wish to say, and I think it is one of those things that really ought to be mended, that so far the Eastern Europeans have never held the Presidency. Now, I do not know any reason why that should have been so. Every year they have one chairman of committee and they have generally produced very

228     REMINISCENCES OF SIR MUHAMMAD ZAFRULLA KHAN

capable chairmen. Why they cannot have the Presidency, I am unable to understand. After all, the President cannot, as it were, take the bit between his teeth and run away with the Assembly. I grant that there are occasions when the President can shift the burden of proof, as it were; there are ways of doing it: he can put a question in such a way that one side would need a majority to win the point rather than the other side. But, a President who is worth being elected does not have recourse to that kind of trick. In electing the President, you should make sure that you know the person and that you can rely on him. In every group there are always plenty of people who are expected to be and would be impartial when holding that high office, both as due to the office and as due to the individual himself.

That is one of the legitimate grievances that the Eastern Europeans have, and nobody has an answer to that. That is only one instance but once a pattern were agreed upon, almost every year the President could be elected unanimously; though there should be a certain amount of consultation behind the scenes whether the individual the group intends to put forward would be generally acceptable.

**Question**: *Without duplicating anything which is covered in your terminal speech as out-going President of the General Assembly, are there any comments you would like to make on the General Assembly as you saw it, the operation of groups within it, the operation of people within it, on the kinds of issues which you had to handle during the 17th Session?*

**Zafrulla**: I think my own experience was somewhat exceptional in the sense, as became very evident during the last meeting, that there was a great deal more cooperation and spirit of give and take and friendliness, among all the sections than I had experienced before. I think it was the result, the culmination, of the process that had been going on. It did not start in that session; I think it had been in operation during two or three sessions, everybody had begun to feel that very difficult questions were coming up, and that it would be of great help to discuss them between the groups behind the scenes. That process had already started but it became much more manifest in the hall itself, on the floor during the Seventeenth Session. Therefore, my only comment is, again, one of gratitude to all my colleagues that they enabled me, as their representative, to give effect to what they themselves were very willing and anxious to do.

## REMINISCENCES OF SIR MUHAMMAD ZAFRULLA KHAN 229

**Question**: *After you ceased to be President of the General Assembly you were, as I think I remember, invited to go to numerous states throughout the world. Is that right?*

**Zafrulla**: I had received several invitations during the Session and some of them were repeats of invitations that I had received earlier. For instance, the North African States; each of them had on several occasions asked me to go and visit them and I have now been able to do so. Then, some others I added myself if I was going to a particular region. I was invited by Foreign Minister Gromyko to visit the USSR. I pointed out to Ambassador Zorin, who delivered the actual invitation on behalf of Foreign Minister Gromyko, that we were then in the fall and running into the winter and that was not the time that one could conveniently make a trip to the USSR and if one did, one would not be able to see very much. He smiled and said, "Oh, no, but in the spring or in the summer." That is how it came about.

So, the two major journeys of that kind that I made, one in January and the early part of February to 11 or 12 - of the Eastern and North African states, and then later, in the middle of the Special Session, as it happened, to Denmark, Finland, the USSR, Poland and Czechoslovakia, were in pursuance of invitations which had been extended during the Session or earlier.

**Question**: *And in each of these visits to the various states were you consulted or did you discuss the role of those particular nations in the United Nations; that is, did you also go as someone who would be advocating or discussing with the foreign offices the United Nations?*

**Zafrulla**: No, I had no particular problems in mind when I started, and I did not make notes: I shall discuss this in Copenhagen or that in Moscow, or this in Cairo or that in Rabat. But, naturally, questions arose; either they wanted to know something from me or I wanted to know something from them. For instance, while I was in Kampala, Uganda, they showed me several of their institutions, took me to their refugee camps for refugees from Rwanda, whom they were trying to resettle, and they related some of their problems to me which were not directly connected with the Assembly but where the United Nations could help. I undertook, not specifically in my capacity as President but as a person who was connected with the United Nations in a certain capacity to assist. Two of their problems involved my stopping in Geneva in my effort to assist them and I was happy to do whatever I could. But my object in these visits was not to have any United Nations problems resolved or to offer my

**230**     REMINISCENCES OF SIR MUHAMMAD ZAFRULLA KHAN

good offices with reference to any particular problem, but just to make contacts, to get to know people, see them, and discuss with them their attitudes, policies, etc.

**Question**: *When you ceased to be President of the General Assembly and returned to your role as Permanent Representative of Pakistan in the United Nations, what sort of tapering-off experiences did you find? Did you find that the wealth of goodwill which you had built up as President of the General Assembly was just part of your growth and friendship within the United Nations or whether people attributed to you a good deal more power and authority than you previously had.*

**Zafrulla**: In the first place, there was no sort of a break with my position as Permanent Representative and then resumption of that position; the two were held together. The Presidency is, of course, a very honourable office, an office of dignity, but it is an honorary office, and in a sense it is expensive both for the holder of the office and for his government. But one carries on in both capacities. As a matter of fact, on one occasion the question arose even with the protocol in the United Nations, whether I could still claim to be the leader of my delegation, and I maintained I could. They said, "True, you are a member of your delegation, but you can't be treated as a leader of your delegation while you are President." I said, "Surely, I am still leader of my delegation." I showed them the rule which says that the President shall not vote but shall appoint a member of his delegation to vote in his place, which clearly implies that while President, he continues leader of his delegation.

I held the two offices together, and so there was no interruption on one side and then resumption on the other; though, of course, there is the descent from the podium, not to go back to the room behind the podium, but to take one's seat where the chief of protocol formally conducts you after the next President has been elected and you take your seat in the hall. The year of the Presidency has helped me a lot in personal relations and otherwise.  The goodwill continues; the friendships won are there; some of them are, I hope for life, and others have been deepened.  The total experience becomes a part of one's personality.

**Question**: *Well, my only point in making that is that you are now leaving the UN for the International Court of Justice to take up another very important official role in the international community* *and the point was only one of academic interest and not practical interest.*

*You did allude to one point, which I don't know whether you want to talk about it in detail, and that is the cost to be borne by the state and by the delegate when he is chosen President of the General Assembly. Do you want to talk about orders of magnitude?*

**Zafrulla**: No, I do not want to. I do not think that is important. But the President has to carry on a great deal more hospitality than he would as merely a member of a delegation or even head of a delegation. Provision has to be made for that. I do not know what happens with other delegations but in my case my government helped. I knew that I would have to do a little more on my own, but how much should be done and at what level and at what cost is an individual matter.

There is a certain amount of official hospitality. For instance, the President has what is known as a Chairmen's lunch every Wednesday, when chairmen of committees meet the President and the Secretariat officers who are working with them to consult on planning the session and the conduct of business and to see how it is running and what adjustments are needed. That is paid for by the United Nations. Every alternate Thursday, the President entertains a score of press representatives in rotation, to keep in touch with the press socially. In turn the press offers a certain amount of hospitality to the President. He receives so much hospitality that he must return it in some way or other.

The Secretary-General and the President give a big reception about the middle of the session, which costs quite a lot of money, but it is the government of the country whose representative the President is who bears his share of the cost.

People have sometimes said to me, "You must receive a tremendous salary as President." There is no question of salary; it is a purely honorary office.

□ □ □ □ □

# INTERVIEW - NOVEMBER 17, 1963

**Question**: *Now, Sir Zafrulla, if we may consider two last points in this discussion of the United Nations General Assembly. The first is that during the League period, certain elder statesmen, people who played an enormous role in the founding and also in the conduct of business, became a group of senior Senators, that is, elder statesmen, and carried over their enormous influence and knowledge and became a body within the body around which all sorts of structural and procedural matters crystallized. Do you think that sort of thing is happening in the UN, as an ex-President, with other ex-Presidents? Do you have the feeling that there is a body of very mature people growing out of this experience?*

**Zafrulla**: That was so certainly during the first 10 years of the United Nations and was not necessarily confined to the President and ex-Presidents; though, of course, they counted. Take a personality like that of the late Senator Warren Austin. He was never President and could not have been because he represented the United States. But he was respected and trusted, and he had those qualities that won people's confidence and affection. I always thought he was much abler and cleverer than people gave him credit for.

There were other people: for instance, General Romulo, Nasrollah Entezam, Prince Wan, from among the Asians: all of them became Presidents. I don't know whether General Romulo exercised much influence in the way of persuading people inside the United Nations, to accept his view, but he was a very persuasive speaker. He had a great command of language and was very eloquent and was held in great esteem. He became President very early, as you know. Then there were Henry Spaak, Lester Pearson, Padilla Nervo and many others.

But it is no longer so; at least not to the same degree. Group influence is now much more prominent that the influence of individuals. At that time, members did not act so much under group discipline, if I might say so; they do it more now, and therefore the individual's influence is less perceptible.

For instance, during the 17th Session, there were as many as nine Presidents present in the Assembly but one did not feel that they were exercising any particular influence, not that the Presidents should form a group by themselves, but they were called into aid much less than would have been the case before if as many as half

## REMINISCENCES OF SIR MUHAMMAD ZAFRULLA KHAN — 233

the Presidents had been available. Also, as time passes, having been President begins to lose the gilt; for one session or two people think, "He has had this experience," but it wears out. My own feeling is that if the individual has to continue in the United Nations after he has been President, he should not continue for too long. If one does continue too long, it becomes a sort of anti-climax.

I have been given the way out by being elected to the Court, but if that had not happened I do not know what the view of our Foreign Minister and our President would have been. My own idea was that I would give up anyway at the end of the present session. It becomes a case of diminishing returns, but that may be a purely individual assessment and may not apply to all, because some people, no matter how long they continue, would always have a great standing and influence.

Nevertheless it remains true that matters are now determined more by group discussion rather than under individual influence. Inside the group, everybody has his own standing, and persuasive qualities count. But the group discipline tends to let the lead to be assumed by the more vigorous, sometimes the more vociferous representatives, and then occasionally the heat is put on so that when the drum begins to beat and that is where wisdom and reason begin to be overborne, and perhaps in this country you would say that is where democracy takes over, but I do not like those aspects of democracy.

**Question**: *Well, can...*

**Zafrulla**: I can mention one instance where I might have been persuaded if I had not been sitting at my desk here at that time and I had been present in the Assembly. You will probably recall, two years ago, when the Foreign Minister of South Africa, Loew, made a speech, which was resented, and Ambassador Cooper of Liberia first made the motion that the speech be expunged from the record, and then the luncheon adjournment intervened and he withdrew that motion, but then moved a censure against the Foreign Minister of South Africa. Our two delegates who were then present in the Plenary, one after the other, came to the telephone and tried to persuade me to let them vote in support of the motion and I said no. I said, "However much we resent the policies of South Africa - we shall condemn them and we shall fight them and shall tear his reasoning to shreds - I cannot accept that he is not entitled to put his

**234**  REMINISCENCES OF SIR MUHAMMAD ZAFRULLA KHAN

case emphatically, whatever case he has to put, and that that should become a reason for either expunging his speech or censuring him.

"But they say he has been insulting." I said, "In the first place, in assemblies like this a great deal of latitude should properly be allowed; people should be able to say things, we should not be too thin-skinned. Secondly, tell me, what is it that he has said which is insulting?"

They came in relays. "Well," one said, "he has said the standard of living, for instance, of the indigenous people in South Africa is much higher than the standard of living in many of the countries of Africa which are now independent and sovereign."

I said, "That may well be true with regard to some of the countries. I have not studied the matter, so I cannot say. But if it is untrue, go and say that it is untrue instead of saying that he must be censured for saying it."

Then the last thing was that one of them rushed up: "A roll-call vote has been called and everybody is saying yes!" I said, "That's no reason for us to say yes." But I confess that if I had been there myself, I might perhaps also have said, yes.

**Question**: *Now, the final point on the UN is the role of the President and the committee chairmen in the selection of the slate for next year. I don't think you should confine your remarks strictly to the case as it is but also the case as you think it might be.*

**Zafrulla**: In the past, very often, not always, the chairmanship of the First Committee, if the functions have been properly discharged has been considered as giving you some claim to the Presidency the following year, provided somebody else has not a stronger claim or some other ground, for instance, regional grouping. That has always counted, and I consider it need not be only the chairmanship of the First Committee but the chairmanship of any committee, if the job has been outstandingly well done, because that shows how the particular individual can manage the business of a committee and interpret rules and see that the committee does not get into a tangle and when it tends to get into a tangle to head it off and that kind of thing. It is a test of those qualities which would help in the Presidency.

So far as the conduct of the business of the committees is concerned, I consider it is a more arduous task than the Presidency. In the first place, a great deal more deference is paid to the President anyhow, and on borderline cases the Assembly tends to support him rather than to obstruct him in the way he wants to go. Therefore, somebody who has come out extremely well from his chairmanship of a committee, so far as individual qualities are concerned, has a good chance to make the grade as President. If it should be the turn of his group and his group puts him forward as their candidate, he would have no difficulty at all.

So far as the Presidency is concerned, there were some Presidents who were so outstanding that when one thinks of the Presidency, their names and their personalities jump to one's mind; and some don't come to one's mind at all; they might have conducted the business well but they did not leave an impress on anything. These are some of those imponderables that one cannot be too precise about, the more time passes the more the judgment of time becomes apparent: Those who are remembered for something or the other, who have left some impression are remembered, the others fade out.

**Question**: *Now, do you think that the President should have a voice in choosing the committee chairmen for the following year, based on his knowledge of the personalities and also the abilities of men?*

**Zafrulla**: No, not only he should not, but he cannot. The view of the President either with regard to the election of the chairmen with whom he will have to work - supposing somebody is quite sure that he is going to be elected President or there is every probability that he will be - or with regard to the year following his own Presidency has no relevance to the election of the chairmen. To some degree a candidate for the Presidency who is reasonably certain of his own election can influence the election of chairmen through his own group. For instance, supposing he is a Latin, he can say to his group, if it is understood that the Latins can have the Presidency that year, "Look, the Presidency is your business also. I have to be in the Chair and I shall have to conduct the business, but if there is any credit in it, it belongs to my country and also it belongs to my group. Therefore, you should make it easy for me, as far as you can. My team will be composed of the Vice Chairmen, so far as the General Committee is concerned, and of the Committee Chairmen, but the Committee Chairmen are really my instruments for the purpose of conducting the business of the Assembly in the committees. I, therefore, hope that both in putting up your candidates and in voting for other candidates, wherever there is a choice, you will exercise it

**236**    REMINISCENCES OF SIR MUHAMMAD ZAFRULLA KHAN

in support of the better man, and if you do not mind consulting me on it, perhaps I could give you some advice." In that way, behind the scenes, he could exercise some influence. But he cannot do even that much if the Presidency is going to be contested, because nobody can arrogate to himself in advance, "I am bound to be elected." That would militate against his being elected.

**Question**: *Well, as a sort of concluding comparative notion of where the President of the General Assembly stands as presiding officer of a great assembly of the world, we have two very different models: the House of Commons, where the President is largely an honorary figure and holds the honour of the House, and we have the House of Representatives of the American Congress, where he holds the agenda, the patronage, the committee assignments and any other number of political plums. One might say that one is almost the strongest possible presiding officer and the other is very nearly the weakest. Where does the President of the General Assembly of the United Nations fit into this spectrum, between the House of Commons and the House of Representatives?*

**Zafrulla**: I would say right of centre; that is, nearer to the Speaker of the House of Commons than to the Speaker of the House of Representatives. He has a little more to do than the Speaker - I don't mean to say that the Speaker hasn't got much to do; he's a very respected figure and convention has become so strong now in Parliament that whatever he directs is carried out. The Presidency is not so well entrenched in the United Nations yet, but it is gradually settling down. Yes, I would say nearer to the Speaker of the House of Commons.

I do want to add that my experience was both revealing and very rewarding, revealing in the sense that I had no reason to expect that I would get such unanimous and continuous cooperation as I did. It really was, in that sense, a revelation to me. Not only that, but I think there was a sort of affectionate response all the time. I am sure on occasion many of them might have felt, "Well, well, he's doing this. We wish he had done the other. But that's alright; he is doing it with goodwill and in our interests."

But it is more than that. When I look back I find that all through the Session not a single point of order was raised. I cannot give any explanation, except that the Assembly must have made up its mind silently and without overt consultation: let us do the best we can. I had some apprehension in my mind that having the reputation - and

## REMINISCENCES OF SIR MUHAMMAD ZAFRULLA KHAN 237

often a reputation has some basis - of being a somewhat standoffish kind of man, I might find it difficult to carry them along, but it was a very rewarding experience indeed.

People have talked to me afterwards and said, "Now, you are free from the strain of the Presidency," but I can say honestly, "I was under no strain at all." The work was so interesting, and then it went along so well, that though my hours of work became long and I had to ask for leave to depart early from dinners that I attended so that I might get enough sleep, it did not require any other adjustment. The consciousness that my colleagues trusted me - and if I might say so here, my response in humility was, "What have I done to deserve their trust?" was more than sufficient compensation for any extra hours of work imposed on me.

**Question**: *This really is much more the House of Commons pattern where part of the lack of tension between the House and the Speaker is that, one, the Speaker puts himself at the service of the house; and two, he doesn't have so much power that it really becomes a contest, a struggle to influence daily items of agenda or committee sponsorship, some obviously, but not so much as certainly would be the case in the House of Representatives in the United States.*

**Zafrulla**: I have no experience of the House of Representatives, so I have nothing to say on that.

I had it in mind all the time that if I had to give a ruling I would not shirk it; I would give my ruling, but I would draw their attention to the rule under which the ruling of a President can always be reversed by a simple majority so as to make it clear that though I had given my ruling I had no personal bias in the matter at all. I think that it was perhaps that impression that the Assembly might have gathered that enabled it to carry on so smoothly. My attitude was that whatever I was doing I would go on doing by the leave and, if possible, with the approval of the Assembly. I think that would help any President, and I am sure the President would always have this attitude.

This might sound irrelevant, but is perhaps worth mention. There are tribal divisions among Muslims, in our country, except that, like in Scotland, for instance, we don't add the name of our tribe to our names, but they're well known. Our tribe is Sahi and my mother's tribe is Bajwa. My mother would sometimes say to me, "My dear, it is well known about the Sahis that left to themselves they will carry on normally and reasonably, but if anybody tries to drive them, they will dig in their toes and will not budge." I think this should be remembered generally with regard to the temper of assemblies also... one should not try to drive them, or anybody for that matter, for then they will dig in their toes. If they feel it is up to them: "This fellow is our representative. We have put him there. He's trying to do his best," they'll take something ever if they should feel, "Well, now we think this is inconvenient, but if he wants it, we shall go along."

**Question**: *I'd like to just turn this question back into the body of the Oral History transcript to 1953, when there were very severe riots which later were investigated by a special tribunal of the Pakistan Government, which concerned the Ahmadiyya Sect of which you were certainly the most prominent public figure at the time, and these no doubt complicated your political life very considerably. They certainly complicated Pakistan's public life very considerably.*

*I wonder if you would like to talk about them briefly. This is obviously a subject which the Munir Report has two volumes about, and you probably just want to give your own impressions, but I think they'd be very interesting for the record.*

**Zafrulla**: There is really nothing that I can add to the excellent report of the Munir Inquiring Committee. Perhaps I might emphasize that the responsibility, though later shared by certain other groups also, was initially that of the group known as the Ahrar. They had from time to time made themselves thoroughly unpopular with the main Muslim body, before Partition as well as after Partition. It was well known that they had been opposed to the idea of Pakistan, so that when Pakistan came their stock was very, very low. They had previously made various efforts to bring themselves into active political leadership and it had become almost a pattern with them, that whenever they wanted to choose a target to rouse Muslim sympathy in their own favour or to win Muslim support, they picked upon something concerning the Ahmadiyya Movement, distorted it and proclaimed, "Here is a great danger for Islam and we are in the vanguard of the defence of Islam."

On this occasion, they were doing two things: one, they were gradually infiltrating into the Muslim League ranks. They had some very effective mob orators, and they began to take part in League elections at the district level. When there was any Muslim League election they would be invited or hired to come and deliver speeches, and this began to attract popular support.

## REMINISCENCES OF SIR MUHAMMAD ZAFRULLA KHAN 239

They were also looking for something on which they could start a general campaign to bring themselves into prominence. Later, certain other factions also joined them. The incident of which they took advantage was that there was an annual meeting of the Karachi branch of our movement, of which my younger brother was President. He was also holding a public office: I believe he was Deputy Custodian of Evacuee Property. He asked me whether I would come to the meeting and speak, and I said I would not mind. My speech was made, although a good deal of opposition had already been whipped up to my speaking at all. The subject and substance of my speech were largely non-controversial. I was not to speak on any doctrinal differences. It was on "Islam: the Living Faith." But the occasion was considered ripe, I suppose, by the leadership of the opposing groups. It was not only the Ahrar by that time; certain other groups had also joined them. As a matter of fact, it had been part of the strategy of the Ahrar that in the beginning they would not take a prominent part in anything but would incite other people behind the scenes. So, a good deal of agitation started almost on the eve of the meeting, to stop me from speaking. Well, I spoke. Later they made the excuse: that in spite of their opposition, I, as Foreign Minister, had spoken in a meeting of the Ahmadiyya Movement, and, therefore, the Prime Minister should get rid of me.

When the agitation grew in volume, I said to the Prime Minister, "If this will ease matters for you, I am prepared to resign." He said, "Today you are prepared to resign. Tomorrow they will say some other of my colleagues should go. I might as well surrender the government to them."

**Question**: *This was Khwaja Nazimuddin?*

**Zafrulla**: Yes. Now that was excellent on principle; yet he would not do anything at all, would not take any action which would stop the agitation. He was, as it were, caught between two winds: one, he was conscious enough of the principle, that if he yielded to the demand, he might as well surrender the government to them, but he had such great respect for the 'ulema that he would not take any step which they might resent.

**Question**: *And also Daultana was probably involved by this time in the Punjab...*

**Zafrulla**: Yes. Daultana professed during the earlier stages that he would stand firm, but the inquiry showed that behind the scenes he was in league with them. Then the time came when he threw up the sponge altogether.

So, the agitation grew in intensity, and, so far as Lahore was concerned, it took on an extreme aspect, mainly on account of Daultana's two-faced policy. Also, I.I. Chundrigarh, who was the Governor, was not a strong man, vis-a-vis Daultana. He was a very nice man, but for one thing he was not well versed in Urdu. He could speak it fairly well -- he was from Bombay originally but he could not read it with any facility and, therefore, when Daultana or anybody else took to him what they represented was an inflammatory matter put forth by the Ahmadiyya Movement, he could easily be misled. On one or two occasions when he gave expression to that kind of feeling to our people: "Well, after all, you are not making it easy. You are doing this and that and people are provoked," it was found that he was absolutely off the mark. Something had been twisted in being represented to him. That became an element of weakness in the situation.

Also, when the crucial time came, when the people became greatly excited and were getting out of hand, he got cold feet.

**Question**: *And the army finally had to come in...*

**Zafrulla**: The army had to be called in, and they came in but not by the decision of the Prime Minister. I had better mention this. After the meeting to which I have referred, which was made the starting point of the agitation, for several weeks I was out of the country. I believe I was here in New York. I had an invitation both from the Egyptian government and from the Iraqi government, to stay a couple of days at each capital on my way back. I had arrived from Cairo at Baghdad when our Ambassador there, Agha Mustafa, who met me at the airport, handed me a telegram from the Prime Minister saying, "You should not arrive in Karachi before the 2nd of February." I was flabbergasted. If a Minister is away, out of the country, I can well understand the Prime Minister saying, "Now, hurry up, we need you here!" but I doubt whether it has ever happened that he has told you must not arrive before a certain date. He might be relieved of his portfolio for some prank that he might have played or for some fault, or because of some revolution that has taken place in his absence, but a Minister, who is still minister and apparently, is to continue, to be told do not arrive home before such-and-such a time, I could not make head or tail of. It also put me in a very embarrassing position. Fadhal Jamali of Iraq, the Foreign

## REMINISCENCES OF SIR MUHAMMAD ZAFRULLA KHAN    241

Minister, was a very good friend of mine. He had insisted that I should stay at least four days in Baghdad, and I had said, I had no time. I could not stay more than two days. Now this added two more days to my stay in Baghdad. What could I say to my host government?

I said to our Ambassador, "This is very awkward. We had better arrange that I should go down to Najaf and Kerbala." He said, "I have already told them you cannot stay in Baghdad for more than two days because you have to go down to Najaf and Kerbala. When you come back you can stay the last at the Embassy, which, incidentally, is a much more comfortable place than their guest house." In those days, except for a few modern houses that had been built, Baghdad was still medieval.

When I arrived in Karachi, I found the reason for the Prime Minister's telegram was that direct action had been proclaimed to take place over this matter on the Friday. Immediately after the Friday service people would issue from the mosques in processions and create a crisis for the government. The telegram meant that I should not arrive in Karachi before this happened, because the Prime Minister was already finding himself in difficulties with his Cabinet. The Cabinet wanted him to take action to stop the direct action, and he was not willing to make a move.

**Question**: *Yes, they would have really focussed on you.*

**Zafrulla**: That was the difficulty, and the Cabinet divided in that way could not prove very effective.

I learnt that on the Thursday evening a Cabinet meeting had been called to decide what to do about this threat of direct action for the following afternoon. The Cabinet sat until 10 or 10:30 p.m. and they could not come to a decision as the Prime Minister would not accept the view of the majority of his colleagues - that he should take action, and the only action that was left to be taken was to arrest the leaders under the Preventive Detention sections. The meeting was adjourned to 10 a.m. next day.

Then, Gurmani, who was then Minister of the Interior, and Amin 'ud-din, who was then Governor of Sind, went together to the Governor's residence where Gurmani was dining that night, and while they were at dinner news was brought to them that the 'ulema having learnt that the Cabinet meeting had been adjourned until 10 O'clock the next morning without having arrived at any decision, had decided to start direct action after the dawn prayers and not to wait till the mid-day service.

So, the Governor of the Province and the Minister of the Interior went to the Prime Minister's residence to insist that the Cabinet should be summoned immediately in view of this development. They arrived there and found the leader of the 'ulema, Maulana Ihtishamul Haq, closeted with the Prime Minister. He had come to warn him of what they were going to do!

So, the Cabinet was summoned, but to that Cabinet meeting Ch. Mohammad Ali, who was then Finance Minister was not invited as he had suffered a heart attack some months before and it was thought best not to disturb him. The discussion went on for a couple of hours until the Prime Minister said, "If you insist upon action being taken against the 'ulema, I shall resign." In the end he banged on the table and said, "All right. Do what you like!" and got up and walked away.

His colleagues did not know whether he had meant: do what you like; whatever you decide will be done; or, if you decide something I do not approve of, I will resign. However, they decided that action should be taken and that the leaders of the agitation should be arrested early the next morning before the dawn prayers.

That was before I came back. The Governor-General, Malik Ghulam Mohammed, was due to leave on a visit to Saudi Arabia for 10 days, and he asked me to tea in the afternoon of the day I arrived back. I went and he said to me: "There is not enough time for me to give you all the ins and outs of the thing. You will find out what has been happening. I am leaving as you know for 10 days and I hope nothing untoward will happen during this period, but I can tell you in two words that I will stand on principle and I would rather receive bullets into my chest than take a stand against principle."

That was all very well, but the Governor-General would be away and the Prime Minister was the centre of power in the parliamentary system, and though his assurance was comforting as far as the Governor-General was concerned, there was not much comfort to be found in the attitude of the Prime Minister.

The Governor-General came back after eight days, and it was then that he began to consider in his own mind - he must have come to a decision either before going or while he was away - that Khwaja Nazimuddin had to go as he would not perform his function! The point was not what decision he should have taken, but he should have taken some decision in the matter and shouldered the responsibility.

Then the change of government took place.

I had to appear as a witness before the Munir Inquiry Committee. Munir had taken the precaution to ask counsel who represented various groups to put in a list of the questions they intended to ask any particular witness, and those questions that he considered irrelevant he disallowed.

Khwaja Nazimuddin, who was also examined, did say in his statement that I had offered to resign but that he had not agreed to it. The representative of the Jamat-i-Islam after he had put to me the questions that had been permitted, put a very silly question to me but while I was muttering my reply - Munir ruled it out. The question was: "Now, what do you consider me? Do you consider me a Muslim or not?" My reply was: "I consider you whatever you consider me."

If Munir had not been so sharp in overruling him and that had not been the last question, I would have insisted that his question and my answer should be recorded.

I have described the question as silly, because the stand of the Jamat-i-Islam was that I was not a Muslim. Counsel asked me, "What do you consider me?" My answer was, "Whatever you consider me." Now, if Munir had said to him, "All right, answer that question" what do you consider him?" If he had replied, "I consider him a Muslim," he would be going against the stand of the party he was representing; and if he had said, "I do not consider him a Muslim," Munir could have retorted: "Then why do you put such a question to him: 'he is not a Muslim in your eyes; what does it matter whether he thinks you are a Muslim or not.'"

These were some of the lighter moments, but all through that period was one of great strain for me and the Movement. On the one hand the Prime Minister said if I resigned I would be weakening his position, and on the other hand, terrible things were happening. I do not want the more extreme aspects to go on the record even here. True, the agitation was directed against the Movement in essence but I was the ostensible target if I had been allowed to go, the thing might have subsided.

## 244 REMINISCENCES OF SIR MUHAMMAD ZAFRULLA KHAN

**Question**: *That brings up one of the most interesting points about all of this, and I think it is one which is hard to sort out and separate from your own principles, and Westerners are not used to thinking in terms of principles in politics. Primarily, one thinks that if Harold Macmillan found himself in a difficult position, he would say, "You are sacked. I personally appreciate your position, but the stability of the government counts on this. Goodbye and good luck." But here you were in an extremely difficult position in which you were given latitude and where the government appreciated your position and yet you had to make every hard decision, because you knew so long as you stayed on that you would continue to be sort of a central symbol which they could manipulate. You knew this must inevitably bring pain to your community.*

*On the other hand, you knew that if you resigned, really the whole credentials of the Movement would have been sullied, I think. These must have been very difficult times.*

**Zafrulla**: There was no question of the credentials of the Movement being sullied in any way at all.

**Question**: *Well, it would really have been backing down in the face of ...*

**Zafrulla**: So far as my resigning or not resigning was concerned, the Movement was not involved. It was just a question of principle. Another demand was that the Movement should be declared a non-Muslim minority.

**Question**: *That's is the important point, yes.*

**Zafrulla**: But even if they had so declared, it would have created some kind of difficulty for us, but that would not make us what we were not, if it came to that. The main thing was: they wanted to get rid of me. I do not think the Movement would have minded one way or the other what I did.

**Question**: *No, but you were the symbol. If they could get rid of you ...*

**Zafrulla**: On the other hand the Movement might - I mean those concerned in the Movement - have felt, "Why does he not resign and make things easier for us?"

**Question**: *But it wouldn't have. By getting rid of the symbol then they could have gone on to the second point.*

### REMINISCENCES OF SIR MUHAMMAD ZAFRULLA KHAN    245

**Zafrulla**: Yet, the following year I decided to resign, not on this issue - this issue had by that time subsided - but on another one.

**Question**: *What has been the position since that time? Is the agitation still remaining, still alive?*

**Zafrulla**: Very spasmodically. In late September and early October of 1958 it was beginning to flare up in view of the impending elections under the then new Constitution. That again shows it was a political weapon. Even a person as sober as Chaudhri Mohammad Ali, having proclaimed that he would stand for election - his party had come to some understanding with the Jamat-i-Islami - one of the planks in his election platform was: It will be my effort to have the Ahmadis declared a non-Muslim minority. Within a week or so of his declaration, martial law came in, a military regime was set up and the Martial Law Administrator, President Ayub, put his foot down and said he was not going to have any nonsense of that kind.

**Question**: *As far as the new law about property goes, the Waqf of property, is Ahmadiyya property under the new law?*

**Zafrulla**: No, it is not. It is liable to be placed under the law and there has been a certain amount of criticism of the administration in the press that by not taking over Ahmadiyya Waqf properly the administration has been favouring the Movement. But as has been explained this is no favour. This Ordinance has been promulgated for the purpose that where the Waqf is being abused and the income is not being devoted to the purposes for which the Waqf was set up, the situation should be corrected. If all the Waqfs were administered as well as the Ahmadis are administering theirs, there would be no need for the Ordinance.

**Question**: *And the whole position of the Aukaf administrator is to take over as little as possible but to jar people to take better care of their trusts. Is Chaudhri Mohammad Ali now in the Nizam-i-Islami Party?*

**Zafrulla**: He's in the Nizam-i-Islami Party, not the Jamat-i-Islam, but they are as elder sister to younger sister.

**Question**: *Has he continued in this new program for Pakistan, to say that he will work against the Ahmadiyya?*

**Zafrulla**: Oh, no. After Martial Law there's been nothing like that. It might flare up again, but so far there has been nothing. They are now so much at loggerheads with each other that they have forgotten

**246**     REMINISCENCES OF SIR MUHAMMAD ZAFRULLA KHAN

us for the moment. If the time should come when it is in somebody's interest to make a show of advocacy of Islam and of defense of Islam, they might start shooting arrows at us again.

**Question**: *What about somebody like Maulana Bashani? Is he ...*

**Zafrulla**: No, no. That's East Pakistan. In East Pakistan there has never been any agitation against us, though we have quite substantial communities in East Pakistan.

**Question**: *Do you? Is this one of the bigger areas?*

**Zafrulla**: East Pakistan? Next to West Pakistan, yes.

**Question**: *About how many Ahmadis?*

**Zafrulla**: I can't give you the exact number, but certainly several thousands and possibly more than 100,000 in East Pakistan.

We are altogether a very small community. Our world figure doesn't go much beyond a million or a million and a half. The largest number is in Pakistan, East and West taken together. The next largest is I think either in India or in Indonesia, and the next largest in West Africa.

**Question**: *Is this a result of missionary work?*

**Zafrulla**: Yes.

□ □ □ □ □

# INDEX

10 Downing Street 98, 267

Abbottabad 38, 43

Ahmadis 7, 245, 246

Ahmadiyya Community 4

Ahmadiyya Movement 8, 83, 238-240

Ahmadnagar 138

Ajnala 155

Albania 192, 193

Alexandria 121

Algeria 186, 207

Ali brothers 7

Ali Sastroamidjojo 203

All India Federation 22

All India Muslim League 6, 36

All India Radio 29

All Parties Muslim Conference 36

Ambassador Amadeo of Argentina 203

Ambassador Binze 227

Ambassador Malalasekra 204, 205

Ambassador Rifai 204

Ambassador Shahi 203

Ambassador Zorin 229

America 1, 56, 127, 129, 133, 189, 207

Amery 127, 132

Amin 'ud-din 241

Amir Ali 6, 24, 135

Amritsar 25, 155

Angola 207

Aranha 182

Archbishop of Canterbury 49, 53, 54

Architecture 18

Asaf Ali 138

Asceticism 87

Assam 11, 12, 48, 76, 115

Assembly 19, 21, 71, 76, 77, 79, 89, 91-93, 95-97, 102, 125, 142, 145, 175, 178, 179, 181-183, 185, 197, 202, 203, 206, 213-237

Atlantic 56, 127, 128, 191

Attlee 10

Austen Chamberlain 53, 106

Ayub 169

Azim Husain's 8

B.N. Rau 178, 187, 197

Baghdad 63, 64, 240, 241

Bahawalpur 9, 162

Bahrain 62

Bakhshi Ghulam Muhammad 180

Bakhshi Tek Chand 154

Balkans 2

Bapuji 100

Basra 62-64, 121

Batala 155, 158

Beaumont 156

Begum Ra'ana Liaqat Ali Khan 167

Begum Shah Nawaz 127, 128, 130

Belgium 120, 124, 133

Bikaner 157

Board of Trade 96-98, 100-102, 105

Boundary Commission 140, 146, 148, 155, 163

Brantford 58

Brindisi 63, 121

British Ambassador 65, 115, 119

British Guyana 129

British Indian Provinces 22

Brown 97, 98, 100, 101, 210

Burma 22, 40, 103, 115, 117, 204

Burundi 208

Cabinet Mission Plan 10, 100, 141

Cairo 63, 64, 126, 127, 139, 229, 240

Calcutta 65, 115-117

Cambodia 192, 204, 206

Cambridge 94, 139, 141, 197, 203

Campbellpuri 9

Cases 2-4, 24, 49, 61, 92, 114, 149-151, 188, 191, 193, 212, 234

CENTO 186

Ceylon 204, 215

Chancellor of the Exchequer 105, 132

Chatham House 56, 136-138

Chaudhari Akbar Ali Khan 152

Chaudhary Rahmat Ali 139, 140

Chaudhri Muhammad Ali 169, 177

Chaudhri Sir Shahabuddin 3

Chaudry Chhotu Ram 8

Christian 90

Chughtai 18

Chungking 114-120, 126, 132

Church of England 83

Cold War 201, 202, 206

Colonel Oliver Stanley 98, 100

Colonel Reitz 123

Colonel Russell 47, 48

Commander-in-Chief 37, 40, 41, 43, 46, 79, 173, 176, 211, 212

Commonwealth 56-58, 95, 96, 99, 136-139, 170

Commonwealth Relations Conference 56, 136, 137, 139

Communal Award 35, 37, 42, 44, 45, 65, 66

Constitutional Reforms in India 4

Copenhagen 86, 229

Corfu 121, 192, 193

Coronation of King George VI 96, 121

Covenant 85, 86, 88

Crete 63

Croft 71

Cuba 206, 207

Danish Muslims 86

Dasuya 155

David Lilienthal 160

Deccan 82, 138

Delhi 9, 24, 29, 30, 36-38, 54, 61, 64, 65, 73, 76, 78, 79, 82, 90, 114, 115, 118, 120, 126, 142, 145-147, 150, 151, 161, 162, 169, 172, 175-178, 198, 210

Delhi Conspiracy 24, 29, 30

Denmark 86, 229

Dennis 182, 183

Denver, Colorado 128

Dhanvantri 26, 28

Dick Casey 120, 121, 126

Din Muhammad 148, 149

Disarmament 202, 203, 206

Doabs 155

# INDEX

Dominion 54, 55, 57, 60, 120, 123, 130, 134, 135, 138, 147, 148

Donald Farms 58, 59

Donald Sommerwell 60

Dr. Ansari 31-34

Dr. Baw Maw 103, 104

Dr. Graham 178

Dr. Judah Magnus 184, 185

Dr. Kitchlew 25-27

Dr. Vishwanath 113

Dublin 57

Duke of Gloucester 124

Dyarchy 3-5, 9, 19

Earl and Countess of Athlone 130

Earl of Derby 98

East and West Africa 86

East Germany 207

Eden 123

Egypt 18, 95

England 1, 2, 15, 19-21, 23, 38, 40, 44, 48, 50, 56, 58, 60, 61, 73, 80, 83, 88, 96, 99-102, 106, 109, 121, 125, 130, 131, 135, 139, 141, 145, 146, 148, 197, 211

Europe 1, 2, 64, 86, 188, 189, 198, 201

Europeans 37, 57, 225, 227, 228

Ex-Italian 173, 186

Fadhil Jamali 182

Federal Court of India 12, 109, 142

Ferdinand 154

Finland 2, 125, 229

First World War 1, 2, 7, 64, 98, 124, 194, 213

Florida 129

Fourteen Points of Mr. Jinnah 33

France 63, 65, 120, 133, 194, 207

Frank d'Souza 94

Frankfurt 86

French Canada 56

Frozepur 155

G.D. Birla 96

Gajenand Sada Shiv Potdar 26

Gander 130, 169

Gaza 63, 64

General Gracey 173

General John Nicholson 9

General McGaw 47, 48

General Romulo 181, 183, 232

General Wigram 46

Generalissimo Chiang Kai-Shek 114

Georgetown 129

Ghulam Ahmad 84

Girja Shankar Bajpai 38, 46, 171, 177

Glasgow 131

Gotebourg, Sweden 2

Government of India Act of 1935 53, 107, 109

Governor General's Executive Council 8, 27, 61

Greek 64

Gromyko 206, 229

Grosvenor House 122

Guatemala 189, 190

Gulmarg 115

Gunther's book 118

Gurdaspur 154, 155, 158

Gurdaspur District 154, 155, 158

Gurmani 162, 241

Gwadar 62

## INDEX

Gwalior 120, 121

H.S. Vatsayana 28

Haiti 182, 183

Hambro 125

Hamburg 86

Harold Macmillan 243, 244

Hasan Ispahani 170

Hilali 169

Hindus 5, 8, 14, 15, 30, 31, 34, 45, 51, 135, 142

His Highness the Aga Khan 6, 50

His Majesty's Government 12, 42, 43, 45, 51, 53, 120, 142, 145, 146

Hitler 64, 106, 120, 125, 133

Holland 120, 133, 194

Holy Roman Empire 90

Honduras 190, 191

Hoshiarpur 152, 155, 158

House of Lords 104, 148

House of Representatives 236, 237

Howard 58

Hydari 47, 48

Hyderabad 47, 82, 83

I.M.S 47, 48

Iberian Peninsula 2

Imam Ullah 112

Imperial Airways 61, 63

Imperial Chemical Industries 116

Inamullah 82, 112

Inayat Ullah 111, 112

India 1-9, 11, 12, 15, 17, 19-24, 27, 29-31, 33, 36, 38, 40, 42-45, 47, 48, 50, 53-56, 58, 60, 63-67, 69-73, 75, 79, 86, 89, 90, 92, 95, 96, 98, 99, 101-105, 107-109, 113, 114, 119, 120, 123-127, 129, 130, 132-138, 140-142, 145-148, 154, 156-161, 163, 168-181, 187, 190, 204, 210-212, 246

Indian 3, 4, 7, 11, 12, 16, 19-22, 25, 37, 39, 40, 47, 48, 53-56, 60-62, 65, 67, 70, 72, 89-91, 93, 95, 97, 98, 101, 102, 109, 110, 114, 120, 132, 135-138, 146, 147, 157, 159, 171, 172, 175, 176, 211, 212

Indian Cases 3, 4

Indian Civil Service 39, 72, 90

Indian Legislative Assembly 97

Indian National Congress 11, 25, 135

Indian Transcontinental Airways 61

Indianization 39, 79, 132, 161

Indonesia 86, 95, 188, 198, 203, 246

Isabella 154

Islam 7, 8, 16-18, 67, 84, 87-89, 106, 112, 238, 239, 243, 245

Islam in India 17

Islam mysticism 18

Islamia College 139

Islamic Republic of Pakistan 16

Israel 181-186

Italy 63, 64

Ivision Macadam 138

Jaisalmer 157

Jalaluddin Rumi 17

Jam of Jawanagar's 62

Jammu 24

Jammu and Kashmir 24, 170

Jawaharlal Nehru 138, 156, 174, 177, 198

Jayakar 53

# INDEX

Jerusalem 184, 186

Jews 88

Jiwani 62

Jodhpur 61, 62, 64

John Foster Dulles 187

Joint Select Committee 23, 53, 56, 60, 61, 67, 109

Jonkheer Von Karnebeck 198

Jordan 204, 215

Juba 126

Judicial Committee of the Privy Council 3

Jullundur 154, 155

Justice Mahr Chand Mahajan 148

Justice Muhammad Munir 148

Justice Teja Singh 148, 149

K.C. Wu 117

Kalka 39

Kanwar Saigh 24

Kanwar Sen 24

Kapurthala 19, 155

Karachi 62, 64, 121, 126, 139, 147, 163, 166, 169, 172, 174, 175, 177, 178, 198, 205, 239-241

Keith Waller 117

Kerbala 241

Khan Bahadur Nadir Shah 39

Khartoum 126, 127

Khilafat Movement 7, 8

Khilafat Movement Conferences 8

Khwaja Abdur Rahim 139, 140, 152, 153

Khwaja Nazimuddin 239, 242, 243

Khwaja Sarwar Hassan 137

Kialing 116

Killarney Hotel 62

King Alfonso XIII of Spain 190

King Edward VII's death 83

King's College, London 1

Kingsley Wood 101

Krishna Menon 172

Kung 117-119

Kunming 116

Kurangi Creek 169

Kusturbhai Lalbhai 96, 97, 99

Kuwait 62

Labour Administration 22

Lady Burns 127, 128

Lagos 126, 127, 130

Lahore 1-3, 6, 13, 15, 16, 24, 30, 38, 40, 51, 69, 70, 73, 78, 88, 112, 113, 139, 143, 145, 148-154, 240

Lahore Government College 1

Lahore High Court Bar 15

Lala Harkishen Lal 5

Lancashire 95, 98-101

Laos 204, 206

Le Bourget 63

League of Nations 19, 55, 58, 125

Leopoldville 126, 127

Liaquat Hayat Khan 9

Liberian delegation 182

Liechtenstein 189, 190

Lincoln's Inn 1

Linlithgow 49, 50, 102, 115, 211, 212

Liverpool 56

London 1, 4, 12, 19, 22, 30, 31, 40, 42, 50, 56, 58, 60, 61, 63, 67, 72, 78, 86, 102, 105, 120-123,

127, 129-132, 136-140, 162, 169-171, 183, 197, 203

Lord Curzon 65

Lord Gort 123, 124

Lord Hailey 129

Lord Halifax 8, 23, 30, 53, 130

Lord Hardinge 53, 65

Lord Irwin 8, 23, 30, 31

Lord Lang 49

Lord Listowel 148

Lord Mountbatten 145-147, 156, 157, 163, 171, 180

Lord Pethick Lawrence 11

Lord Radcliffe 148

Lord Reading 53

Lord Robert Cecil 58

Lord Sankey 52

Lord Sinha 37

Lord Templewood 23, 53, 148

Lord Wavell 138

Lord Willingdon 8, 28, 37, 43, 49, 61, 69, 73, 80, 211, 212

Lord Wovell 12

Lord Zetland 65, 66

Lucknow Pact 45, 66

Lyallpur 112

M.C. Setalvad 154

M.S. Aney 132

Madame Chiang Kai-Shek 114

Madras 37, 44, 47, 67, 70, 93

Maginot Line 124

Maharaja Gaekwar of Baroda 96

Maharaja of Kapurthala 19

Maharajah of Indore 162

Major Ganapati 47

Malik Ghulam Mohammed 242

Mao Zedong 118

Marquis of Salisbury 53, 58

Marseilles 121, 122, 126

Master Tara Singh 145

Maulana Bashani 245

Maulana Mohammad Ali 7, 22

Maulana Shaukat Ali 7

Medina 88

Mediterranean 63, 64, 139

Mein Kampf 64, 133

Miami 128, 129

Mian Mumtaz Daultana 154

Mir Maqbool Mahmud 56

Moffat 59

Mogul rule 81

Monasticism 87

Mongi Slim 203, 205, 214

Mont Tremblant 120, 126, 127, 129-131, 139

Montagu-Chelmsford Scheme of Reforms 3, 4, 19

Montgomery 152

Montreal 56, 129-131

Morocco 173, 186

Moscow 117, 118, 169, 229

Mosques 18, 86, 241

Mozambique 207

Mr. Alexander 11, 136

Mr. and Mrs. Baldwin 103

Mr. Edwin Samuel Montagu 4

Mr. Gandhi 7, 23, 30-35, 100, 132, 133

# INDEX

Mr. Jinnah 9, 10, 12, 22, 33, 36, 102, 142, 146, 147, 150, 151, 162-166, 168

Mr. Nehru 12, 157, 161, 162, 171

Mrs. Dunlap 58-60

Mrs. Ross 60

Mrs. Starr 59, 60

Munir Inquiring Committee 238

Murray White 128

Musa Abbas Ali Beg 6

Muslim Nationalism 18

Muslim Renaissance 18

Mutiny 9

My Mother 55, 81, 82, 85, 237

Najaf 241

Natal 128, 129

Nawab Sir Allah Bakhsh Khan Tiwana 143

Nawab Liaquat Ali Khan 96

Nawab Muzaffar Ali Khan Qizalbash 143, 144, 181, 245

Nawab of Bhopal 146, 147, 162

Nawab of Chhatari 22

Nawab of Dacca 6

Nawab of Mamdot 144, 151-153

Netherlands 188, 194, 195, 198

Neville Chamberlain 53, 98, 105, 106

New York City 1

New Zealand 103, 138

Newfoundland 130, 169

Nicaragua 190, 191

Nietzsche's 18

Nigeria 126, 127, 130

Nisar Ahmad 152

Nizam-i-Islami Party 245

Norfolk House 124, 132

Northwest Frontier 51

Nottebahm 188, 189, 193

Ottawa Conference 95

Ottawa Trade Agreement 73, 95, 96

Pakistan 1, 5, 10, 11, 13, 15-18, 40, 86, 93, 96, 136, 137, 139-142, 145-147, 149, 151, 155-161, 163-166, 168, 170-178, 180, 181, 186, 187, 196-198, 201, 205, 210, 212, 214, 224, 230, 238, 245, 246

Pakpattan 152

Palace Hotel 62

Palestine 173, 181, 183-185

Parliament 19, 23, 53, 146, 179, 191, 211, 236

Pathankot 150, 158

Patiala 9

Peninsular and Oriental Company 2

Permanent Undersecretary of State of the Board of Trade, Mr. Bro 97

Persian Gulf 64

Philip Noel Baker 60, 170

Phillip Jessup 129

Piccadilly 30

Pinhorn 61

Political career 19

Portugal 190, 207

Powells 57

President Roosevelt's New Deal 56

President Truman 183

Prestwick 130, 131

Princely States 22, 163

Princess Alice 130

Prof. Wayne Wilcox 1

Prophet 84, 89, 112, 196

Pseudo-mysticism 19

Pundit Nanak Chand 51

Punjab 3, 5-9, 11-16, 19, 21, 30, 37, 38, 41, 44, 45, 51, 52, 67-69, 81, 96, 113, 140, 142, 143, 145, 146, 148, 150, 154-156, 158, 159, 163, 172, 239

Punjab Legislative Council 3, 19, 21, 30, 38

Quebec 56, 120, 126

Queen Mary 130

Quetta 166

Qur'an 81, 87, 88, 196

R.A. Butler 125

Rahon 155

Rajputana 64, 157

Ram Chandra 38-40, 46, 47

Ramaswami Mudalior 56

Ramsey MacDonald 22, 23

Rangoon 168, 169

Reed 38-40, 46-48

Religion 81, 87

Retreat 39, 82, 111, 122

Ritz Hotel 30

Romanov dynasty 2

Rotterdam 188

Roundtable Conference 22, 23, 28-32, 37, 44, 47, 50-53

Royal Commission 19, 20

Royal Institute of International Affairs 56, 136

Rural Interests 14

Russia 125, 127

Rutba Wells 63, 64

Rwanda 208, 229

S.S. Arabia 2

Sahibzada Nusrat Ali 152

Sardar Abdur Rab Nishtar 168

Sardar Muhammad 9, 112

Sardar Muhammad Hayat Khan 9

Sarojni Naidu 23

Satyamurthi 93

Scandinavia 67, 86

Scheduled castes 34-36

Scheme for Partition 10

SEATO 186

Security Council 168-174, 176-179, 192, 193, 219, 222, 223

Shaffi 170

Shah Wali Ullah 17

Shakargarh 155, 158

Shamsul Ulema Maulvi Mir Hasan 17

Shanghai 117

Shannon 169

Sharifa 83

Sharjah 62

Sheikh Abdullah 180, 181

Sialkot 1-3, 16, 83, 84

Sikhs 5, 8, 14, 51, 142

Simla 19, 38, 39, 41, 46, 72, 82, 90, 111, 113, 155

Simon Commission 20

Sind 42, 51, 64, 65, 88, 241

Sir Akbar Hydari 47

Sir Ali Imam 37, 67

Sir Allan Burns 127

Sir Allan Parsons 48

# INDEX

Sir Aziz-ul-Haq 132

Sir Aziz-ul-Haq 132

Sir B.L. Milter 45

Sir Datar Singh 96

Sir Donald Boyd 30

Sir Edward Benthal 96

Sir Eric Mieville 43, 61, 73

Sir Evans Jenkins 13, 156, 157

Sir Fazle Hussain 3, 5, 6, 8, 13, 15, 19, 21, 27, 29, 37-39, 42, 43, 45, 47, 51, 61, 67-69, 71, 72, 74, 79

Sir Findlater Stewart 98, 124, 132

Sir Firoz Khan Noon 105

Sir Frank Noyce 38, 73, 76, 77, 80

Sir Frederick White 97

Sir George Abel 156

Sir George Shuster 48, 49

Sir Gilbert Laithwaite 49

Sir Girja Shankar Bajpai 38, 171, 177

Sir Gopalaswami Ayyangar 170, 171

Sir Hari Singh Gour 47, 53

Sir Harry Haig 43

Sir Henry Bourdillon 127

Sir Herbert Emerson 69

Sir Homi Mody 101, 102, 132

Sir Horace Seymour 119

Sir Jagdish Prashad 72

Sir James Crarer 29

Sir James Grigg 49, 73, 76, 132

Sir Jeremy Raisman 134

Sir John Beaumont 110

Sir John Thompson 54

Sir Joseph Bhore 71, 72, 76-78, 89, 90

Sir Khizr Hayat Khan 8, 10, 13, 141-143, 145

Sir Launcelot Graham 42

Sir Lyman Duff 130

Sir Maharaj Singh 137

Sir Malcolm Hailey 68, 122

Sir Maurice Gwyer 109

Sir Muhammad Habibullah 37, 67

Sir Muhammad Iqbal 15, 16

Sir Muhammed Shafi 6, 13, 22, 67

Sir N.N. Sarkar 73, 80, 81

Sir Olaf Caroe 120

Sir Owen Dixon 176, 177

Sir Parshotam 96, 97

Sir Parshotam Das Thakar Das 96, 97

Sir Patrick Spens 158, 159

Sir Philip Chetwood 43, 46, 79

Sir Ramaswami Mudaliar 132

Sir Said Ahmad Khan 68

Sir Shah Sulaiman 109

Sir Sikander Hayat Khan 8, 9, 142

Sir Stafford Cripps 11, 136

Sir Syed Sultan Ahmed 22

Sir Tej Bahadur Sapru 53

Sir V.T. Krishnamachari 132

Sir Zafrulla Khan 1

Sirdar Shaukat Hayat Khan 154

Slansgate 23

Somalia 173

South Africa 42, 103, 123, 137, 208-210, 233, 234

Southampton 122

Sri Prakash 93, 94

Srinagar 28, 162

St. James's Palace 22

St. Petersburg 2

Stanleyville 126, 127

Sultan of Turkey 7

Sun Fo 119

Sun Yat-Sen 119

Supreme Court 29, 45, 110, 114, 130, 149, 187, 212

Sweden 2, 194, 195

Switzerland 62, 63, 67

Syed Amir Ali 6, 135

Syed Amir Ali Musa Abbas Ali Beg 6

Syed Amjad Ali 169, 186

Syed Bashir Ahmad 127-129

Syed Muhammad Shah 152

Taj Mahal Hotel 97

Thailand 192

The drunken Duchesses 56

The Hague 86, 167, 188

The King 44, 50, 103, 104, 191, 212

The Kuomintang 117

The Reconstruction of Religious Thought in Islam 16, 17

Tribunal 24-28, 158, 159, 238

Trivedi 156, 157

Trygve Lie 182

Tunisia 173, 186, 203

Turkey 7

Unionist Party 5, 6, 8, 9, 14, 19, 21, 51, 142

United Nations 163, 168, 170, 173, 179, 181, 183, 185-187, 193, 197-203, 206, 207, 213, 214, 216, 217, 219, 223-226, 229-232, 236

University Law College in Lahore 3, 24

University of Toronto 56

Uttar Pradesh 7

Vallabbhai Patel 148

Viceroy, Lord Chelmsford 4

Viceroy's Executive Council 6, 36, 37, 67, 89, 110

Vincennes 123

Waldorf Hotel 129

Walton Airport 149

Warren Hastings 37, 211

Washington 130, 170, 183, 186

Wedgewood Benn 23

Weightage in representation 20

West Pakistan 5, 11, 146, 157, 159, 160, 246

White 23, 24, 50-54, 97, 103, 109, 128, 209, 210

White Paper 23, 51-54, 109

Whitehall 97

Winston Churchill 53

Yangtze 116

Yudhishtar Raj Wadheva 56

Zafar Ullah 112

Zhou Enlai 118

Zira 155, 156, 158